MW01290730

The Ark of Millions of Years
Volume Two

2012 and the Harvest of the End Times

2nd Edition

by

E. J. Clark & B. Alexander Agnew, PhD

Cover design by Phillip Franklin

Bloomington, IN

authorHOUSE®
Milton Keynes, UK

AuthorHouse™
1663 Liberty Drive, Suite 200
Bloomington, IN 47403
www.authorhouse.com
Phone: 1-800-839-8640

AuthorHouse™ UK Ltd.
500 Avebury Boulevard
Central Milton Keynes, MK9 2BE
www.authorhouse.co.uk
Phone: 08001974150

First published by AuthorHouse 8/27/2007

ISBN: 1-4259-1593-0 (sc)
ISBN: 1-4259-1594-9 (hc)

Library of Congress Control Number: 2006900887

Printed in the United States of America
Bloomington, Indiana

This book is printed on acid-free paper.

Table of Contents

The Dedication

To my wonderful husband who accompanies and makes it possible for me to travel the world in search of new archeological finds, even though he hasn't the foggiest idea of what he is looking for or looking at. I also want to again dedicate the writing portion of this book to my beautiful cat, Youshabel, who always lies by my side whenever I write. **--E.J. Clark**

The world is changing so quickly, it sometimes overwhelms me. I'm not sure how to dedicate this book, except to focus my love on the human race. We are probably the most amazing and incredible creatures in the universe. One thing is for sure. Many races throughout our ages have thought we are interesting, because they have traveled to this Earth from distant places in the galaxy to observe us and interact with us. That is not always a good thing. I am more convinced than ever that we are not alone. How does that fit into my training or my senses? I can't describe it. I doubt you can either. But, that does not change the truth of it. And, in my opinion, before December of 2012 we will have evidence of off-worlders that will shake most religions and traditions to the dust. You feel it the same as I do, but this feeling is one of the main reasons why I have dedicated myself to getting this book out 12 months after the first volume. This story must be told, and it must be told with all the facts and correlations right now.

My wife, two sons, and two daughters have been more supportive than I can describe. They have addressed boxes as we've shipped your books. They've come to countless book signings and lectures and late-night expeditions into the mysteries of the universe through the eyepiece of a telescope outside in the cold. They have endured hundreds of hours of discussions about ancient calendars, civilizations, and planning meetings for travel to remote spots of the Earth. To them, I cannot express enough gratitude.

OK. This isn't an Oscar acceptance speech. I just want to say, "Thank you," to all the readers who have bought Volume One and written me such wonderful mail. Without hearing of your experiences of growth and wonder, I doubt I would have had the will to complete this book.

Peace,

--Brooks A. Agnew

Corrections

In Volume One there are four typos that we would like to correct as follows:

1. On page 7...no. 19. *The Holy Bible*, is a library of sixty-four books......should read, *The Holy Bible*, is a library of sixty-six books etc. (we actually knew that)

2. On page 242..2nd paragraph...should read, The spiritual earth (female principle) united with the temporal earth (male principle). (remember the correct gender when referred to throughout book)

3. On page 276...last two lines of third paragraph should read as follows: Perhaps this is the tunnel or cave from which Y-Okib derives it name. Your authors believe that this particular pyramid site is a good candidate for the location of the Yucatan Hall of records.

4. On page 324, top paragraph, last line...(see also page 280 for Yucatan hall of records) Page 280 should be page 276

The Forewords

The Ark of Millions of Years, **Volume Two,** is a continuation of some of the chapters from **Volume One,** but the main and most important chapters will deal primarily with the End Times. Your authors believe that we have uncovered new information that no-one else has found pertaining to the End Times and particularly the Mayan 2012 End Time date. We are the generation that prophets, seers and revelators all spoke of when they used the words **"in that day"** to refer to the End Time generations of **"this day."** That we are living in the End Times is no doubt; it is in the door. This book will "open the eyes of your understanding" on the End Times, in a way that no other book will. Its message is not one of doom, but "to prepare" for a great fulfillment of prophecy that will **shortly** take place. Three Great Ages are winding down; the sickle has been reaping and the *Harvest* is almost complete.

As with Volume One, Volume Two is non-denominational. Volume One was about the creation of the earth, its birth, and ancient history. The future world was broadly addressed. Volume Two will deal mostly with End Time details and the ultimate destiny of this planet as seen through the application of the missing **"Key"** known as the Union of the Polarity. The **"Key"** is the secret to understanding the creation's destiny and to the understanding of the *Bible. Revelation* is unlocked. Readers will still find the reference chapter, **The Beginning**, in Volume One to be equally as helpful in Volume Two.

I almost forgot to mention that since the writing of Volume One, Brooks and I, and our spouses, did travel to England and Scotland. We visited Stonehenge, Roslyn Chapel, and saw the Stone of Destiny. Brooks had to return to the U.S. but I continued on and saw Hadrian's Wall, Avebury, and the British Museum. Later, we all went to Mexico and visited the archeological sites of Tula and the magnificent ruins of Teotihuacan. Of course, we also spent much time in the Museum of Anthropology in Mexico City. I plan to see Machu Picchu in Peru next year, providing "the good Lord willing and the creeks don't rise."

-- E. J. Clark

I used to think that life was moving fast. When I reached the age of forty it was as if they shortened years to about nine months. Then I hit fifty. I don't think it's so much my age as it is the quickening of events that occur on the Earth today. We have just come through an amazing five years.

The millennium aged and passed away. The sun began emitting different energy, more flares, and more violent solar storms. Mars is closer than at any time in my lifetime. What an amazing red jewel to behold in the night sky above my home in the country. We can watch surface exploration from our own screens anytime we want. We have landed on moons, touched a comet for the first time, and felt our own Earth rumbling as if reacting to painful fleas upon its skin.

In the last year alone we have had 25 tropical storms, some of which turned into the most powerful hurricanes we can measure. There were also six major earthquakes that killed hundreds of thousands of people and left that many more exposed to a killing winter. We have had tidal waves. We have also heard the groanings of ancient volcanoes threatening to awaken with sulfuric revenge. Our planet has warmed like other planets in the solar system, but we still don't know why, or if anything can be done by man to stop it. We see the signs of a sudden and cataclysmic ice age upon us and, as in times of old, this realization is used by those engorged with greed and lust for political power to enrich themselves at the expense of everyone.

We have wars and rumors of wars like never before. The current world war has ghosts for soldiers who accomplish their merciless goal of killing every man woman and child who will not forsake God and bow down before them. And it is not just the defensive soldier who is not safe. It is the very most innocent, tender, and loving people who are peacefully sharing quiet joy with one another shattered across the streets of rubble like a social asteroid pounding into the very soul of humanity.

We were taught as youths that the things we have read and studied over our lifetimes about these times were coming, even though at the time they seemed so distant and surreal. Now that we are all living in the future, the sounds are more moving. The smells are more pungent. Sorrow and fear are inescapable.

As we walked the ruins of ancient peoples this year gathering our photographs and perfecting our study, it was as if we could feel the dedication of the builders to their faith. The Mayans, Aztecs, and Olmecs not only learned great knowledge from their teachers, the Nephilim, they acted upon that knowledge and built the most magnificent cities and temples. Standing on the temple of the moon looking North down the Street of The Dead, I was overwhelmed with the scope of their work. The entire country of Mexico cannot muster the manpower and funds it would take to restore and maintain these beautiful alabaster structures, yet the ancients in this city did it with a population on barely 200 thousand.

As I felt the same breeze and looked at the same moon and stood in the same spot that perhaps thousands of ancient explorers experienced, I wondered why so many modern civilizations believe so strongly that we are not alone in the universe? How could these ancient scientists and writers know of distant planets, spacetime portals to other dimensions, and the relationship of matter to energy? How did they know of the Earth's 26 thousand year axial precession? Why did they think the end of this age, in December of 2012, would be so cataclysmically important for us that we needed their record to understand it and prepare for it?

Well, the answers are in this book. The effects these ancient people had on the universe were lost for many hundreds of years. But the hope of their existence is not lost. In the early 19th century many of these truths were restored to the Earth. Although these truths fell on a deaf and stiffnecked people for nearly a hundred years, by the early 20th century these ruins began to be unearthed. The words that had been preserved, their translators martyred, are now being read by you and millions of others. This most recent expedition taught me that the process of uncovering and maintaining these mighty edifices is a never-ending process. The wilderness reclaims these ancient structures with a fertile dust every Spring, which blooms into life and attracts more dust the next year. Within less than 5 years, the structure looks like an ordinary hill again and needs to be re-excavated.

But, we saw a monumental effort to express to the world, and perhaps to other worlds, that they were a people that clearly understood where they came from, why they were here, and where they were going from here. We most certainly do not have all the details of how they built these unbelievable structures. We do understand their date keeping systems.

The things we reveal in this book will change the very foundations of your life. You will discover things about yourself, your thoughts, and your potential that were once believed to be impossible. You'll know they're true. You won't be able to deny your heart as you read. There is so much more power and glory yet to be displayed in the human race. That is why you will also read about a change that has been evolving. Did I say evolve? Yes.

The next evolution of mankind is about to take place. The ancients saw it. They wrote about it. They gave us a timetable for its occurrence. They also told us it wouldn't be easy. They tried it too, and destroyed themselves before they could reach critical mass. They too had their evil combinations that sought to destroy innocence and consume everything on the Earth. They came to the edge, more than once, and ended in destruction instead.

The human race is nearing that threshold again. Will we pass over into the new realm of peace and prosperity? Will we be able to read the signs left by our predecessors and choose a different future for our race? The future is in flux, my friends. It is not chosen for us. We have complete control over who we will become and to what potential we will aspire.

My hope is that millions will read this volume of our work and look at the future with different music. I hope they will see joy and peace. I hope they will quietly lay their battle axes down and walk back to their families and realize that there is enough of everything for all. I hope the reader learns that we are not alone in the universe, and that our relatives care about us. Whether you consider them divine or not changes no truth. If you can't transcend the need to have faith in something, then have knowledge instead. Know who you are. Know where you came from. Know what you can become. Look upon the knowledge we have carefully inked on these pages and choose life.

--Brooks Agnew

Special Foreword by Dr. Nick Begich

Brooks Agnew has been a friend for many years, and I was please to be asked to prepare a few remarks regarding his current work coauthored with E.J. Clark. Knowledge is a gift from God as is the wisdom to apply it in a manner that lifts people up rather than pressing people down. Things that stimulate thinking, questioning and initiation of the uniformed, start with the active search for truth; a search toward which this book will surely contribute. In seeking the truth much is learned, and what is learned often defies the conventional or accepted. This book promises to awaken those who are asleep at the wheel of life and stimulate others to begin, reactivate, or recognize the search that our life on earth requires – a search for our own identity in the context of all creation.

Over the years I have studied science, religion and philosophy among other things of interest to me. I have always been particularly drawn to, and fascinated by, the history of humankind on Earth. My life has been dedicated to the search for truth and to its disclosure once found. In that search many paths are followed and, by the grace of God, our own truths are realized, our birthrights as humans discovered, and our call toward stewardship over the creation recognized.

***The Ark of a Million Years*, Volume II** is an outstanding work destined to be controversial and thought provoking in bringing forward a combination of ideas supported by historic and archeological records that will cause every reader to look deep and reflect on the "truths" we now accept. The book is focused on many aspects of the "coming age" that many are sensing is at hand. From the traditions of ancient peoples from around the world, and a review of the evidence, correlations are made that connect ancient societies in ways that are rarely reported. These connections are often ignored because they do not fit the current model of human history created by the "gatekeepers" of knowledge. History has also shown that time reveals all truth. For those of us who believe that we are at a crossroads and are seeing the clashing of good and evil play out in the world of human and spiritual interactions, this book is a must read.

Dr. Nick Begich

Author

The Polarity Union

This chapter is a continuation of the chapter *The Union of the Polarity* in Volume One.

The vital missing key to understanding the creation is the knowledge of the union of the polarity. This vital key of knowledge was lost about 6,000 years ago and ultimately its loss resulted in the great chasm between creationists and evolutionists   causing many to stumble into unbelief. Many believe that there is no God and feel the *Bible* is a collection of myths that cannot be proven as fact, until the restoration of the vital missing key through the first volume of the book, ***The Ark of Millions of Years.***   There is no possible way that we can fully understand the creation without the vital missing key. Your authors would like to point out some of the many topics and questions that the vital key solves that have plagued Christians, religious theologians, other faiths, and scientists for generations. The restoration of the ancient knowledge is a religious and scientific break thru in understanding not only the creation but biblical scriptures as

1

well. Below are some of the topics that the vital missing key, called the union of the polarity answers.

1. The union of the polarity defines and clarifies the *Genesis* creation texts of two creations, the spiritual and temporal earths.

2. By clarification of the *Genesis* creation texts the locations of both the spiritual and temporal earths become quiet clear.

3. The return of the vital missing key reveals the ages of the two earths. One was created in 6,000 years of man's time or 6 days of God's time and was called the first or original creation; the other came forth as the result of the "Big Bang" and the natural process of evolution over 4 billion 500 million years ago. As a result of the union of the polarity we can now safely say that the earth has two ages.

4. The vital missing key reveals the ancient origin of Noah's family of which one branch became known as the Hebrews. The Jews have long insisted that they were not from around here which claims are supported by the vital missing key of knowledge.

5. The vital missing key reveals that the flood of Noah was indeed universal.

6. The vital missing key reveals how the ark of Noah managed to hold all the animals without having to be the size of the state of California.

7. The vital missing key reveals that all biblical events from Adam to Noah occurred on the spiritual earth.

8. The vital missing key reveals how Noah and his entourage arrived here on this planet.

9. The result of the union of the polarity reveals that this earth is now a living thing with spirit as well as all living things on it; everything living has a spirit, has a name.

The book, ***The Ark of Millions of Years,*** however answers even more questions, the result of studying ancient sacred and historical texts as seen in the light of the restored vital missing key of knowledge known as the union of the polarity. Below are a few answers that the book reveals.

1. The book describes how the great universes are designed and some of what they contain.

2. The book reveals the concept of multiple universes long known to the ancients as the visible and invisible creations.

3. The book reveals the interaction of these universes to each other.

4. The book gives new theories to spinning black hole formation of space-time warp tubes.

5. The book defines the "skins" of Adam and Eve as being skins of spiritual flesh to house their souls.

6. The book defines what the Fall was…the literal falling of the spiritual creation through multiple dimensions to unite with this planet called the union of the polarity.

7. The book reveals the ancient names of the two earths.

8. The book gives the ancient history of the two creations.

9. The book relates how man was created or formed on the spiritual creation and how man was evolved and then genetically re-engineered on this planet.

10. The book reveals the creators of each creation.

11. The book defines the names of the 2 floods, the flood of Deucalion and the flood of Oggyes that have long been misunderstood.

12. The book reveals why the ancients on the spiritual earth and on the temporal earth (till the time of Moses) lived so long.

13. The book reveals where Heaven is located.

14. The book follows the books or manuscripts given to Adam to present day where about or location of these writings.

15. The book reveals the irruptions of the Nephilim (fallen angels) on both planets and why they corrupted mankind.

16. The book reveals where the bones of Adam and Eve were reburied on this planet.

17. The book tells how the Nephilim still affect us in present days.

18. The book reveals the names of the 2 races of men on the temporal earth along with the Nephilim and their giant off spring for a total of 4 races.

19. The book in general further clarifies many biblical stories that were considered biblical myths. Opponents of the *Bible* have long criticized these stories as being myths and the *Bible* historically untrue. However, the restoration of the vital missing key of knowledge will prove them wrong.

20. The book gives detailed accounts of who the giants were and evidence of their world wide occupation.

21. The book explains the meaning of the ancient Star of David symbol, knowledge long lost by the Hebrews; probably lost during the many dispersions of the Israelites.

22. The book reveals why Christ was born on this planet.

23. The book tells more about the great cataclysm of 9, 600 B.C. that nearly destroyed this planet of which few people are aware.

24. The book tells who the Cro-Magnon man was and why skull sizes of men diminished after the great cataclysm of 9,500 B.C., which has long perplexed anthropologists.

25. The book explains the meaning of pre-Christian crosses that has long perplexed religious theologians.

26. The book reveals more about the Sphinx of Egypt as to who and why it was built.

27. The book explores many ancient megalithic sites, such as Stonehenge and Avebury, as to who built them and for what purpose.

28. The book explores the many megalithic stones cites of the world, including the pyramids, as to who built them and their purpose.

29. The book addresses the ancient history of the Earth prior to 10,000 B.C., and fills in the missing years of 10,000 B. C. forward to 7,000 B.C., even delving fearlessly into forbidden archeology.

30. The book teaches the reader how to read and interpret ancient symbolism (spirals, columns, circles, crosses, vortexes etc.) on sites built by the ancients.

31. The book explains the symbolism of the "dragon" or "serpent" seen anciently word wide in motifs on temple walls, drawings, etc.

32. The book reveals the possible site of the Yucatan Hall of Records.

33. The book reveals the possible source of Hapgoods Maps showing the Polar Regions without ice and the Bering Strait connected.

34. The book reveals what the Templar's were really looking for and found.

35. The book reveals the blood lines of Columbus and what he was really seeking.

36. The book reveals the reason why the US really won its independence from England that has long perplexed historians.

37. The book presents a new theory as to what the continental division was in the days of Peleg.

38. The book identifies who the mysterious Votan and Quetzalcoatl were.

39. The book explains the Life Force (electromagnetic energy) and ley lines as viewed and used by the ancients.

40. The book reveals the visits of the pre-mortal Christ and the Shining Ones on this planet in ancient times, along with Votan, faithful soldiers, and probably other grandsons of Noah.

41. The book presents explanations of the Mayan end time date of December 21, 2012, along with world wide end time prophecies.

42. The book tells of the future destiny of this planet....its spiritual return to where it was created.

43. The book reveals a great sign that manifested in the heavens on November 8, 2003, and possible explanations for its appearance.

44. The book restores the ancient vital missing key of knowledge, called the union of the polarity, back to the world in fulfillment of an ancient Jewish prophecy found in the *Zohar,* that the knowledge would be restored in the End Times.

These are only a few answers *The Ark of Millions of Years, Volume One* reveals. There are many more too numerous to recall at this moment of writing. At one of our book signings a minister of the gospel made the statement, "If your book answers just one of these questions it will be a monumental break thru." Furthermore, the claims made in our book are well documented from reliable sources that are hard to refute.

One question that persistently arises at book signings and radio interviews is **"Why doesn't the *Bible* contain more of this knowledge."** This is a very good question to ask and rightly so. It shows us that our readers and listeners are paying close attention to what we have written and are presenting at book signings and are listening to our radio interviews. The answer is quiet simple. It is because the ancient knowledge was purged, cleansed or removed deliberately from the *Bible* texts. How do we know this? We will explain. First of all everyone will agree that the *Bible* is a Jewish record. There are many other ancient Jewish records, including the *Dead Sea Scrolls* and *The Nag Hammadi Library*, of which every record contains an abundance of evidence of the union of the polarity, which we document from in our book. But, when you come to the *Bible*, a Jewish record also, it suddenly has only a hint here and there which leaves you hanging and wanting to know more. If all other Jewish records contain an abundance of the ancient knowledge and the *Bible*, also a Jewish record, contains only a hint here and there, it quickly becomes quiet evident that it was purposely removed. Why was it removed? Well, we can only surmise. Perhaps they didn't understand the ancient knowledge and removed it, deeming it unreliable. Some was lost through translation. The removal could have been politically motivated. However, some of the ancient knowledge was retained in the biblical texts because removal would further confuse the text to the point of making "no sense" unless the content remained as written. We point this out in the book when it applies to what ever we are documenting. Then there was the first church council of Nicea, held in 325 AD, called by Constantine and attended by 300 bishops. Assembled groups of bishops decided matters with no facts whatsoever. They would simply agree among themselves whether something was true or not and it was adopted. At the conclusion of the meeting, Constantine issued the decree if any opposed the agreed on doctrines, the penalty was death by beheading! Much was probably removed at this meeting and understandably never opposed. After the death of Constantine, there were dozens of church councils, each reversing the decrees of the other and oftentimes excommunicating each other's groups. It has even been suggested that Constantine and Eusebius, a bishop of the church, destroyed all earlier copies of the gospels, and then produced a new set of gospels which are the basis for all Christian belief today! Perhaps this is why there are no early copies of gospels found in Rome. There is no doubt whatsoever that the original manuscripts considered for inclusion into the *Bible* were tampered with and altered. Therefore it becomes quiet evident that the plain and precious truths concerning the union of the polarity have for the most part been removed, but enough evidence has survived in the scriptures to reconstruct the story from other Jewish writings.

Even in today's times translation has become a problem. There are many modern day translations of the *Bible* and they all differ further adding to the confusion of correct meaning and intent. Of all the translations of the *Bible*, there is only one that is deemed the most accurate. It is Ferrar Fenton's ***The Holy Bible in Modern English.*** It is translated into English direct from the original Hebrew, Chaldee and Greek, first published in 1903. It has been in and out of print over the years and fortunately in print once more.

One more point we wish to make is that the *Old Testament* is a history of the Jews; it is their record. *Genesis,* from the creation of Adam to the Flood of Noah, deals primarily with their history and origins, not the origins of man on this planet, the temporal earth. However, *Genesis* does give a confusing brief account of the spiritual and temporal creations which are clearly not definitive. Not knowing

10

about the union of the two earths makes *Genesis* more difficult to understand. The **vital** key of creation, the union of the polarity, is the missing piece of the puzzle to understanding the *Bible*. Once this is understood, then the entire creation is easier to comprehend.

Did the union of the polarity actually happen? The ancient scriptures and writings say it did, including the *Bible,* which retains bits and pieces of the ancient knowledge. It was foretold in an ancient Jewish prophecy found in the *Zohar,* that in the End Times or last days the ancient knowledge would be restored and the knowledge would fill the whole Earth before the Lord returns to renew the Earth. The restoration back to Earth of the ancient knowledge, known as the vital missing key of creation, was even heralded by a great planetary alignment known as the Star of David, Seal of Solomon or Grand Sextile shown on the front cover of Volume One on November 8, 2003, just as the text of the book was finished, even to the very day of completion. The alignment was even more noticeable because it occurred during a full lunar eclipse, which is extremely rare. The earth was centered in the alignment as pictured. This alignment is the ancient symbol of the union of the polarity. The return of the ancient knowledge answers **all** the questions that have plagued mankind concerning the creation. What further proof do you need?

Another question that often arises during radio interviews is **Can you prove scientifically that the union of the polarity occurred?** Yes. When the two planets came together, they formed a circumbinary planet we now call earth. The two bodies were of different spectra, different dimensions, different vibrations like a circle of

11

fifths in music, or standing wave modulations in physics. Because of this harmony, they formed solid matter in this dimension in this time at this probability moment in space. Consider a bucket full of marbles. Although it may be full to the brim with marbles, nearly another bucket of water could be added to it, without it overflowing. Two massive quantities have come together and now occupy the same container. This is a very common event in space. We observe the event as coalescing binary neuton stars pulling at one another like two ice skaters grabbing hands as they skate past each other. Coalescing is the process of merging together. The resulting ripples in space-time produced by this event's gravitational waves have been measured by radio   telescopes and most recently by the **LIGO** system—Laser Interferometer Gravitational Wave Observatory. It appears that these *coalescing* actions are easier to detect with the more dense neutron star than with ordinary planetary captures, because gravity is a very weak force and dissipates like all radiation with the square of the distance it travels. Extremely dense bodies, like neutron stars or even black holes, make an intense enough wave radiation to survive this dissipation, and thus reach our detectors here on Earth. The fact that this union of the polarity event occurs in binary neuton stars is proof that this type of event does occur in space. If it occurs in this physical dimension then it could occur in another dimension as well or even physically coalesce, in this dimension, with a spiritual creation as spirit and matter are attracted to each other.

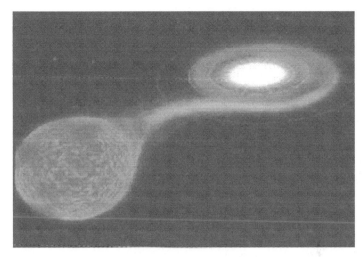

Coalescing Binary Neutron Star, one stripping the other of its mass

To the utter amazement of the authors, as we continue our research for this book, having the knowledge of the vital missing key and applying it where applicable has resulted in clearer understanding of the history and destiny of this planet. We think the upcoming chapters, *The Tower of Babel, The Holy Tongue,* and *The End Times* are good examples of this application, so sit back, kick your feet up, relax and enjoy a good read.

The Star of David

Readers are referred to the chapter, *The Union of the Polarity,* Volume One for the beginning knowledge and symbolism of the six pointed star pictured below.

The Star of David or the 2-Dimensional MerKaBa

The Star of David, the Creator's Star, or Magen David (Shield of David), is a six-pointed star formed by two interlocking equilateral triangles. The Shield of David gets it name from the tradition that David carried a hexagram-shaped shield during his defeat of the giant Goliath. Later, tradition has it that the now King David flew it on his banner, making it the symbol of his kingdom. From where did David get this symbol? The symbolism has much more ancient roots. It was first designed by Noah, Shem and Abraham, to illustrate the union of the polarity to their descendants and to others of the Hu'man Race. The knowledge was preserved through Abraham's lineage until the time of David, when he made it his national symbol. The symbol was a reminder of their ancient divine origin. When it became King David's national symbol, it was often referred to as the King's Star. His son, King Solomon wore a six-pointed star signet ring, called the Seal of Solomon. According to tradition, the ring possessed magical properties that Solomon used in Kabbalistic magic.

The symbol, with the upward-pointing triangle, the symbol of the temporal earth (fire), and the downward-pointing triangle, the symbol of the divine spirit earth (water), represents the descent of the watery divine into fiery matter or the union of the polarity. Where these two meet in the center of the Star, a unifying point of balance and beauty is reached, the origin for the Yin and Yang symbolism and origin of the name, the Creator's Star. The ancient symbol would have been lost to the world had it not been preserved in the Kabbalah. In Kabbalistic magic, the form of the hexagram is employed for its magical and protective properties.

Today, it is a strong symbol of Jewish identity, and remained so even during the dark days of Nazi persecution when Jews were forced to wear a yellow hexagram as an identifier. Modern day Jews view the six points of the star as representing a day of the week with the center corresponding to the Sabbath. The Star was incorporated into the flag of the State of Israel (below) in 1948.

The Flag of Israel

The Star of David has also been found in cosmological diagrams in Hinduism, Buddhism, and Jainism which suggest they have a common origin. This has long puzzled scholars as to where the common origin originated. Lacking the knowledge of the union of the polarity, the origin of the symbol would still remain a mystery. Most likely, the children of Abraham, by his second wife and concubines, carried the knowledge with them when they departed to the East with gifts that their father had given them. From them the knowledge spread and was incorporated into Eastern doctrine.

The planetary Grand Sextile alignment is another heavenly symbol (signs in the sky) denoting a remembrance of the union of the polarity. The rare magnificent planetary show as seen the night of November 8, 2003, occurred during a full lunar eclipse. If you drew imaginary connecting points to the planets in the alignment, a Star of David would be formed with the earth located in the center of the star. This particular alignment was last seen when it heralded the birth of King Solomon. Because Kabbalists view this sign as a heralding sign of an important event, your authors believe that it heralded the return to earth the lost knowledge of the vital missing key of creation, called the union of the polarity, restored in our first book, ***The Ark of Millions of Years,*** Volume One. The Star of David, after all, was the symbol of the union of the polarity. The event was viewed world-wide.

It seems that only a few viewers of this spectacular event took notice and regrettably, even fewer knew of its symbolism. Were all the Kabbalists and astronomers asleep at the wheel? Your authors were aware of the approaching event three months of its occurrence, and furthermore we understood its symbolism. CN News did make a brief announcement of the heavenly event, only mentioning the full lunar eclipse. Present day astronomers are the finest the world has even known but unlike the ancient Magi, who were astronomers as well, they lack ancient prophecy knowledge concerning the cosmos which the Magi possessed. The Magi could link prophecy with the signs in the sky. It is unfortunate that this ability appears to have been lost because astronomers could have alerted the world, much earlier than your authors writings of Volume Two, about the significance of the upcoming Mayan world end time date of 2012. However, your authors believe it is better late to be forewarned than never warned at all.

The Ark of the Covenant

One of the most mysterious relics in the *Old Testament* is the Ark of the Covenant also called the Ark of the Testimony and the Ark of Jehovah. The well known account of the ark first appears in *Exodus* 25:10-22, where Moses is instructed by the Ever-Living to speak to the children of Israel to make Him a sanctuary that He may dwell among them and to make an ark of shit-tim wood, which is interpreted to be acacia wood, a tree known throughout Egypt and the Near East. Shittem is pronounced *Shee-teem* in Hebrew. The tree is a hard wood that endures well and takes on a high polish. The purpose of the ark was to house the testimony which Moses was about to receive from the Ever-Living on Mt. Sinai.

Moses was commanded by the Ever-Living to come up to the cloud covered Mt. Sinai where he remained for forty days and nights. While Moses was there he received very comprehensive instructions of how His sanctuary was to be made and how to construct the ark of acacia wood overlain with pure gold which was to be topped by two Kerubim of gold. After the Ever-Living had finished communing

19

with Moses on Mt. Sinai, the Ever-Living gave Moses two tables of testimony, tables of stone, written with the finger of the Ever-Living. The well known event discloses that Moses came down from the mountain and broke the stones in anger upon seeing the idolatry of the Israelites.

Exodus 35:31-33, and 37:1-29, disclose that the Ever-Living chose Bezaleel, by name, to construct the ark according to the instructions given to Moses. The instructions were very explicit and Bezaleel constructed a golden ark according to the pattern given him. The measurements of the ark were given in cubits and would be approximately 45 inches in length, 27 inches in width, and 27 inches in height (*c.* 113 x 68 x 68 cm), using 18 inches as a cubit standard. If using the variable 22 inch cubit measurement, it would be 55 inches long, by 33 inches in width and height (*c.* 140 x 84 x 84 cm). It could be either of the two measurements or even something in between. The above measurements are approximate.

Leen Ritmeyer is probably the world's leading expert on the archaeology of the Temple Mount and the most recognized archaeological architect in biblical archaeology. Several years ago, in the March/April 1992 issue of *Biblical Archaeology Review*, he presented evidence demonstrating three stages in the development of the ancient Jewish Temple Mount. He reconstructed the original Temple Mount of Solomon and the Second Temple Mount's Hasmonean addition and Herodian expansion. His research confirmed the traditional view that the first Jewish Temple once sat directly above the famous Rock, known in Arabic as es-Sakhra for "rock," beneath the Moslem shrine Haram el-Sharif, known to the world as the Dome of the Rock. Ritmeyer also presented convincing evidence of the location of the Holy of Holies and believes that he has identified the exact location where the Ark of Gold once sat inside the Holy of Holies. The place can now be identified as the rectangular depression in es-Sakhra, that measures 2 feet, 7 inches by 4 feet, 4 inches or 1.5 by 2.5 cubits, the same dimensions as the Ark of the Covenant. E. J. Clark has visited the Dome of the Rock or the Noble Sanctuary (Haram el-Sharif) located on the Temple Mount. She has seen the rectangular depression in es Sakhra whereon the Ark of Gold once rested in the Holy of Holies.

The box construction as mentioned above was made of acacia wood that was gold plated inside and out with pure gold. Its top was bordered by a gold crown edging all around that prevented the lid from slipping off. The lid was a thick slab of solid gold. On each corner of the long end of the ark was a gold ring through which staves of acacia wood overlaid with gold passed to bear the ark. On top and in the center of the gold lid of the ark was a solid gold mercy seat that was covered high by spreading wings of the solid gold images of two Kerubim with their faces one to another and toward the mercy seat. Ferrar Fenton's translation of the *Holy Bible in Modern English* says that the Kerubim (cherubim) were the Divine Watchers (Re Fenton's translation p. 4).

Another translation error found in the *Bible* is, instead of the word cherubims, the word cherub should have been used. The word "cherub" comes from the old Semitic "kerub," meaning to ride and is correctly pronounced "qerub." Both 2 *Samuel* 22:11 and *Psalm* 18:10, state: "He rode upon a cherub and did fly." *Ezekiel* 9:3 refers to God riding on a cherub stating: "And the glory of the God of Israel was gone up from the cherub, whereupon he was, to the threshold of the house." From the above verses we can deduct that the cherubs were some sort of flying devices, a mobile heavenly throne, associated with flight.   *Exodus* 25:18-19 has it partly corrected stating: "And thou shalt make two cherubims of gold" corrected in verse 19 to: "And make one cherub on the one end, and the other cherub on the other end:" The verses in the *Bible* concerning the construction of the mercy seat indicates that the Kerubs and mercy seat were fashioned together or all connected together as one piece.   The Septuagint and other old texts do not make this error referring instead to cherubs in lieu of cherubims. What this all boils down to is that the use of any graven image was forbidden by God, unless God made an exception in this case. To use an angelic representation on the top of the ark would be in direct violation of this order.   However by the time of Solomon's temple this directive seems to have been lost. The problem is further compounded by using the word "cherubim" as a plural from of "cherub."   This would mean, according to *Old Testament* translations, the word "cherubims" constitutes a double plural, which is impossible.

Here again, it seems that we do not fully understand the meaning of the word "cherub" (Kerub) or know exactly what they looked like and furthermore, the knowledge was lost early. There is an illustration in Volume One, page 431, of a winged disc. It may be that winged discs were an Egyptian depiction of the mobile heavenly throne. One can never forget the haunting imagery of Ezekiel's vision where he explained: "Then I looked, and, behold, in the firmament that was above the head of the cherubims there appeared over them as it were a sapphire stone, as the appearance of the likeness of a throne....And when I looked, behold the four wheels by the cherubims....and the appearance of the wheels was the color of beryl stone. As for their appearances, they four had one likeness, as if a wheel had been in the midst of a wheel. When they went, they went upon their four sides; they turned not as they went, but to the place whither the head looked they followed it....And when the cherubims went, the wheels went by them; and when the cherubims lifted up their wings to mount up from the earth, the same wheels also turned not from beside them" (*Ezekiel* 10:1-22). In *Ezekiel* 1:1-28, he adds even more, describing noisy rotating rings, lights issuing bolts of lightning, and a great whirlwind which came out of the north spouting fire. Likewise in the *Apocryphal Book of Abraham* 18:11-12: "Behind the being I saw a chariot which had wheels of fire, and every wheel was full of eyes all around, and on the wheels was a throne and this was covered with fire that flowed around it." Here we have another description of a heavenly fiery chariot that spits fire similar to what Ezekiel envisioned and what we today would describe as a UFO. We must be prepared to accept the fact that God may indeed drive a flying saucer or travel in some sort of winged interdimensional chariot. So until we learn exactly what a "cherub" is or what it looks like, most biblical scholars generally accept the traditional angelic watcher representation.

After Moses breaks the tablets of the testimony, the Ever-Living directs him to place them in the Golden Ark as found in *Exodus* 25:16: "And thou shalt put into the ark the testimony **which I shall give thee.**" Bold type added for emphasis. These tablets of stone are the ones that the Ever-Living made and gave to Moses.

Later, the Ever-Living orders Moses to return to Mt. Sinai. This time the Ever-Living was not going to give a new set of tablets to Moses. Instead He said to Moses as found in *Exodus* 34:1: "Hew thee two tablets of stone like unto the first: and I will write upon these tables the words that were in the first tables, which thou brakest." Moses is even ordered by the Ever-Living to bring another ark with him, one of simple wood as disclosed in *Deuteronomy* 10: 1-5: "Hew thee two tablets of stone like unto the first, and come up unto ME into the mount; and make thee an ark of wood. And I will write on the tables the words that were on the first tables which thou didst break and thou shalt put them in the ark......And I turned myself and came down from the mount, and put the tables in the ark which I had made; and there they be, as the LORD commanded me."

The *Torah* makes it perfectly clear that there were two arks, one golden and one made of wood, and two sets of stone tablets, the broken stones that God gave and the stones that Moses cut. The broken stones were placed in the wooden Ark and the stones that were cut by Moses were placed in the Golden Ark. This is confirmed in the *Talmud, The Tabernacle,* chapter Vll as follows: "There were two arks, one which abode in the encampment, and one which went forth with them to war, and in it were the broken tables, as is said, 'And the ark of the covenant of the Lord went.' But the one with them in the encampment contained the roll of the Law." The wooden Ark is the one which was carried forth into battle while the Golden Ark remained behind in the Tabernacle encampment and did not go into battle, except in the days of Eli when they were punished for this and it was captured. Another reason why the Golden Ark was probably left behind is because it was extremely heavy to carry due to all the gold clad wood and thick solid gold slab lid. It is estimated that it would have weighed over a ton. Not all agree that there were two arks. A different view is given in Yerushalmi Sotah, *lac. cit.,* according to which there was only one ark which served as a receptacle for the two sets of the two tables, for the scroll of the *Torah,* and for the presents offered by the Philistines (1 *Samuel* 6:8). Since neither ark has been located at our present writing, it is difficult to prove whether there were more than one but it does stand to reason that because of the extreme weight of the Golden Ark that perhaps there were two. The answer may be found in Ginzberg's *Legends of the Jews,* page 643, where the following states: "The Ark consisted of three caskets, a gold one, the length of ten spans and a fractional part; within this a wooden one, nine spans long, and within this wooden one, one of gold, eight spans long, so that within and without the wooden was overlaid with the golden caskets." This writing says that the ark consisted of three nested arks, two golden and one wooden; one ark, three parts. Ginzberg continues, "The

Ark was an image of the celestial Throne,......so that even during the march it was spread over with a cloth wholly of blue, because this color is similar to the color of the celestial Throne." The covering was called an "atonement cover" and referred to as a "veil" in the King James Version. It was never carried uncovered.

The mercy seat is the covering of the Ark defined in the Septuagint as a "lid." It is the top lid made of pure gold. Fine or pure gold was used for the Ark because it symbolized what is divine, lasting, incorruptible, pure, precious, and glorious. It is the most precious metal available on earth suitable for the presence of God. The space between the two cherubs is where God communed with Moses. It was where He manifested His presence among His people. Moses erected the portable Tabernacle, or "Tent of Meeting" and placed the Ark along with other religious articles inside. A veil covered the Ark and another veil curtain, called the veil of the tabernacle, shielded and separated it from the golden altar placed directly in front of it. The veiled room containing only the Ark was called the Holy of Holies and the room containing the gold altar of incense, the sacred lamp stand, and table of shew-bread, was called the Holy Place. The tent rooms were surrounded by the Outer Courtyard. The Outer Courtyard (Telestial Glory), the Holy Place (Terrestrial Glory) and Holy of Holies (Celestial Glory) were rooms and area that symbolized the different degrees of glory (Re Volume One, *The Heavens*, page 36). The tent walls of the tabernacle were made of eleven curtains all connected together by means of golden clasps or pins called taches, creating the appearance of a single drape over the tabernacle. The eleven curtains represented the early belief of eleven heavens or universes of the creation (Re Volume One, *The Heavens* and *The Eternal Heavens* chapters, *Exodus* 36:15). We are assuming that the Ark remained "nested" at all times except when necessary to carry the lighter wooden Ark into battle and perhaps for some other religious functions. There simply isn't any information to be found as yet that might shed some light on the "inner Arks." Your authors speculate that the inner gold Ark may have contained the *Divine Book of Wisdom* later called *The Jerusalem Scrolls* by the Templars. These scrolls were passed from God, to Adam, to Enoch, to Noah, to Shem, to Abraham, to Isaac, to Jacob, to Levi, to Moses, to Joshua, and then to Solomon, who learned most of his wisdom from them (Re *The Garden of Eden, The Arrival of Noah, The Books,* Volume One). The cloud of the Lord rested over the Tabernacle, probably above the Ark, by day and manifested as pillar of fire by night. When the cloud lifted up, it was time to pack up the Tabernacle, the encampment and move on (*Exodus* 39-40).

The Levitical priesthood began with the tribe of Levi and proceeded through the sons of the family of Aaron. The Lord chose Aaron to become His first high priest. And so that Aaron and his sons would not be overworked, they were assigned assistants who were called the Levites but functioned as priests (11 *Chronicles* 29:24). The priests and high priest were required to wear ceremonial apparel as cited in *Exodus* chapter 28. Other than the family of Aaron, there were three other family lines in the tribe of Levi (*Numbers* chapter 4): the Kohathites, who maintained the furniture, vessels and veil of the

Tabernacle; the Gershonites, who maintained the coverings, hangings and doors of the Tabernacle; and the Merarites, who maintained the supports, including the planks, bars, and cords of the Tabernacle. Any other tribe that touched the holy things would die instantly. The principal duty of the high priest was to officiate on the holiest day of the year, the Day of Atonement. It was only he who could enter the Holy of Holies to "draw near to God." According to the *Zohar*, it was customary to tie a rope on one leg of the high priest before he entered the Holy of Holies to drag him out should he be killed by the Ark. On the Day of Atonement, the high priest dressed in his ceremonial priesthood garments, entered the Holy of Holies and sprinkled the blood of the bullock over the top and before the mercy seat of the Ark as a sin offering for himself. After he came forth from the Holy of Holies, he again entered and sprinkled the blood of the goat of the sin offering for the people upon and before the mercy seat. The blood of both animals was sprinkled with the finger of the high priest seven times (*Leviticus* 16:6,14,15, 30).

Whenever Moses and his followers made acceptable animal sacrifices to the Lord, fire came out from before the Lord and consumed upon the altar the burnt offerings and the fat which times when all the people saw, they shouted and fell on their faces (*Leviticus* 9:24). The fire which emerged from the Ark was preceded by a "glow" described in the *Bible* as the "glory of the Lord." While the Ark of the Covenant was in this state it was dangerous and could not be controlled as witnessed by the nephews of Moses:

"And Nadab and Abihu, the sons of Aaron, took either of them in censer, and put fire therein, and put incense thereon, and offered strange fire before the Lord, which he commanded them not. And there went out a fire from the Lord, and devoured them, and they died before the Lord" (*Leviticus* 10:1-2).

Louis Ginzberg's *Legends of the Jews,* contains many records of ancient oral traditions pertaining to the Ark, traditions and records that refer to "fiery jets" or "sparks" that leap spontaneously from the cherubim and upon occasion burned or even destroyed nearby objects. During the intermittent appearance of a "cloud" between the cherubim, the Ark was considered so dangerous that even Moses dared not approach it. At such times, the Israelites believed that their holy relic was possessed of demons.

During the Exodus, the Israelites and Hebrews were clearly not on a journey of friendly migration but one of invasion and conquest to claim the Promised Lands given to them by the Lord. There were many battles with certain indigenous tribes they encountered such as Canaanites, Amalekites, Edomites, Midianites, and the like during their journeying. They were successful with relative ease against their adversaries because they possessed something their enemies did not, the most powerful and deadly of all known weapons, the Ark of the Covenant.

It was necessary to follow strict procedures in handling of the Ark by only the Levite priests who wore special clothing devoid of any metal and who carried the Ark bare foot. The Ark was so dangerous that it was carried a mile in front of the journeying mass of people. On page 643 in Ginzburg's *Legends of the Jews,* he writes: "it was through the Ark that all the miracles on the way through the desert had been wrought. Two sparks issued from the cherubim that shaded the Ark and these killed all the serpents and scorpions that crossed the path of the Israelites and furthermore burned all thorns that threatened to injure the wanderers on their march through the desert." Jewish legends relate that even carrying the Ark was a very dangerous task because the relic contained so much power it was known to jerk suddenly into the air, without warning, dragging its bearers with it. On several occasions it was recorded that the violent jerking of the Ark flung the priests to the ground and even emitted sparks that killed them. *Numbers* 11:1-3, record that during a rest in the Exodus journey the Ark caused the deaths of more than a few Levite Ark bearers:

"And when the people complained….the fire of the Lord burnt among them, and consumed them that were in the uttermost parts of the camp. And the people cried unto Moses; and when Moses prayed unto the Lord, the fire was quenched. And he called the name of the place Taberah: because the fire of the Lord burnt among them."

It seems as if Moses was the only one who could control the Ark. When the wooden Ark was set forward in battle Moses would direct its actions saying:

"Rise up, Lord, and let thine enemies be scattered; and let them that hate thee flee before thee. And when it rested, he said, Return, O Lord, unto the many thousands of Israel" (*Numbers* 10:35-36).

The Ark had the ability to levitate. In the Holy of Holies it levitated itself several fingers width off the ground and remained thus off the dirt floor. Jewish legend tells of an account of one such battle whereon Moses directed the Ark into battle. The account describes the Ark as first uttering 'a moaning sound' then raising up off the ground it rushed towards the enemy, catching them by utter surprise, who in their terror were plunged into complete disarray and slaughtered on the spot. In a short while, the results of all these battles made the Israelites very powerful and feared as reflected in *Joshua* 2:24:

"Truly the Lord hath delivered into our hands all the land; for even all the inhabitants of the country do faint because of us."

Upon the death of Moses, leadership of the Israelites and the secret to controlling the Ark was passed to Joshua, his successor. Joshua had respect for the Ark and knew its destructive capabilities in so much that when he built an altar unto the Lord in Mount Ebal he followed the instructions of Moses in building an altar **of whole stones, over which no man hath lift up any iron** and offered thereon burnt offerings unto the Lord and sacrificed peace offerings. No metal could be brought too close to the Ark. Apparently the Ark's energy source was attracted to metal, similar to electricity; in essence the Ark could arc. The Ark performed another miracle similar to that of the Red Sea for when the priests bearing the Ark waded into the Jordan River, during its highest flood of waters, the waters parted and stood on heaps on either side and the people passed over on firm dry ground to come against Jericho. It was the power in the Ark that brought the invincible twelve foot thick walls of Jericho tumbling down. The Ark was ritually housed in an old Canaanite sanctuary when not carried into battle.

One hundred fifty years after the death of Joshua and in the days of Eli, the Israelites carried the Golden Ark, instead of the wooden Ark, into battle against the Philistines where the Israelites were defeated. It was carried the second time during the next encounter where God punished Israel for this by allowing 30,000 Israelite soldiers to be killed and the Ark to be captured by the Philistines. The Philistines carried their trophy to Ashdod and placed it in their own temple beside a statue of their god, Dagon. The next morning they discovered their statue had fallen face down on the ground. Replacing their statue upright the same thing happened the following day only this time the statue was smashed into bits and the head and hands were severed from the trunk. Those not killed by the Ark's emission rays suffered terrible afflictions. Seeing such troubling events, the Philistines decided to move the Ark to the town of Gath, but shortly after the Ark arrived the citizens suffered a widespread pestilence of cancerous tumors which caused such a panic that the Ark was quickly taken to Ekron, where another outbreak of tumors quickly occurred while, at the same time, the city began to under go a deadly destruction causing panic and civil uproar to the point that the Philistine leaders were told that the Ark must go. The Ark was quickly loaded upon an ox cart along with a peace offering of gold and jewels and sent off un-manned to the nearest Israeli occupied town which was called Bethshemesh. The Philistine chiefs escorted the ox cart, following at a safe distance to the territory border, and then allowed the ox cart to proceed on it own. The cart eventually stopped in a field of a local farmer named Joshua. He recognized the Ark and immediately called together a large crowd who made a sacrifice on a nearby stone. The Ark was removed from the cart and it was opened. Those who had crowded around to look inside were immediately struck dead. The artifact was then removed to Kiriathjearim for safe keeping at the house of Abinadab whose son, Eleazar, was appointed its care taker and guardian. Here it remained for twenty years.

When David became King of Israel, he put the Ark back into action and defeated the Philistines in a series of battles. He decided to bring it to Jerusalem in order to celebrate his victories over the Philistines on a specially made cart. During this journey the Ark swayed and Uzzah inadvertently put forth his hand to steady it and was killed on the spot. David, fearing the Lord, would not take the Ark into the city of David but carried it aside into the house of Obededom the Gittite (2 *Samuel* 6:3-10). After three months had passed, King David, following the safety precautions laid down by Moses, brought the relic into Jerusalem where it was placed in a portable tented tabernacle, similar to the original one.

When Solomon, the son of David, became king he set about building a new home for the Ark described as a temple but resembling more of a protective vault. Mount Moriah was chosen for the temple site because according to Jewish tradition it was the place where Abraham sought to offer up Isaac as a sacrifice in obedience to the Lord's command, later revered as a holy site. Its top was leveled and immense walls were built on megalithic foundations. No expense or effort was spared for the House of the Lord. The walls were of hewn stone, overlaid, as was the ceiling, with gold. All the ceremonial vessels, ten candlesticks, 500 basins, and all the sacrificial utensils were of solid god. The entire temple was overlaid with gold on the inside, including the floors. It took ten years to build.

The Ark was placed in the veiled dark chamber of the Holy of Holies on a massive stone slab known as the Sketiyya, or Foundation, the rectangular depression in es-Sakhra. Shortly afterwards the house was filled with a "cloud" that prevented the priests from carrying out their duties and as happened in the past "fire" erupted from the Ark. The dedication ceremony lasted for two weeks during which 22,000 oxen and 120,000 sheep were sacrificed.

"Then spake Solomon, The Lord said that He would dwell in the thick darkness. I have surely built thee an house to dwell in, a settled place for thee to abide in for ever" (1*Kings* 8:12-13).

So it was, when the celebration was over, the massive Temple doors were closed and the Ark was hidden from all except the Levite priests through many generations of Solomon's successors. It was never taken into battle again and only used for ceremonial purposes. In the subsequent reigns of Kings Manasseh and Amon, the Ark was taken to a Levite sanctuary and later it was returned to its former abode by King Josiah of Judah. This was over 360 years after Solomon built the Temple and shortly before the first invasion of Jerusalem by Nebuchadnezzar of Babylon around 597 B.C. Numerous Hebrew texts relate that prior to the invasion it was secreted away and hidden by the prophet Jeremiah.. This is validated by the fact that it appears that Nebuchadnezzar's troops didn't take the Ark or the venerated Stone of the Covenant/Stone of Destiny as inventories of plundered items as given in 2 *Kings* 25:13-17 and *Jeremiah* 52:17-12, fail to list them and the book of *Jeremiah* 3:16, suggests that he did hide the Ark in the following verse:

"The ark of the covenant of the Lord: neither shall it come to mind: neither shall they remember it; neither shall they visit it."

One thing for sure, the *Bible* and other Jewish records are consistent in stating that the Ark was hidden in the reign of Josiah so as not to be seized by the Babylonians. We know through Jewish records that Jeremiah rescued King Zedekiah's daughter, Tamar (Tea) and brought her to safety to Ireland. He also rescued the anointing stone/Stone of the Covenant before the second Temple was demolished and carried this venerated stone to Ireland where it became known as *Lia Fail*; the Stone of Destiny. Recently both of your authors viewed this stone which is now housed in a vault with Scotland's crown jewels in Edinburgh Castle. If we are to believe that Jeremiah rescued the Stone of Destiny then he most likely rescued and hid the Ark of the Covenant too. The big question is where did Jeremiah hide the Ark? For all the Indiana Jones Ark hunters, we have narrowed down the many theories as to what happened to this sacred relic to four possible locations to consider as follows:

1. **Axum, Ethiopia.** In the *Kebra Negast* or *Glory of the Kings* , a well known account of the Queen of Sheba's visit to King Solomon is recanted in more detail than given in the *Bible*. After a prolonged visit she returned back to her county pregnant with Solomon's child. She bore him a son, said to be in the very likeness of his father and named him Menyelik (son of a wise man). When Menyelik was twenty years old he visited his father in Jerusalem who instantly recognized him. Solomon loved his son and afforded him much honor in so much that after one year the Elders became jealous of him and insisted that Menyelik be returned to his county. Solomon

agreed on one condition that the first born sons of all the Elders should be sent to accompany him, about 12,000 sons total. Among these was Azarius, the son of Zadok the high priest of Israel. Azarius conspired with other first born young men to steal the Ark and when they left Jerusalem with several wagon loads of goods, the Ark was hidden in the bottom of one of the wagons. A covered wooden box was left in its stead in the Holy of Holies. It is said that an angel of the Lord helped them in this endeavor. Azarius did not disclose to Menyelik what they had done until they were far away from Jerusalem. Menyelik replied, "They could not have secreted the Ark unless God had willed so bold of a venture." He carried the Ark to Axum, Ethiopia, and said that it would remain there until the second coming of Christ.

When Zadok discovered that the Ark had been stolen, he fainted. According to the record Solomon had to revive him but it was too late to catch up with the thieves. The *Kebra Negast* relates that the Ark levitated the wagons, animals, and all traveling with Menyelik one cubit off the ground and that they flew on the wings of the wind, crossing land and sea without harm, stopping only to rest. An angel accompanied them. King Solomon and Zadok were embarrassed by the obvious theft of the Ark and decided it was in the best interest of all to not reveal that it had been stolen, so they conspired a cover-up based on that it was the will of God. Solomon and Zadok made an exact duplicate copy of the Ark, installed it in the Holy of Holies, and passed it off as the original. This is further verified in 1 *Kings* 8:9, when it states that Aaron's Rod/the Rod of God and the pot of manna were no longer in the Ark. These were items that couldn't be duplicated and because the Ark was a fake copy is probably why it was never used in battle during Solomon's reign, although his reign was a peaceful one. Solomon in despair over the loss lamented, "The glory of the Lord has now departed Israel and entered Ethiopia."

When Menyelik returned home, his mother abdicated the throne in favor of her only son and he became the first emperor of Ethiopia. Having learned the secrets to controlling the Ark from his father, he put the Ark back into use. He invaded the lands of the Nubians, Egyptians, Arabians and Indians. He attacked the peoples to the west, south, and east of his country and prevailed. The Ark fought the battles for the Ethiopians as it did for the Israelites and they emerged victorious every time; many peoples were blotted out and whole districts laid waste. When not in battle the Ark rested in the Holy of Holies in St. Mary of Zion Basilica, built in 372 AD., in Axum. Twelve hundred years later it was removed and hidden again with the threat of a Muslin invasion which occurred in 1535. The ancient church was burned to the ground by fanatical Muslim armies of Ahmed Gragn. One hundred years later the Ark was brought back in triumph and installed in the new second St. Mary of Zion Church where it remained until 1965, when Haile Selassie, a 225th direct line descendant of Solomon, had it moved to the new and more secure chapel where it remains guarded today. No one has seen the ancient relic in years and when it had been displayed, it was covered. The Ark is regarded as too dangerous, too powerful, and too sacred for public display. A priest guards it night and day, allowing no one to venture near; he appoints his successor when near death for a life time calling.

Makeda was the name of the Queen of Sheba. On her departure from Israel, Solomon gave her many gifts among which was a motorized boat (yes, we said a motorized boat) and an airship like the one King David passed to his son, Solomon (Re Volume One, page 316). She promised Solomon that her country would serve the God of Israel and so it did and today Axum remains the oldest Christian State in Ethiopia and the first Christian State in the history of the world.

Assuming this story is true, then King Josiah and Jeremiah hid the duplicate of the original Ark. Finding the one they hid would confirm whether or not the *Kebra Negast* story is true. It is also entirely possible, as some archeologists believe, that only the inner wooden Ark was taken to Ethiopia. There are several different stories in circulation of how the Ark got to Ethiopia but most all agree that it was spirited out of the Jerusalem Temple by godly priests. Ark hunters next look in:

2. The caves under Temple Mount.

By and far this is the most popular theory of the Ark's location. An alleged secret chamber is purported to have been carved out of bedrock and reached by a carved tunnel under the First Temple built by King Solomon. The entire Temple compound has many caves, cisterns and tunnels, some which have been explored and some that are sealed off.

In 1981, a number of Israel's leading rabbis supposedly cleared selected rock-carved tunnels and chambers beneath the Temple Mount, working in secret for about 18 months. They were convinced that another 18 months would take them to the chamber holding the Ark, when they were discovered. Their efforts were halted by the Israeli government due to religious and political pressure from the Moslem/Arab sector. Many Jews believe that it still remains hidden or buried in the secret chamber.

Ark hunters, the Templars may have beaten you to it when they explored the many tunnels and caves under Solomon's Temple, looking for the "flying scrolls" or as later called the *Jerusalem Scrolls*. It is Templar tradition that they found the scrolls and the most prized treasure of all, the Ark of the Covenant. This fact is confirmed in Laurence Gardner's book, *Lost Secrets of the Sacred Ark,* page 279-80, quoted as follows: "….a verbatim extract can be given from a ceremonial address by a Knight Grand Commander of the Chivalric Order of the Temple of Jerusalem to a Masonic Templar Chapter of the Grand Lodge of Scotland in 1990. This took place at the 12th-century Cistercian chapel of Newbattle Abbey in the Lothians. The Lodge was specially convened to celebrate the 20th August feast day of the Templars' original patron and protector St. Bernard de Clairvaux, and the relevant text is as follows:

In 1127 Hugues de Payens received word that he must come back to his native France to take part in the proceedings of the Council of Troyes, headed by none less than the Cardinal

Legate of France: Pope Honorius 11's personal representative. However, the power behind the cardinal, whose word was law and total obedience, was the abbot Bernard de Clairvaux of the Cistercian Order. Hugues de Payers was related to Bernard and to the Count of Champagne, but he did not come back to his cousins empty handed-far from it. Trunks of ancient books were given to St. Bernard, together with the prize of all, the Ark of the Covenant."

Hugues de Payens was one of the Poor Knights of Christ/ Knights Templars who spent seven years searching in the ruins of Solomon's Temple looking for the "flying scrolls." St. Bernard's own records indicate that the relics were placed under the Count of Champagne's military guard for its journey through France and Burgundy. Journey to where? The records fall silent. Some Ark hunters believe that it was carried to Britain, some to the Abbey of Clairvaux in Aube, France. Others believe it was hidden in one of the Templar's French strong holds of Rennes-Les-Chateau, Gisors Castle, Stenay, or Languedoc. It has even thought to be hidden in a mountain, named Pech Cardou, in the Rousillon region of southern France. If it was taken to England or Scotland, then it may have been returned because it is believed, and there is a preponderance of evidence, that the Ark was in the Templar's Temple Chapter House in Paris, April 1147. Later it may have been spirited away to England or Scotland when the Templars fled Paris, France, in advance warning of Phillip the Fairs assault, in 1307. It appears that William Sinclair had the trunks of scrolls in his home, Roslyn Castle while Roslyn Chapel was being built. After a castle fire, he built vaults under his castle where the trunks of scrolls were stored. Since he died before Roslyn Chapel was finished, could these scrolls still be there in a vault? Roslyn Castle is still possessed by the Sinclair descendants. The property is private and not open to the public. Your authors recently visited Roslyn Chapel in Scotland. The symbolic evidence found there is overwhelmingly suggestive that perhaps the chapel was built to house the *Jerusalem Scrolls* and the Veil of Veronica. Some think that these scrolls and Veronica's Veil are concealed in an underground vault under the chapel or hidden in the Apprentice Pillar. It does seem that wherever the scrolls were taken in the past, the Ark went there too. But, there is mounting evidence that William Sinclair took only the trunks of scrolls and maybe Veronica's Veil to Scotland, and that the Ark remained safely behind in France in the protective hands of others.

Associated with the Templars was another secret society called the Priory of Sion, believed to be another branch of the Templar monks. The Templars were warrior monks. This organization claims to be the guardian of the Ark and will return the Ark to Israel when the times are right. The problem is that no-one knows anything about this mysterious society, supposedly still in existence. Could it be that the Priory of Sion is the Great Prior, a Benedictine Cisterian Order in 1147, who were present at the Paris, France, Chapter House when the Ark was displayed in 1147? Could it have been secretly housed in the Paris Templar compound and later in the Chartres Cathedral, during those years? St. Bernard de Clairvaux was the "protector saint" of the Templars. He founded the Cisterian order of monks and helped to found the celebrated order of the Knights Templars, wherefore he fervently endorsed the Templar's quest for sacred religious artifacts, particularly the Ark and the Holy Grail. Hugues de Payens, his cousin and a Poor Knight of Christ/Templar brought the Ark and scrolls to him for their protection. St. Barnard also endorsed the sacred geometry in gothic cathedral building and was especially involved in seeing that the sacred geometry was employed at its finest in the building of the Chartres Cathedral. Why the finest, if not to house the Ark and other sacred relics. There is a small stone relief carving, on a northern portal column of the Gate of the Initiates at Chartres that shows the Ark undergoing transportation, along with an inscription that translates to "Here is sent the Ark of the Covenant." It may not be there now but it once was secretly housed there in the past. The word "priory" means a monastery or convent. Have the Cisterian Benedictine Monks been in possession of this ancient artifact all along? If we are right, then the Ark could now be stored in any one of their monasteries, world-wide. It was and still remains the perfect hiding place.

Because America was the prophesied New Jerusalem, some Ark hunters believe that the Ark and scrolls were sent there. It does appear that the Founding Father's of America did have access to some of the knowledge found in the *Divine Book of Wisdom/Jerusalem Scrolls* from which the U.S. Constitution was drawn based upon the new found principles of freedom and democracy to establish a

New World Order. The sacred relic could be in America as there are Chapter Houses of the Benedictine Order in many states.

3. Hid in a Mountain

Maccabees 2:1-8, states that the prophet Jeremiah, being warned of God, ordered the Tabernacle and the Ark to go with him, as he went forth into the mountain, where Moses climbed up, and saw the heritage of God. When He came to the mountain, Jeremiah found a hollow cave where he laid the Tabernacle, the Ark, and the altar of incense, and then sealed the cave entrance so good that those who followed him could not find it. Jeremiah commented saying, "As for that place, it shall be unknown until the time that God gathers his people again together, and receive them unto mercy." Is Mount Nebo--now in Jordan, across from the Dead Sea--the final resting place of the Ark, concealed in a cave? According to local tradition, Jeremiah is buried on Devenish Island in Loch Erne in western Ireland and that he brought the Ark of the Covenant to Ireland, himself. Did he return to the sealed cave, remove the relics and take them to Ireland? If he did, the trail grows cold. He did bring the Stone of Destiny, currently housed in Edinburgh Castle, Scotland.

There is another fact that must not be overlooked and it is that the Egyptian king, Shishak, took **all** the treasures of Solomon's Temple during the reign of Rehoboam. All means all (11 *Chronicles* 12:9). There after, each time the Temple was renewed, after a desecration, duplicate copies of the treasures were made. Did they make copies of the fake Ark again and again? Jeremiah makes it quite clear that copies of the Ark had been made not just once but frequently as found in *Jeremiah* 3:16: "The Ark of the Covenant of the Lord; neither shall it come to mind;.......**Neither shall it be made any more**." It appears that fake copies of the fake Ark were made until the time of King Josiah when it was hidden permanently. Upon the death of King Josiah, the political scene was in turmoil for a long period of time which subsequently resulted in loss of memory of where the relic was hidden; even to what it looked like. Without a pattern to follow, the Ark was never re-made. We are now looking for a copy of the fake Ark that was copied many times previous from other fake Arks which were copied from the fake copy of King Solomon's Ark! Complicated ain't it? Ark hunters, there is yet another mountain of sorts to consider.

Ron Wyatt, now deceased, was an Indiana Jones hunter of biblical sites and sacred relics. He claims to have dug down into the mount or hill known as Golgotha or Calvary and accessed a tunnel leading to a chamber where the Ark and other temple artifacts were hidden. Ron determined, at the time of the crucifixion, "the rocks were rent" from an earthquake and that a crack was formed connecting the site of the crucifixion to the chamber containing the Ark. At the time of the crucifixion the blood of Christ went down through that crack and onto the mercy seat of the Ark. He believed that God had arranged for the Ark to be hidden in that chamber hundreds of years before Christ died. To date his account has not been proven to be a fact. His many accounts and explorations can be viewed on line at the Ron Wyatt website. He has been labeled a fraud by some factions but your author E. J. Clark, who knew him personally, found him to be a very humble, honest, Christian man who like herself was a "seeker of knowledge." We think that Ron was only trying to "prove" the *Bible* by finding biblical sites and relics and certainly not for compensation. He financed most of his trips out of his own personal funds.

4. In Heaven

In chapter 11:19 of *Revelation*, John sees the Ark in vision and reports what he saw, "And the temple of God was opened in heaven, and there was seen in his temple the ark of his testament: and there were lightnings, and voices, and thunderings, and an earthquake, and great hail"

This scripture leads many Ark hunters to believe that it has been taken into heaven but there are others who believe that the earthly Ark was merely a copy of the one in heaven. Ark hunters, we never promised finding the Ark would be easy.

Conclusion:

Recovery of either of the two lost Arks would be the greatest archaeological discovery of all time. The fact that two Golden Arks, each weighing over 1 and ½ tons, simply disappear into thin air without a trace indicates that they are hidden and not destroyed. Ark hunter E. J. Clark believes that the original Golden Ark is indeed in Axum, Ethiopia, and that the many times copied Golden Ark is in the protective hands of The Priory of Sion, alias the Cisterian Benedictine Monks. The artifact could be hidden in any one of their monasteries or it may still be in an underground vault at Chartres Cathedral. We bet they do not know it is a copy of the many times copied fake Arks, which were a copy of the fake Ark of King Solomon. Once the word gets out, they just might produce it. Then at long last, we could finally see what a cherub looks like. The Priory of Sion assures us that they will return the Ark when the time is right. Is this not the right time since the Ark they possess is only a copy and can never be used by the Jews in their future temple? Even the return of the copy would bring many souls to repentance and salvation. After all, wasn't that the intended purpose of the sacred relics, to bring men unto God?

The Tower of Babel

From the King James Version (KJV) of the *Holy Bible, Genesis* 11:1-9, translates as follows:

"And the whole earth was of one language, and of one speech.

And it came to pass, as they journeyed from the east, that they found a plain in the land of Shinar; and they dwelt there.

And they said one to another, Go to, let us make brick, and burn them thoroughly. And they had brick for stone, and slime had they for mortar. And they said, Go to, let us build us a city and a tower, whose top *may reach* unto heaven; and let us make us a name, lest we be scattered abroad upon the face of the whole earth.

And the Lord came down to see the city and the tower, which the children of men builded. And the Lord said, Behold, the people *is* one, and they have all one language;

49

and this they begin to do: and now nothing will be restrained from them, which they have imagined to do.

Go to, let us go down, and there confound their language, that they may not understand one another's speech. So the Lord scattered them abroad from thence upon the face of all the earth: and from thence did the Lord scatter them abroad upon the face of all the earth."

From Ferrar Fenton's translation of *The Holy Bible in Modern English,* the same account reads as follows:

" All the country was agreed for settled objects. But some of them marching from the East arrived at a plain the Bush-land, and halted there. Then each said to his neighbour, "Come, let us set to work making bricks, and see that they are properly burnt;   and bricks shall serve us for stone, and petroleum for mortar."

So they agreed, "We will build here for ourselves a City and a Tower whose top shall reach the sky; thus we will make a Beacon for ourselves, so that we may not be scattered over all the surface of the country." But a Chief came down to inspect the city and the tower which the sons of men had built; and the Chief said, "You see all these people are united in the same purpose, and having begun to do this they will not be restrained from anything they determine upon. I will go down and frustrate their designs, so that one will not listen to another's proposals."

So the Chief scattered them over the surface of the whole country; and they abandoned the building of the city. They therefore called its name Babel because it was there that the Chief confused the designs of all the country. Thus from there the Lord scattered them over all the surface of the land."

Ferrar Fenton's foot notes give more insight to his translation as follows:

"The word Jehovah, commonly translated Lord, was originally used as a title of honour for nobles or governors as shown in *Genesis*, Cb, xviii. v. 13, and elsewhere, as in *Exodus*, Ch. iv. v. 24, where the title is given to the chief of a tribe, who attempted to murder Moses; and was not reserved as a synonym for God until after the promulgation of the Law from Sinai. In this passage it is evident it did not mean the Supreme Being, and to translate it as if it did misleads the reader." F.F.

Since Ferrar Fenton's translation is considered the most accurate translation of *The Holy Bible*, having been translated into English direct from the original Hebrew, Chaldee and Greek, the meaning of those scriptures changes dramatically from those we have traditionally accepted. Prior to receiving the promulgation of the Law from Sinai, God was addressed as "THE EVER-LIVING." So where did the story of the "confusion of languages" creep in? We believe that it is somewhere in between. One must examine other writings, sort out the many myths, and read in between the lines to find out the whole truth before jumping to wrong conclusions. After researching many records, the following scenario emerged; one that we would like to present as follows:

All the records that we were able to access do agree that Noah and his people came from the East and settled on the plain of Shinar/ Shumir/ Shumer, or Sumer, ancient Sumeria. This area is identical with Babylonia or Southern Mesopotamia, now modern day Iraq. Shumer may be a Sumerian form of Shem. The word "Shumer" was pronounced *Shumi* or *Shum*, later interpreted in the Hebrew tongue as "Shem." This is not to be confused with Samaria, an area in ancient Palestine between Judea and Galilee, known today as the West Bank region.. Ferrar Fenton foot noted that "Shinar" signifies "bush-land." Archaeology dates the origin of the Sumerian civilization to ca 4500 B.C. This area was first peopled by Turanian tribes. Around 3000 B.C., tribes of Semites invade and become its rulers. These Semites would be the people of Noah. There is archaeological evidence, during this time period, that the area was invaded by a superior race of people who brought with them advanced technology in farming, tools, construction, metallurgy, and writing. New grains, such as barley and wheat, were introduced in farming and new farming techniques were developed such as irrigation and the use of the plow. They were cattle, goat and sheep raisers as well as fishermen. The use of wheeled vehicles, the sailboat, and the potter's wheel were all of Sumerian origin. From earliest times Sumerian architects made use of the arch, dome, and vault which was probably introduced to Greece and Rome from contact with Babylonian cities. Using clay tablets to inscribe upon, they devised a system of cuneiform script and pictograph writing that was used all over the ancient civilizations of the Near East and western Asia, including India, and eventually brought to Europe. In the field of mathematics the Sumerians devised a decimal system which probably was a prototype of the Hindu-Arabic decimal system currently in use today. They formulated the earliest concepts of algebra and geometry. They were the first to pave roads, the first to have a postal system, the first to make a magnifying glass, the first to have public libraries, the first to found a public university, the first to have public schools, the first to write literature (poetry, epics, hymnals, medical texts) and the first to have a complex sewer system with flushing toilets. Legal and ethical concepts with moral ideals were developed and written down by the Sumerians. They were the first to spell out in writing law codes so that no misunderstanding could happen, basically inventing law which became the foundation for their central government and future governments throughout the world. Essentially these concepts were identical with those of the Hebrews. The Sumerians even mapped the heavens. They had scale maps of our solar system; knowledge that we didn't have until the 20th century. They had electric batteries, may have had electric lights and had the knowledge to electroplate gold. It seems the Egyptians may have learned this technology from contact with Noah's people. In commerce, a system of weights and measures were developed and used until the Roman period. Last but not least, they brewed beer. As to physical appearance, these early Semites were fair skinned, tall and slender. They called themselves the Sag-gi-ga, which meant "the black-headed ones."

As previously discussed in Volume One, we estimated the union of the polarity occurred around 4800 B.C. By the time Noah and his family arrived to the plain of Shinar, 800 years had passed. During those years Noah's family had multiplied greatly, even to the fifth or sixth generation of descendants. Their numbers could have easily reached a million or more. It was a slow migration over a number of years, gradually leaving the eastern mountainous regions of ancient Armenia, where the ark had rested, into northern ancient Babylonia (Iraq), maybe into Arabia, and lastly into Southern Mesopotamia. There is much evidence to suggest that the ancient Sumerians and Noah's people were one and the same. This of course, will move the time line much further back than previously thought by biblical scholars.

It appears that Noah and most of his descendants spoke the Archiac Sumerian language. Was this the pure "Adamic" language that was spoken on the spiritual earth? It very well could be, recognizing that some change would have occurred over a period of 800 years. Sumerian was not a Semitic language; neither was Noah a Semite. The descendants of Shem were Semites. The Semitic languages developed through Shem's descendants, the result of mixing with other cultures who spoke other languages. Some of Shem's descendants were most likely bilingual, speaking the Semitic ancient Akkadian tongue as well as Sumerian. Over a period of time, the Semitic Akkadian language gradually replaced Sumerian as the main spoken language of Sumer. Language is a strange thing. It is not static but is always in perpetual change; it is always evolving. Sumerian is an unclassified language which has so far resisted all attempts to relate it to any known living or dead language. Maybe this is because the language came from another world, the spiritual earth, and was brought here by Noah (Re *The Brave New World*, Volume One, p. 470).

Genesis 11:1 records: "And the whole earth was of one language, and of one speech." This verse is misleading. The Jews had a peculiar style of writing, that is well known by biblical students of scripture. Even though the verse translates as "whole earth", the intent and meaning was different from a Jewish stand point during ancient times. The Jewish intent and meaning of the same verse would read, if it were written in today's times as: "And the whole region was of one language, and of one speech." Another example of this style of writing that appears many times in biblical scriptures is "And all the people were killed." The Jewish intent and meaning would be: "And all the people in the region were killed," or "As far as I know, all the people were killed." This peculiar style of writing is also found in *The Book of Mormon*. The important thing to remember is that language has changed, even as to intent and meaning, and is continuing to do so. Employment of the peculiar literary style of writing has caused much confusion in non Jewish literary circles.

Historians know that prior to the Tower of Babel, there were various different tribes of people in many foreign lands that spoke different tongues. This is an established fact which consequently has caused countless numbers of people to view the Tower of Babel as a myth.

Returning to the story. Noah and his descendants have migrated to the plain of Shinar. The whole region now speaks one language and one tongue, the Archaic Sumerian language. Families paired off into tribes and were scattered over all of the region but remained in relative close proximity to each other. It is said that the families couldn't bear to depart from each other and "scatter" as God had commanded nearly 800 years previous. Because they now lived in Sumer, they were called Sumerians.

Among the descendants of Ham was Nimrod, the grandson of Noah, son of Cush. His father Cush had married his mother at an advanced age and Nimrod was the beloved and only son of his old age. Cush may have been credited to have been his father but he was a giant son of the Nephilim born to his mortal mother. Nimrod was his Hebrew name but current thinking is that he was the Babylonian king called "Gilgamesh." Your authors are in agreement with his true identity. The *Dead Sea Scrolls* identify Gilgamesh as being two thirds god and one third human, which makes him a demi-god. Being a giant offspring, he was endowed with incredible strength, size and cunning. *Genesis* 10 describes him as a "mighty hunter before the Lord." Besides being a mighty hunter, he was also known as both a conqueror and builder of cities after the great flood of Noah. He built cities all over the ancient Near East and perhaps throughout the entire known world in order to restore civilization back to the world following the flood of Noah. He was truly a "mighty man," one of the giant off spring of the Watchers who possessed the inherited nature of perversion, idolatry, and evil inclination. The *Book of Jasher* discloses that after Nimrod had joyfully returned from one of his many battles, victorious, "his brethren, together with those who knew him before, assembled to make him king over them, and they placed the regal crown upon his head. Afterwards he advised with his counselors to build a city for his palace, and they did so. And they found a large valley opposite to the east, and they built him a large and extensive city, and Nimrod called the name of the city that he built Shinar." A tower was to be built in the city to act as a beacon to draw the dispersed tribes into the city from time to time. The city and tower was to act as an unification point or central government for all the tribes. Noah may have approved of the endeavor. In Volume One, page 480, we wrote that Francis Nunez de la Vega, Bishop of Chiapas, stated that he saved a partially burned book purported to be written by Votan (grandson of Noah) where he wrote the following: " that he saw the great wall, namely the Tower of Babel, which was built from earth to heaven at the bidding of his grandfather Noah." The *Book of Jasher* further discloses that Nimrod reigned in the earth over all the sons of Noah, and they were all under his power and counsel.

The *Book of Jasher* states additionally that it took about six hundred thousand men many years to build the city and the tower. Some mud bricks, used in the construction of the city and tower, had to be burnt by fire to make them strong; others were sun baked. This method of construction was slow and labor intensive.

The *Book of Jubilees* (in use 200 B.C.-90 A.D.) contains one of the most detailed construction accounts found anywhere in building of the Tower.

"And they began to build, and in the fourth week they made brick with fire, and the bricks served them for stone, and the clay with which they cemented them together was asphalt which come out of the sea, and out of the fountains of water in the land of Shinar. And they built it: forty and three years were they building it; its breadth was 203 bricks, and the height (of a brick) was the third of one; its height amounted to 5433 cubits and 2 palms, and (the extent of one wall was) thirteen stades (and of the other thirty stades)." (*Jubilees* 10:20,21, Charles' 1913 translation)

According to Ferrar Fenton's translation, the city and tower was never finished. A great chief, most likely Shem, didn't approve of the undertaking. Perhaps it was too costly in man hours, or maybe he remembered God's command to "scatter," and feared a severe judgment from THE EVER-LIVING if they failed to do so. Shem would have viewed their failure to obey THE EVER LIVING'S command as a rebellion against God. Regardless of the reason, he felt compelled to frustrate their designs to the point that the workers threw up their hands and simply walked off the job. Some time later, when the tribes still refused to "scatter," THE EVER-LIVING confused their tongues and then they obeyed the command to "scatter." Into foreign lands of another people, who already spoke different languages, they migrated as given in the Table of Nations in *Genesis*. Their purpose was to restore civilization that was lost during the 9,500 B.C. cataclysm, provide an uncorrupted bloodline for the Messiah to be born into, and to bring to the people of this planet the knowledge of their Creator, the one true God, THE EVER-LIVING. There after the tower was called Babel, referencing to babbling, because the confusion of languages occurred in that region around it. An account is given in the *Book of Jubilees* that God overturned the tower with a great wind. Abandoned, the partially built city and tower fell into ruin but not for long.

Afterwards, the *Book of Jasher*, chapter X1 records that Nimrod built four cities. The first city he named Babel, in memory of the 1st city and tower; the second was Erech, the third was Eched and the fourth was Calnah. After Babel was built, Nimrod lived there and renewed his reign over the subjects and princes who now call him (Nimrod) by a new name, Amraphel. Nimrod was his Hebrew name. His Sumerian name was Amraphel and his Babylonian name was Gilgamesh. Ferrar Fenton's translation of the *Bible* lists the four cities of Nimrod as Babel, Ereck, Akad, and Kalinah in the Bush-land. The KJV of *Genesis* 10:10 lists the four cities as Babel, Erech, Accad, and Calneh. It is believed that Babel is the city of Babylon. Calneh is believed to be Calno (*Isaiah* 10:9) and Canneh (*Ezek.* 27:23), the modern Niffer lying in ruins as a lofty mound of earth on the east bank of the Euphrates, about 60 miles south east from Babylon. Akad or Agade has yet been undiscovered. Biblical Erech/Ereck was known as Unug to the Sumerians and called Uruk today. Iraq derives its name from Uruk. To the Greeks it was known as Orchoe and to the Arabs, Warka. The ancient city is located about 140 miles south east from Bagdad, situated east of the present bed of the Euphrates. These four cities were the first of Nimrod's kingdom. From there he went to Assyria and built Nineveh, Calah, Resen, and Rehoboth (*Genesis* 10:8-12). Adding to the confusion is the well known King List that lists the first three Sumerian dynasties after the Flood as those of Kish, Erech, and Ur, in that order. Historians have learned from Sumerian epics and hymnal lore that the last two kings of the Kish dynasty, Emmebaraggesi and his son Agga, were contemporaries of Gilgamesh, the fifth ruler of Erech, with whom they fought bitter battles for supreme rulership over Sumer. Cuneiformists generally accepted that the two first dynasties of Kish and Erech overlapped

The original city of Shinar has not yet been discovered or identified in Babylonia. However, there is strong evidence that the city of Shinar/Babel was not Babylon, as commonly believed, but rather rebuilt as the far older Eridu south of Ur, where there is a very large ruin of an abandoned ziggurat. Ziggurats were a product of Sumerian architecture. The one pictured below is a typical example of the pyramidal building style. It is believed, with some certainty, that the Tower of Shinar/Babel was a ziggurat.

The Ziggurat (credit Sir Leonard Woolley)

All of Nimrod's cities had a ziggurat. Most were built on immense scale. The inner core of construction was sun-baked bricks with the outer façade made of fired glazed bricks in different colors. They could be shaped as a square, rectangle or oval. It was not a place of public worship or ceremonies but a temple, in the beginning, accepted as a House of God and tended to by priests. Each city took great pride in their religious center. The seven tiers symbolically represented the structuring of the cosmos; each tier representing one of the seven heavens or universes, knowledge that Noah and his family brought to Shinar.

Nimrod's wife was named Semiramis. She and Nimrod corrupted the religion of Noah by introducing the worship of other gods after the sons and grandsons of Noah were scattered. It is evident that some third generation and generations beyond remained in Shinar to carry on Sumerian traditions and language. The God of Noah was replaced by the worship of many Babylonian gods. Semiramis started the worship of Babylonian gods in Sumer and Nimrod enforced the belief. They were the source of all pagan religions in the world. Nimrod was an evil king who was only benevolent to his subjects if they paid tribute to him.

On April 29, 2003, the BBC News announced that archaeologists in Iraq believe they may have found the lost tomb of King Gilgamesh-the subject of the oldest "book" in history. The following is the news story:

" *The Epic of Gilgamesh* written by a Middle Eastern scholar 2,500 years before the birth of Christ commemorated the life of the ruler of the city of Uruk, from which Iraq gets its name. Now, a German led expedition has discovered what is thought to be the entire city of Uruk including, where the Euphrates once flowed, the last resting place of its famous King. "I don't want to say definitely it was the grave of King Gilgamesh, but it looks very similar to that described in the epic," said Jorg Fassbinder of the Bavarian department of Historical Monuments in Munich, as he told to the BBC World Service's Science in Action programme."

"In the *Epic of Gilgamesh,* actually a set of inscribed clay tablets, Gilgamesh was described as having been buried under the Euphrates, in a tomb apparently constructed when the waters of the ancient river parted following his death. "We found just outside the city an area in the middle of the former Euphrates river the remains of such a building which could be interpreted as a burial," Mr Fassbinder said. He said the amazing discovery of the ancient city under the Iraqi desert had been made possible by modern technology. "By differences in magnetisation in the soil, you can look into the ground. The difference between mud bricks and sediments in the Euphrates river gives a very detailed structure. This creates a magnetogram, which is then digitally mapped, effectively giving a town plan of Uruk." He added, "The most surprising thing was that we found structures already described by Gilgamesh. We covered more than 100 hectares. We have found garden structures and field structures as described in the epic, and we found Babylonia houses. The most astonishing find was an incredibly sophisticated system of canals. Very clearly, we can see in the canals some structures showing that flooding destroyed some houses, which means it was a highly developed system. [It was] like Venice in the desert."

It was during the reign of King Nebuchadnezzar 11 (605-562 B.C.) that the ancient city of Babylon was rebuilt, its awe inspiring beauty and magnificence surpassing all ancient cities of its time, taking eighty eight years to build. Its famous hanging gardens were proclaimed one of the seven wonders of the ancient world. Like modern day Budapest, Babylon was built on both sides of the Euphrates river. In ca. 670 B.C., Nebuchadnezzar wrote:

"A former king built [the Temple of the Seven Lights of the Earth], but he did not complete its head. Since a remote time, people had abandoned it, without order expressing their words. Since that time earthquakes and lightning had dispersed its sun-dried clay; the bricks of the casing had split, and the earth of the interior had been scattered in heaps. Merodach, the great lord, excited my mind to repair this building. I do not change the site, nor did I take away the foundation stone as it had been in former times. So I founded it, I made it; as it had been in ancient days, I so exalted the summit."

Inside the city, a ziggurat called the Etemenanki interpreted to mean "the temple of the creation of heaven and earth" was constructed. It was one of the largest ziggurats ever built and was dedicated to the Babylonian god Marduk. In 440 B.C., the Greek historian Herodotus wrote:

"Babylon's out wall is the main defense of the city. There is, however, a second inner wall, of less thickness than the first, but very little inferior to it in strength. The center of each division of the town was occupied by a fortress. In the one stood the palace of the kings, surrounded by a wall of great strength and size: in the other was the sacred precinct of Jupiter Belus, a square enclosure two furlong [402m] each way, with gates of solid brass; which was also remaining in my time. In the middle of the precinct there was a tower of solid masonry, a furlong [201 m] in length and breadth, upon which was raised a second tower, and on that a third, and so on up to eight. The ascent to the top is on the outside, by a path which winds round all the towers. When one is about half-way up, one finds a resting-place and seats, where persons are wont to sit some time on their way to the summit. On the topmost tower there is a spacious temple, and inside the temple stands a couch of unusual size, richly adorned, with a golden table by it side. There is no statue of any kind set up in the place, nor is the chamber occupied of nights by any one but a single native woman, who, as the Chaldeans, the priests of the god, affirm, is chosen for himself by the deity out of all the women of the land."

Herodotus may not have actually seen the tower himself but nevertheless wrote of it. He erred in saying that it had eight tiers instead of seven tiers. Their god, Marduk, was a fallen son of God, one of the Nephilim. Women, chosen by Marduk, were brought nightly to the temple and taken to the top room of the ziggurat where they had sexual intercourse. Babylonian writings firmly state that these beings took on bodily form and walked among men "in the days when gods walked upon the face of the earth." Furthermore the Babylonian writings say with certainty that "their eyes beheld them." Each city of Sumer/Babylonia had their own personal god and ziggurat dedicated to them where the same nightly activities took place between their nephilim gods and mortal women. Each ziggurat had priests who attended to the ever beck and call of these nephilim gods whose wishes were their command. Stories about their gods, once considered myths, may in fact be actual as recorded and believed by Herodotus, a credible Greek historian that earned him the title, "The Father of History." There is enough evidence in biblical accounts to say that it did happen.

By word of mouth the accounts of the magnificence of the Etemenanki ziggurat was spread by traders and visitors to the city and in time became wrongly associated with the original Tower of Babel, it (the Marduk ziggurat) being located in Babylon; Babylon and Babel being associated. Babylon is from the Akkadian word Bab-ilu which means "gate of the god," and has nothing to do with confusion of languages. Constant war and turmoil virtually emptied the city of Babylon in 275 B.C. By 141 B.C., the city was in complete desolation and ruin. Saddam Hussein partially restored part of the city and apparently the foundation base of the Marduk ziggurat has been discovered.

Even though the Sumerians developed one of the earliest civilizations on earth it wasn't until the middle of the 19th century that anyone knew that they had preceded the Babylonians. No one suspected that the Sumerian language preceded Akkadian or the Babylonians had adapted and later modified the Sumerian writing, agriculture, and religious systems. Noah's people restored civilization to the earth following the great cataclysm. It is incorrect to say that Noah's people, the Sumerians, invented or developed some of their technology; correctly stated they brought this technology and knowledge with them. They had already formulated all the attributes of civilization when they arrived on the scene. The source of their wisdom was *The Divine Book of Wisdom*, the "flying scrolls" of Adam. Subsequently, today's society can trace much of what we have achieved to far earlier "roots" in Sumeria, the "civilized land," or as the Sumerians called their land, Ki-en-gi, the "place of the civilized lords."

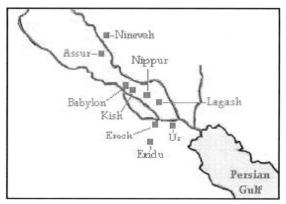

The Lands of Ancient Sumer

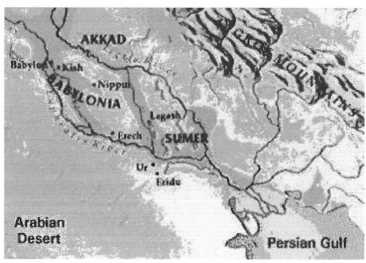

Lands well-developed by Temporal mankind long before Noah ever arrived did not, however, have a complex written language capable of supporting trade, astronomy, and medicine.

Gilgamesh the demi-god holding a lion. Stone relief from the Palace of Sargon 11.

The Holy Tongue

The Holy Tongue is the pure Adamic language that Noah and his family spoke. In the beginning, when God created Adam, he gave Adam a language that was pure, perfect, and undefiled. It was the language spoken on the spirit earth and according to the *Zohar* Volume One, page 256, was the celestial tongue of the Gods.

The *Book of Moses* 6:5-6, says: "And a book of remembrance was kept,…in the language of Adam, for it was given unto as many as called upon God to write by the spirit of inspiration; And by them their children were taught to read and write, having a *language which was pure and undefiled.*" Whenever men called upon the Lord in the Holy Tongue, they were empowered because it is the language that can fully express the purpose of the heart and thus help to the attainment of the desired goal; hence it was deemed a far superior tongue over others in that respect. For that reason it was also referred to as the sacred language.

Previous to this writing the Adamic language was unknown and believed to be extant since the confusion of the languages. True, on this earth the language is dead but your authors are 100% sure of its identity and that **we are the first in the world to identify the Holy Tongue; it is our claim to fame**. Without the knowledge of the vital missing key, which is the union of the polarity, it may have been impossible to learn or at least very difficult to locate and identify the language. We do not know what Noah and his children called the language, other than the Holy Tongue, but linguists have identified and named it **Archaic Sumerian.** Previous to this chapter, in *The Tower of Babel* chapter, we explained how we arrived to this conclusion. When Noah and his entourage arrived on this planet, they brought with them all the attributes of civilization already formulated, among which was a written form of the language they spoke.

Laurence Gardner, in his book, *Genesis of the Grail Kings,* said this about the written form of the Sumerian language: "It appeared in a complete and composite form, **as if from another world,** in the style known as cuneiform (wedge-shaped). Bold type emphasis added. Laurence Gardner doesn't realize how right he was when he penned the above statement. The spoken and written form of the language did come from another world, the spiritual creation and was brought here by Noah (Re *The Union of the Polarity,* Volume One).

What is Sumerian? Sumerian is the language spoken initially by Noah in ancient times. Over time the language became corrupted (changed) and is now distinguished into the following four periods: Archaic Sumerian, Old or Classical Sumerian, New Sumerian, and Post-Sumerian. Archaic Sumerian covered a period from when Noah first arrived to this planet about 4800 B.C. down to about 2500 B.C. The first Sumerian records make their appearance in Sumer about 3100 B.C.

The Old or Classical period of Sumerian covered the period from about 2500 to 2300 B.C. During this time period the sources are much more numerous than the time period previous and are represented mainly by the records of the early rulers of Lagash. These records consisted mainly of business, legal, royal and private inscriptions, and administrative texts, both private and official; including incantations.

When the Semitic Akkadians became the dominating political power in Babylonia, during the period of the Sargonic dynasty, a definite setback occurred in the progress of the Sumerian language. During this time the Akkadian language was used extensively throughout the entire area while Sumerian was confined to a small area in Sumer proper. A brief revival of the language occurred during the third dynasty of Ur, then the New Sumerian period came to an end about 2000 B.C., when the third dynasty of Ur was destroyed by invading Semites who then established their own dynasties of Isin, Larsa, and Babylon. These dynasties were called the Old Babylonian period and it was during this period that Babylon reached the zenith of her glory as the capital and the most important city in Mesopotamia, resulting in the Sumerians losing their political identity and gradual disappearance of their spoken language. Their written language however continued to be written until the end of the use of cuneiform writing. This was the last period of the Sumerian language, called Post-Sumerian.

It was during the Old Babylonian period and early Post-Sumerian times that the written form of Sumerian blossomed into rich Sumerian literature found in their hymns, lamentations, myths, epics, incantations, rituals, proverbs, and royal inscriptions, as well as legal and administrative texts which many times were written bilingual, in both Sumerian and Babylonian languages. One of the last rulers of Assyria, King Ashurbanipal, even boasted of being able to read the difficult language, as late as the 7th century B.C. As difficult as the language apparently was, it did continue to be studied in the Babylonian schools much like Latin was continued to be studied in modern times, and both continued to be spoken in religious ceremonies. All knowledge of the Sumerian language as well as the written cuneiform writing disappeared around the time of Christ. In a few centuries the memory of the name of Sumer had disappeared; vanished from history until the early part of the 19th century when it was rediscovered through the decipherment of cuneiform writing. Scholars, after sifting through countless Babylonian texts, became aware of the existence of another written language different from Babylonian. At first it was designated Scythian, later Akkadian, and finally after much research and new knowledge that came forth, it was named correctly, Sumerian.

What are the language characteristics? Because your authors are not linguists, we have elected to document from free use internet website as indicated. For more detailed study of the language there is much available in the online book stores. We were surprised to find dictionaries available for both Babylonia and Sumerian in the online stores.

It appears that the written form of the language was in constant change during the early periods. If Noah's language and writing system was so advanced, why does the written form seem so primitive? Noah's language and writing system was far advanced of the civilization they came to. Not all of Noah's descendants could read and write the more complicated original system, so it appears they devised a simpler system that all could understand with little or no formal education.

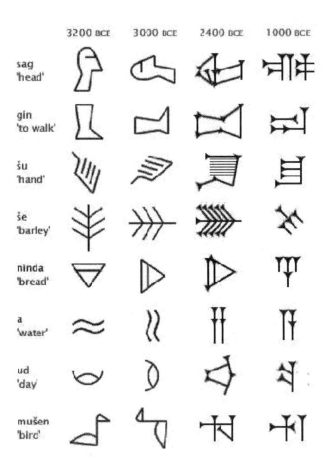

Samples of these cuneiform changes are illustrated above, taken from www.ancientscripts.com/sumerian.

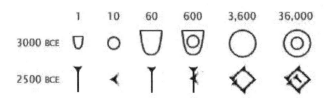

The sexagesimal part of this system, shown above, survives in the modern era in units of time (seconds and minutes) and of trigonometry (360 seconds).

As the written form evolved so did the language change from Archaic Sumerian to Post-Sumerian. We don't know if anyone today can speak the language correctly but some details in characteristics are known as follows, taken from the website www.ragz-international. com/sumerian_language.

"The distinctive sounds (phoemes) of Sumerian consisted for four vowels, a, i, e, u, and 16 consonants, b, d, g, h, k, l, m, n, p, r, s, s, s, t, z. In Classical Sumerian, the contrast between the consonants b, d, g, z and p, t, k, s was not between voiced (with vibrating vocal cords) and voiceless consonants (without vibrating vocal cords) but between consonants that were indifferent as to voice and those that were aspirated (pronounced with an accompanying audible puff of breath). The semivowels y and w functioned as vocalic glides.

In the noun, gender was not expressed. Plural number was indicated either by the suffixes-me (or-me + esh), -hia, and –ene, or by reduplication, as in kur + Kur "mountains." The relational forms of the noun, corresponding approximately to the cases of the Latin declension, include: -e for the subject (nominative), -a(K) "of" (genitive), -ra and –sh(e) "to," "for" (dative), -a "in" (locative), -ta "from" (ablative), -da "with" (commutative). The Sumerian verb, with its concatenation of various prefixes, and suffixes, presents a very complicated picture. The elements connected with the verb follow a rigid order: modal elements, tempo elements, relational elements, causative elements, object elements, verbal root, subject elements, and intransitive present-future elements. In the preterite transitive active form, the order of object and subject elements is reversed. The verb can distinguish, in addition to person and number, transitivity and intransitivity, active and passive voice, and two tenses, present-future and preterite.

Several Sumerian dialects are known. Of these the most important are eme-gir, the official dialect of Sumerian, and eme-SAL, the dialect used often in the composition of hymns and incantations (see also cuneiform)."

The picture below is an illustration of cuneiform script taken from the Wikepedia, The Free Encyclopedia website.

Cuneiform Script

The children of Noah spoke Archaic Sumerian. They carried the language as given in The Table of Nations in *Genesis* to the different nations to which they were scattered who spoke different tongues. These scattered tribes were assimilated into other nations who eventually adopted the language and customs of their adopted country. Noah's children were scattered so that they could restore civilization and knowledge to the children of the temporal earth, having survived a great cataclysm and to bring knowledge of the one true God, THE EVER-LIVING. Not only was knowledge replenished but the animals and plants on the ark replenished the earth with new species.

In the *Book of Mormon* there is an account found in the *Book of Ether* 1:32-43, of the son of Jared with his brother and their families who were at the great tower at the time the Lord confounded the languages. Jared prayed unto the Lord to not confound the language of their families and of their friends. The Lord had compassion upon Jared, their friends and their families, and upon the brother of Jared; therefore he did not confound the language of Jared. Jared spoke the Holy Tongue. Jared, his brother, their families and friends were led by God to build barges and cross the ocean to the New World. They came to what is now called Central America approximately 2,800 B.C. (Re *The Giants* Volume One, pp. 363-373, for a more detailed account). After arriving to the New World, the new immigrants were called collectively, the Chichimecas. At least one branch of the Chichimecas, were the family and friends of Jared who spoke the Holy Tongue on this continent. It may have become extant with the extermination of the Giants who probably irrupted in the family of Jared.

There were other families, besides those of Jared, his brother, their families and friends, who came with them to the now Central American continent who spoke other languages. Of the twenty-four families who came, there is the possibility that at least twenty of those families spoke another tongue. By 2600 B.C., the oldest known language developed into what is known as Mam. It seems to have replaced or at least became the dominant language of that period. The U Mamae were named in Guatemalan (1554) writings as a group of people, who came with the first settlers. Maybe Mam was their spoken tongue or the language was named after them (Re Volume One, p. 360). The other tongues appear to have become extinct. Mam is still spoken today mainly in Guatemala.

Short Chronology of the Mayan Languages

2600 BC	Mam
1800 BC	Huastec
1600 BC	Yucatecan
1400 BC	Lacandon
900 BC	Chontal
750 BC	Tzeltal
400 BC	Tojolabal
200 BC	Quiche
100 BC	Kekchi

Perhaps the find of the century is the extraordinary discovery of two items near Lake Titicaca and Tiahuanco, Bolivia. Around 1958/60, Don Max Portugal Zamora, a Bolivian archeologist, learned of the existence of a libation bowl and a monolith statue that had been discovered by a Bolivian peasant farmer but was not shown until the year 2000. The bowl was named the Fuente Magna Bowl.

Fuente Bowl (front view)

Fuente Bowl (inside view)

The Fuente Bowl with Sumerian Cuneiform writing

The statue is called the Pokotia Monolith. Archeologists were stunned to find Sumerian writing on each of these objects. The artifacts have both cuneiform writing and Proto-Sumerian writing symbols on them.

Pokotia Statue (left). Detailed cuneiforms (above)

The only civilization known to have used both types of writing at the same time were the Sumerians. Anthropologist Mario Montano Aragon states "that the bowl shows itself to be the transitional period between ideographical writing and cuneiform. Chronologically, this leads us to the 3500/3000 B.C., Sumerian-Akkadian period." The

Pokotia statue and Tiahuanco monuments share similar headdresses and rib impressions along the chest area (Re *The Nephilim Evidence*).

Mario Montano has found linguistic evidence that supports the Sumerian presence in Bolivia. He has found startling linguistic evidence that indicates a Sumerian substratum in the Aymara and Quechua languages spoken in Bolivia, Peru, Northern Chile, and parts of Argentina. Sumerian terms in the Aymara language and Sumerian writing on the Fuente Magna Bowl and Pokotia statue make it obvious that the presence of a Sumerian civilization was formerly widespread in South America. It has been speculated that the Sumerians were there to mine tin and perhaps they were but in Volume One, pages 478-479, we wrote of Noah's grandsons, led by Votan, along with the "shining ones," who were directed by divine command to come to the Americas and restore civilization. Myths from the Andes tell us that this group of people came and settled among the people of Lake Titicaca some time after the Flood of Deucalion. This same group of people traveled and lived all over South America. They were able to do so because they lived for hundreds of years. The twelve "shining ones" were angelic disciples of the pre-mortal Christ, who accompanied them. Christ was known to the Aymara-Quichua speaking people as Viracocha. Noah's grandsons, Christ and the angelic "shining ones" spoke Archaic Sumerian called the Holy Tongue. They were the ones who brought the Sumerian presence to the South American people anciently. It is said that this group of people, the "shining ones," and Viracocha, brought agriculture, animal husbandry, medicine, metallurgy, writing and knowledge of the one true god to the South American people. It is evident from the style of writing found on the artifacts, that the bringers of knowledge came early (3000 B.C.). It is entirely possible that trade routes to the Old World were established as well, furthering a greater Sumerian presence. After all, some other grandsons of Noah were given the divine decree to go and remap the world following the great cataclysm. These maps were used extensively by all sea faring nations to cross the oceans (Re *Volume*. One, p. 477).

In addition to the above Sumerian finds, Moseley published a number of inscribed Moche/Mochica bricks (North coast of Peru 100 A.D.) and a Tiwanaku portrait head whose characters are identical to the Pokotia writing. These finds suggest that the Sumerian language continued to be spoken for an extended period of time in the Andean countries. Science is just now catching up.

The Sumerian language characters are compared to the Dravidian (India) and Mande (West African) languages. They show affinity in grammar and vocabulary. This is because at one time cuneiform was used to write: Hurrian, Hittite, Elamite, Akkadian, Sumerian, etc., therefore it is not surprising that the Sumerians, Minoans, Indus Valley people, Libyco-Berber people and Mande used the same writing. This brings us to the case in point that archeologists have tentatively identified Olmec symbols, found near the Olmec site of La Venta, Mexico, as Mande. It is not known for sure if the symbols are a form of writing and no decipherment has been made. The findings are still under study and are inconclusive to date. It is our opinion that linguists should look for Sumerian linguistic evidence in Mexico and Central America from 2700 B.C. to 500 A.D. If the Sumerians were present in South America during those years, there is high probability that they had a presence, at least a trading presence, in those countries as well. Even with the limited linguistic knowledge that your authors have, we have discovered a few word similarities between Maya and Sumerian/Akkadian language listed on a comparison chart below.

Sumerian/Akkadian	Maya	English Equivalents in both languages
A	Ha	Water
ABBA	BA	Father
BALA	PAL	Companion, also Pal
KUN	KIN	Daybreak, Day, Sun
NANA	NAA	Mother
SAR	ZAC	White
TAB	TAB	To place, to add, to be, to join, to write

Note: The letter Z in Maya is pronounced as an S sound, so ZAC would be pronounced SAC.

The Incas used beam scales of balance, like those of ancient Rome. They also used the decimal system and the old Sumerian sexagesimal system of measurement by six, twelve, and sixties. The decimal system is over 4,000 years old. Furthermore, the Incas had taken the decimal system from the ancient people of Chimu who had long been subjected to them. The Chimu had been familiar with the decimal system centuries before the Incas appeared which further collaborates our writings in Volume One that the Sumerian bringers of knowledge came to the ancient people of South America in remote times and restored knowledge and civilization.

Recently, while visiting the Museum of Anthropology in Mexico City, your authors made this remarkable find in the Olmec Room. The museum states that the Olmec civilization was made up of many different tribes and cultures. We found this stone head bust, pictured below, of a man, wearing a hat almost identical to the Tiahuanco statues. The Pokotia statue, found in Tiahuanco with Sumerian writing and dating to 3,000 B.C., also wears a similar style hat (refer to pictures in *The Nephilim Evidence*). This finding indicates an early Sumerian presence during Olmec times in Mexico.

Circa 2,000 B.C Sumerian Hat on Olmec head found in La Venta region of Mexico

During the millennium, it appears that men will once again have the ability to speak and write the Adamic language called the Holy Tongue. In that day the Lord says he will "turn to the people a *pure language*, that they may all call upon the name of the Lord, to serve him with one consent" (*Zephaniah* 3:9).

The Nephilim Evidence

This chapter is a continuation of *The Giants*, Volume One.

Much has been written, in other books as well as *The Ark of Millions of Years*, about the Nephilim and their giant offspring, but little has been offered as to what they looked like other than descriptions. These beings walked the earth with mortal men in ancient times as attested in early Sumerian, Assyrian, Egyptian, Hebrew, Greek, and Roman writings. Besides writings, much in oral traditions has also survived to present day times that acknowledge these beings were seen face to face by their ancestors, that they knew and served them as their gods. Not only did they write about these beings, but in some instances they drew or carved pictures of them on temple walls, tombs, pillared columns, and mountain sides. We have also included some drawn pictures that depict a belief in a particular god. Since there were no cameras around in those days to record their existence, the early civilizations resorted to the next best thing—stone or metal engravings. We believe that anthropologists and archeologists have misidentified some of what we are about to present or were at loss as to what the pictures or drawings represent.

Let us begin with the Gate of the Sun in Tiahuanaco, Bolivia.

The Gate of the Sun in Tiahuanaco

On the Sun Gate are many tiers of carved winged figures, some human-headed and some with heads of condors, tigers, and serpents. We believe them to be carved pictures of the Nephilim who were called Elder Gods. According to legend, the Elder Gods built Tiahuanaco in remote times past. Those with animal and bird heads probably were a symbolic representation of something associated with their name or ability. Below is a drawn copy of two of those images found on the Sun Gate.

Condor-Headed Nephilim on right

We believe the hand held staffs represent the Life Force creative power. The staff held by the condor-headed Nephilim, is divided which shows the twin nature of the creator, twins or opposite forces (yin and yang). We believe whoever made the carved images deified them as feathered serpents or creators. The Elder Gods were viewed as creators. When they mated with mortal women in that region, the results were giant offspring. There are a few surviving monolith statues which we believe to be "snap shot" pictures of their giant children. These monoliths are 23 feet high as pictured below. Archeologists call them simply "the idols."

Statue of Child of the Elder Gods

Note square head, eyes, and mouth. The right hand (hand on reader's right side) held object appears to be a book or scroll, the other a knife like object. The images appear to have a Sumerian influence (Sumerian hat style) that could be because the grandsons of Noah, the 12 shining ones, and Viracocha (pre-mortal Christ) were in

Tiahuanaco, re- establishing civilization to the survivors of the great cataclysm of 9,500 B.C.

Near-by is another 23 foot statue, called "El Fraile" pictured below. Note same hat style.

Statue of Child of the Elder Gods

Side View of Statue of Child of Elder Gods

In Nazca Peru, the famous "Owl Man" or the "Astronaut" is a drawing of a giant 98 foot figure of a man pointing to heaven with one arm raised and the other arm pointing to the ground. We believe that this could possibly be a picture of one of the giant offspring, maybe waving to an Elder God, in the region in ancient times, as pictured below.

The Owl Man

In Sumeria, the first evidence of female goddesses appears. There were female watchers who came to the temporal earth. Some mated with mortal men and others mated with male watchers, the Nephilim. In order to differentiate between male and female Nephilim, we wish to "coin" a new word for Webster. From this writing forward the female Nephilim will be called the nephertali. Pictured below is the Sumerian nephertali, Inanna (winged figure). Every large city in Sumer consecrated at least two temples to her worship. Note her size in comparison to the lion where rests her foot.

Akkadian Seal ca 2334-2154 B.C.

**The wingless Nephilim god of the sun, Utu,
seated on his throne found on the tablet of Sippar.**

Note his giant size in comparison with mortal earth men. His Akkadian name was Shamash. He was also called the god of justice or law. Nothing evil could escape his all seeing eye. All large centres, such as Babylon, Ur, Nippar, and Nineveh, had a temple dedicated to him.

Next is an Assyrian hawk headed Nephilim god. Note the similarity to the condor headed Nephilim god on the Tiahuanaco Sun Gate. This god was later known under the names of Thoth and Hermes. He has a pinecone in his hand, sprinkling purifying dust or symbolically transferring authority to kingship. Museums call these images Genii or protective spirits. Practically all the Nephilim are shown with a bucket in their hand. What the purpose is or what is contained in it is unknown, maybe the sanctifying dust?

Pinecones also represent regeneration or rebirth. Practically all civilizations associate pinecones with their gods. Even the Pope in Rome carries a pinecone symbol on his staff.

Winged Nephilim holding a pinecone in his right hand and his *bucket* in his left.

**Nephilim Elder God Holding a Deer. Panel from palace
of Sargon 11, Ninevah (720 B.C.), British Museum**

Assyrian Nephilim Elder God

Egyptian Statue of Winged Nephertali Isis

Next is the Nephilim Assyrian Elder God Ea, the fish god, known under the Akkadian name, as Enki, and who later would be known to the Greeks as Oannes. Enki was the main god of the Sumerian city of Eridu. Ea was responsible for teaching everything that is human to Homo sapiens; he was the source of all wisdom. Every

evening he retired to the sea. Enki may have even been an air-breathing fish being, similar to a dolphin. Note the hand held buckets which appear to be the signature identification of

The Assyrian Elder God Ea.

Nephilim as practically all pictured Nephilim are shown carrying the "pocket book."

Oannes, holding his bucket with the pinecone in his hand.

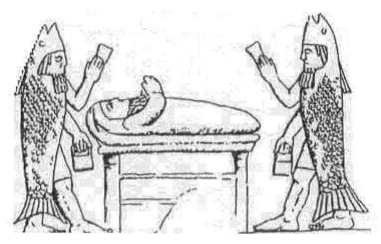

Oannes portrayed by Persian priests. Notice the bucket in the right hand.

Egyptian Nephilim God, Ra with ankh in right hand. The rod in his left hand is used to commute dimensional energy into the initiate. The ankh has been shown to greatly enhance this vibration. It's form is identical to the chakra energy lobes in the human body.

Although not pictured with wings, Ra does have a hawk head similar to the condor headed winged Nephilim found pictured on the Gate of the Sun. Could they be one and the same? Most probably, YES.

Indian Nephilim God, Rama

In Dorset England, the Cerne Abbas Giant is carved on a hillside in solid lines from the chalk bed rock. He measures 180 feet high and carries a huge knobbed club, which measures 120 feet in length. The figure dates to the 17th century but its style and proximity to an Iron Age earthwork suggests a much earlier origin.

Folklore tradition is that the figure is of a Danish giant who had led an invasion of England from the coast. He had fallen asleep on the side of the hill, and the local villagers had taken advantage of his slumber and cut off his head. They then drew around his prone body in the manner of a gigantic police chalk line, to show his size and where he met his doom. To view an actual photo of the site, just type in Cerne Abbas Giant on your search engine. The picture below is a drawn copy of the actual site.

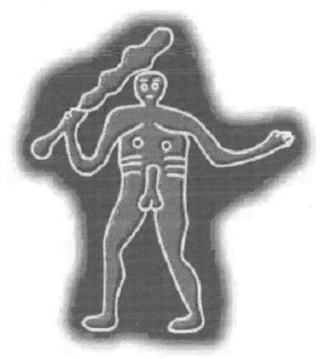

Cerne Abbas Giant

Nephertali Isis with her bucket pocketbook in her left had and her serpent rattle in her right hand. She is the Egyptian goddess of fertility and wife of Osiris. Shaking the rattle was said to be the lullaby force in nature, bringing it back into balance when things became unstable.

While visiting Mexico City in November 2005, your authors went to the ruins of Teotihuacan. Our driver, an Aztec descendant, took us to a part of the ruins seldom seen by tourist where we made this remarkable find, pictured below.

Winged Nephilim Aztec God with Pocket Book at Teotihuacan, Mexico.

The above picture literally changes everything previously thought about the Aztec gods. It shows that the Nephilim were present in Mesoamerica. Apparently the same thing that happened in Babylonia was happening in Mesoamerica as well. These fallen angels were being worshiped as gods. The indigenous people were building temples to them in every city and providing them with mortal women of their choice. It happened all over Mesoamerica with no consideration to tribes whether Aztec, Mayan, Olmec, Zapotec, etc. They all were worshipping the fallen host of heaven and giants were being produced as documented in Volume One (Re *The Giants* Volume One).

Ruins of Teotihuacan, Mexico. Standing on the Temple of the Moon, looking down the Street of the Dead. The grassy dust reclaims the smaller structures in only three years old.

The following stone picture is rather unusual in that it shows a Nephilim god, with his pocket book, encircled by a dragon (Life Force?) His headdress is also unusual. Object was found in the La Venta region of Mexico, now in Mexico City Museum of Anthropology.

Nephilim god with pocket book found in La Venta region of Mexico. He appears to be in the act of "flying" in a machine, driven by the life force.

The picture above shows a Nephilim god with stylized wings in the act of beheading an enemy. They taught all manner of warfare, murder, and human sacrifice to the children of men. Object displayed in Mexico City Museum of Anthropology

E.J. Clark making close examination of Aztec/Mayan Nephilim god with his pocketbook. Notice the butterfly breastplate. This statue is on display in the Mexico Museum of Anthropology.

An <u>outstanding</u> archeological treasure found in the Mexico Museum of Anthropology! A Nephilim *teaching circle*. The students appear to be in the act of praying, while the Nephilim hold their Zodiac constellation plates and tell the story of creation. Note the obvious difference in size between the Nephilim, with their stylized wings, and the people.

A replica mural carefully repainted outside the Mexico Museum of Anthropology depicting multiple Nephilim gods with fringed carpet stylized wings. These figures were originally painted with a mold that turns red when mixed with water. The large number of winged beings, and the widespread use of feathers by human dancers and priests in imitation of these beings, is clear evidence of their prominence in ancient America.

This picture was made by the authors. Because of the gradual vaulting of the ceiling and poor lighting, the images are the best we could get under the circumstances. The original murals are to be found in the Mayan ruins of Bonampak.

E.J. is touching the *pocketbook* of the Tula Giants—offspring of the Nephilim—atop the temple. Archaeologists have named them the Atlantes, believed to be protective spirits of dead warriors. The fact is, they were giants and warriors, which made them easy to worship for a people that averaged 5 feet in height.

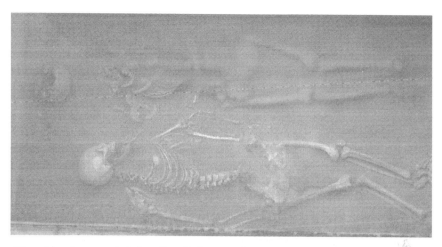

The stone box containing the skeletons of a husband and wife in the Aztec ruins of Cuicuilco Mexico City were found under an altar in a nearby pyramid. He was over 7 feet tall and was said to be able to knock a horse to the ground with one blow of his fist.

Our driver was a direct descendant of Aztecs. He testified that the ancient Aztecs were a very tall race. After mixing with local indigenous peoples, and centuries of poor diet, the overall height has dropped to around 5 feet 6 inches.

The evidence presented in this chapter is only a hundredth part of what is available to witness world wide. We were not able to survey some countries such as China, Africa, Tibet, and the Middle East. With what we have written here, one would think the proof irrefutable and incontrovertible. Yet, these claims may not fit the established interpretation of anthropology in the modern world. Search the items out for yourself, and you will see that we are right. Truth is truth.

The Spiraling Life Force

This chapter is a continuation of the chapter, *The Interaction of Universes*, Volume One.

A brief review: The spiraling Life Force is a name for the etheric energy substance that travels through the dimensions in spirals and was called the etheric "water" of the cosmic ocean. It is this all pervading, omnipresent substance that exists in inexhaustible quantities, extending through the immensity of space that is the light, the life, and the power of all things.

Almost all ancient cultures had a name for this energy substance. To the medieval magicians it was called "Astral Fluid," to the Kabbalists "Fiery Water," the "Life Force," "Spiraling Life Force," "Serpent Fire," and "Solar Spirit." The Polynesians called it "Manna." The Hindus refer to this substance as "Prana" and the Chinese refer to it as "Chi" (pronounced Ki by the Japanese). It was known to the Egyptians as "Ka." The American Indians referred to the Life Force as Orenda (Iroquois), Wakan (Sioux), and Manitou (Algonquins).

The Mayans called it the "Plumbed Serpent." To the Hebrews it is called the "water of life," and Christians call it the "Holy Spirit." Today's scientists approximate it with electro-magnetic energy, which is actually a densification of the "Life Force" but similarly travels in spirals.

In *The Interaction of Universes,* Volume One, we established that the Life Force energy was generated by gigantic rapidly rotating generator stars located in the highest spiritual universe in the fifth dimension. The energy is then channeled down to the lower universes, both spiritual and physical, passing through filters or curtains that separate the great universes. The veils act as a filter to channel the correct amount of energy required for that universe. Without the filtering veils, the energy is so strong that it could destroy universes. It is what keeps all that is contained in the great universes in sync.

Every thing in our universe receives energy from the Life Force, including our earth. The ancients knew that this form of energy entered our planet at certain energy conductive points called "vortexes" or "dragon lairs." These collecting points then dispersed the energy around the planet throughout a "world grid" network of energy channels called dragon lines, dragon paths, straight paths, spirit paths, or ley lines. These vortexes where the spiraling energy was strongest were often identified with inscribed recurring spirals somewhere upon the site. Ex: Carved on a cliff or carved on temple blocks. In the illustration below, the powerful vortexes are the dark dots with ring like spokes radiating outward like a wheel, connecting to the light colored ley lines and heavy black lines. The heavy black lines are energy lines that seem to be naturally generated, although as yet, not understood.

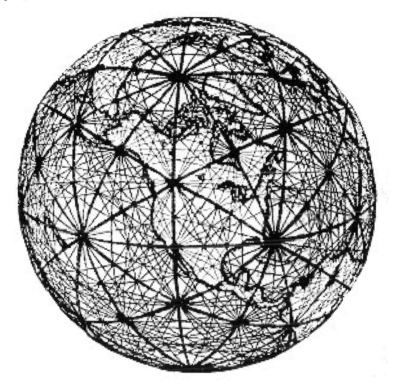

The World Grid Energy Network

Now the most amazing thing, outside of the Life Force itself, is the Tzolk'in *Dreamspell* calendar because it has the ability to time and measure the Life Force frequency. Within the cycle of the 260 day Tzolk'in *Dreamspell*, there is a 13 galactic cycle associated with the "galactic tones" and a 20 day solar cycle associated with the solar tribe/day glyphs. These two smaller cycles rotate together and overlap to form the 260 day cycle. This is the cycle of 4th dimensional time, which comes into the solar system from the galaxy. It runs concurrently with the Mayan Long Count 365 day cycle of the year, to create 4th dimensional time as it applies to this solar system. In other words, time is a frequency that can be measured. In theory, time travel might be possible by utilizing or accessing the correct frequency or "galactic tones" in the universes. Think of the "galactic tones" as cosmic highways of rapid transit into the future or past by traveling on frequencies. Essentially this is what shaman or priests have done when they opened an interdimensional portal in a vortex and may be the mode of travel in those individuals who have had an out of the body experience (OBE's). These individuals have simply "tuned in" to the time travel frequency, whether by accident or intentional.

Dr. Jose Arguelles is considered by some to be a pioneer in new interpretations of the Mayan Tzolk'in calendar which work was published in *Dreamspell,* a book he co-authored. It is important to note that the ancient Tzolk'in calendar is not the same as the 13 moon *Dreamspell* Tzolk'in calendar, although both offer a 260-day calendar. Dr. Jose Arguelles decoded the Sacred Calendar of the Maya and in so doing made the discovery of the 4th dimensional codes of time. In a work created with the assistance of his wife Lloydine, known as the *Dreamspell*, they reveal these codes and correlate the current Gregorian calendar to the cycles of time identified in the Sacred Calendar of the Mayans. The modern interpretations of Dr. Argüelles are both cosmic and spiritual which incidentally agree with our writings in both books. Indeed, his work is a modern application of ancient science. Labeled a New Age author, his work is often dismissed because the Maya did not use his form of calendar, however in our third up-coming book, now in writing stage, we offer evidence that new age thinking is nothing more than resurrected ancient thought that the Maya did understand. Dr. Arguelles writes:

"The *Dreamspell* Count based on the Gregorian calendar synchronization date of July 26, is a precise expression of the prophetic tradition of the Chilam Balam - the Jaguar priests of Lowland Yucatec Maya. The Quiche or Mayan Long Count represents the chronological order of time...as such, it is a linear [expression] of the Tzolk'in....The purpose of the Chilam Balam Count was to establish a basis for understanding that there exists a synchronic order of time, completely apart from what is usually referred to as the Long Count, the linear count of days (B.C. 3114 – A.D. 2012). The synchronic order is complementary to this linear interpretation, but introduces the human to the radial order of the higher dimensions... The two counts, actually constitute a prophetic alliance....There is no conflict....The Law of Time embraces both systems in the higher fourth-dimensional order of truth."

The users of the *Dreamspell* calendar, both ancient and modern, understand that the Life Force travels through the dimensions in waves or cycles of pulsing energy and throughout the cosmos in cycles of 13. This is the reason the ancients considered the number 13 "sacred." The energy travels on a timed frequency, known as "galactic tones", from 13 millennia to 13 micro seconds and beyond. If you convert the "galactic tones" or frequencies into music, one could literally hear the music of the spheres playing throughout the universes. Some people have the ability to hear the earth's "galactic tones" and have reported hearing a steady, pulsing, low frequency hum. Attempts to locate the hum were futile and unexplained. These reports are world wide and many have been thoroughly investigated as to cause, but to date remain unsolved. The *OM HUM*, is a low frequency hum done by Tibetan Buddhist priests and is the replicated sound of the Life Force energy known to Buddhists as Prana. OM is the primal vibration out of which all things came forth and into which all things will be absorbed at the end of a cosmic cycle, every atom vibrates with it.

Aura's are manifestations of the Life Force energy that surround, encompass and permeate all living things. The human aura is Life Force energy similar to a force field protecting and vitalizing every cell in the body. Everyone sighted can learn to see auras around any living object, providing they are taught the technique of how to see them. Sensitive finger tips can even feel this energy, when moved over a human body.

The disciplines of Yoga awaken the Kundalini (Life Force or Dragon) from its seat at the base of the spine which kindles the serpent fire. Through meditation the serpent fire can easily move up the spine, through seven major chakras or vortexes, in spirals like the serpents of the caduceus, uniting at the top of the head producing balance or polarity union thus spiritual enlightenment can be attained by the Life Force stimulation of the inner or third eye, sometimes referred to as the spiritual eye, located in the forehead.

The ancient Tzolk'in calendar uses a system of 13 galactic cycles or pulses. The 13-day pulse cycle builds up like a wave for the first 5 to 6 days and then peaks on days 7, 8, and 9. Day 8 is referred to as the crown of the 13-day pulse of the Life Force and is a preferred day for ceremony and Shamanic activity in many of the Maya lands. Utilizing days that are Life Force charged are advantageous for the success of planting crops, when to travel, when to harvest, when to make business deals etc. A distinguishing difference between the ancient Tzolk'in calendar and the *Dreamspell* calendar is that users of the *Dreamspell* calendar say it is the "natural time" of things in this universe that promotes harmony and spiritual well being. Furthermore, they say users of other calendars are not in sync with the natural order of things, causing planetary harmonic discord or chaos resulting in the loss of spiritual consciousness. The *Dreamspell* does not utilize days favorable for planting of crops, times to harvest, when to travel, days for business deals etc. as does the ancient Tzolk'in calendar.

A modernization of the *Dreamspell* Tzolk'in calendar, by Jose Arguelles, produced a "loom," as it is called, of 52 black squares, each representing a heightened energy pattern, known as *galactic activation portals.* Jose, believed the black square configurations closely resemble the DNA double helix of human genetics, which admittedly it does, but your authors believe it also is a "snap shot" picture of the spiraling Life Force energy that travels in waves. The DNA double helix design depicted below in the shaded portion of the calendars is found woven in Mayan, Toltec, and Zapotec blankets. The pattern and design of the DNA double helix woven into their blankets has been in use for at least 2,000 years. The first illustration is the old *Dreamspell* Tzolk'in calendar version and the second illustration is the modern updated version.

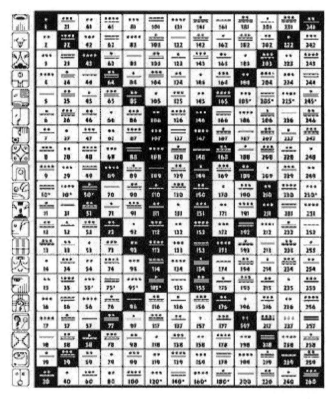

The Day Glyph Table of the Dreamspell Tzolkin Calendar

The Sacred Mayan Tzolkin

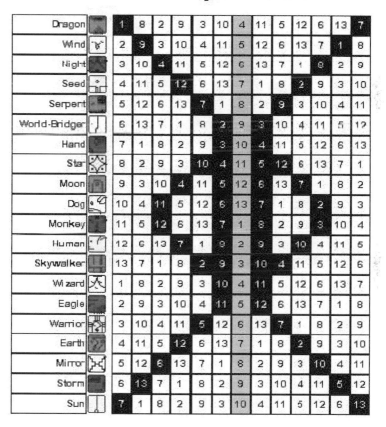

Dragon	1	8	2	9	3	10	4	11	5	12	6	13	7
Wind	2	9	3	10	4	11	5	12	6	13	7	1	8
Night	3	10	4	11	5	12	6	13	7	1	8	2	9
Seed	4	11	5	12	6	13	7	1	8	2	9	3	10
Serpent	5	12	6	13	7	1	8	2	9	3	10	4	11
World-Bridger	6	13	7	1	8	2	9	3	10	4	11	5	12
Hand	7	1	8	2	9	3	10	4	11	5	12	6	13
Star	8	2	9	3	10	4	11	5	12	6	13	7	1
Moon	9	3	10	4	11	5	12	6	13	7	1	8	2
Dog	10	4	11	5	12	6	13	7	1	8	2	9	3
Monkey	11	5	12	6	13	7	1	8	2	9	3	10	4
Human	12	6	13	7	1	8	2	9	3	10	4	11	5
Skywalker	13	7	1	8	2	9	3	10	4	11	5	12	6
Wizard	1	8	2	9	3	10	4	11	5	12	6	13	7
Eagle	2	9	3	10	4	11	5	12	6	13	7	1	8
Warrior	3	10	4	11	5	12	6	13	7	1	8	2	9
Earth	4	11	5	12	6	13	7	1	8	2	9	3	10
Mirror	5	12	6	13	7	1	8	2	9	3	10	4	11
Storm	6	13	7	1	8	2	9	3	10	4	11	5	12
Sun	7	1	8	2	9	3	10	4	11	5	12	6	13

**The Day Glyph Table of the Dreamspell Tzolkin Calendar
with the names added**

The following illustrations are a few of the many that symbolize the spiraling Life Force.

The Galactic Butterfly

The above illustration was named the Galactic Butterfly and woven into blanket designs by the Maya, Toltec, and Zapotec peoples. Recently it was renamed the Hunab Ku which is a Mayan term for the principle of intelligent Life Force energy that pervades the entire universe.

Swirling Life Force Symbols. These are the oldest crosses known to man and appear in every civilization ancient or modern.

Spiraling Life Force Energy Symbol

An American, John Worrel Keely, the Father of sympathetic vibratory physics, stated in the late 19th century, "Ether is dynamic vibratory energy." Keely wrote in 1893: "Everything is space, and space is everything. This space is ether (Life Force) vibratory energy. There is no dividing of matter and force into two distinct terms, as they both are one. Force is liberated matter. Matter is force in bondage" (Pond, 1996, p. 90).

Keely even invented machinery which was driven by the Life Force energy, but his theories and inventions were opposed by organizations with vested interests, to which he eventually gave up. He was a man far ahead of his time.

There is a phenomenon currently being experienced by many people world wide. This is the feeling that time has speeded up, yet the clock still ticks to the rate of 60 minutes per hour and 24 hours in a day. The sensation manifests as " time is flying by," " there isn't enough hours in the day," " is it Christmas already ", or " where has time gone." It is a sense of things speeding up and not enough time to get things done. It is hurry to work, hurry to drop the kids off to school, hurry to get home, hurry this and hurry that, hurry, hurry, hurry. Time is running out sensation etc. And, it seems that the older you get, the more noticeable this phenomenon becomes.

The following is your author's explanation for what is occurring. The Life Force energy is dynamic vibratory energy. It is very much in motion and this motion always follows a vortex path. It moves in a vortex or spiraling fashion because the vortex provides least resistance to the flowing motion. As all spiraling vortexes do, they accelerate in speed, like water going down a drain. The Life Force energy enters our universe from other dimensions. It is the mysterious, elusive substance that scientists have dubbed "dark energy." As this energy flows into our universe, it fills space between existing unseen matter. As space between existing matter becomes "filled up," expansion of the universe occurs. At some points in the universe, the expansion is occurring at the speed of light. Instead of dissipating, some of this energy returns back to other dimensions and some is converted into "dark matter," light, and heat. The real culprit causing our planet to "heat up," may be the Life Force energy converting into heat because the entire universe is experiencing a "warming period." Galaxies and solar systems do not expand because of gravitational forces preventing it. Furthermore, its not that the galaxies are moving, its that the space between them is expanding and it is indeed expanding as scientist have observed from the red shift.

The Prophet Mohammed apparently was aware of the expanding universe. The Qur'an says in Surrah Dhariyat, ch. 51, verse no. 47:

" We have created the expanding universe."

The spiraling energy is not measurable or observable to us at a physical level, because it is an implicate structure existing at a hyper-dimensional level but our bodies feel or have the sense of acceleration because the Life Force is part of us, even our blood flows in a spiraling motion through our veins. As the spirals tighten or weave in their flow, throughout the universe, the energy speed accelerates. The more energy pouring into our universe, the greater the acceleration, and the faster the expansion. Here is where it gets interesting. The acceleration and expansion may be interacting with the Time Frequency, causing it to speed up as well. It is the interaction with the Time Frequency and the acceleration of the Life Force energy that we are experiencing which gives us the illusion that earth time, as we measure it, is speeding up. Aging human bodies become more attuned to the vibratory energy from many years of interaction experience, thereby the phenomenon is more noticeable the older they become.

Today, scientists are realizing that there is some kind of bizarre form of fundamental energy that pervades space and interacts with matter that is, in effect, gravitationally repulsive. In fact, WMAP has confirmed the existence of a dark energy that acts like anti-gravity, driving the universe to accelerate its expansion. NEWS FLASH! Since ancient times, practically all cultures have known about and have given different names for this very same all pervading energy that we call the Spiraling Life Force.

In all probability, the anti-gravity portion of this form of energy was used to levitate heavy objects in ancient times. Apparently Keely rediscovered the secrets of the vibratory energy and invented machinery that could be driven by its power. Edward Leedskalnin, in the 1930's, claimed to have re-discovered this form of energy. With only primitive tools, he raised and set blocks of stone weighing many tons. Single handed he constructed a complex known today as the Coral Castle, in Florida. He cut and moved blocks greater than those used to build the Great Pyramid, without electricity. For some unknown reason, he refused to share his knowledge with the world, taking his secret to the grave. Vast wealth and riches, beyond compare, await the man or woman, who can once again re-discover how to unlock the secrets of the Life Force energy.

Whether by accident or fate, E. J. Clark recently met a scientist in Puerto Rico who claims to have re-discovered and harnessed this form of energy. In fact, he has a patent pending. E.J. told him (he wishes to remain anonymous) " I have just written a chapter on the Life Force energy and now I'm talking to the one who has harnessed it.

What are the odds that I would run into you, apparently by accident, in Puerto Rico?" Over several days, a flurry of information and ideas were exchanged. If indeed his discovery is patented, we are sure it will revolutionize everything we use in modern civilization.....
and.... **we do mean everything.**

The Wheel of Time Untime

This chapter is a continuation of *The Future World* from Volume One.

Did the ancient Maya, Toltec, or Aztec of Mexico and Central America and the North American band of THE THUNDERBOLTS Cherokee of northern Tennessee and Kentucky share a similar calendar device for measuring time? The Cherokee called this device the WHEEL of TIME UNTIME. The following is an ancient account of this device:

"And brought among the people was the WHEEL of TIME UNTIME, the calendar of the Cherokee, wheels upon wheels, markings upon markings, TIME UNTIME."

From the legend we learn that the Cherokee, at one time, apparently had a wheel like calendar device, maybe with moving parts, to measure time. The problem is no evidence has ever been found thus far, that any ancient civilization on the North American continent ever had such a device, with the exception of the Aztec

Sun Stone   and Native American Medicine Wheels, noting both had no moving parts. Yet, the Cherokee legend suggests other wise. From this point forward we will refer to the WHEEL OF TIME as the WHEELS OF TIME or in the plural as more than one wheel was probably involved. In theory, if such a device did exist, the **Wheels of TIME** moving forward could measure the present time and future calendrical and astrological events. Again, in theory, if the wheels were moved backward as the undoing of time, past events such as eclipses, could be recalled on a certain date, thus the name of **TIME UNTIME.** By counting the number of revolutions of each wheel, it could be possible to project thousands of years into the future and into the past. For example, some Maya monuments record the dates of events 90 million years ago, while others predict events that will take place 3,000 years into the future. By looking at the markings that coincided with each notch on the wheels, future events could be predicted and past events could be recalled. In addition to tracking days, such a device could also be employed to measure cosmic time based on cycles of the planets, sun, and stars. If such a marvelous device did exist in ancient Mesoamerica, it would explain how their astronomers were able to track and keep extremely accurate measures of time. Just because archeologists haven't found such a device, doesn't mean that they didn't exist. Rather, they are waiting to be discovered.

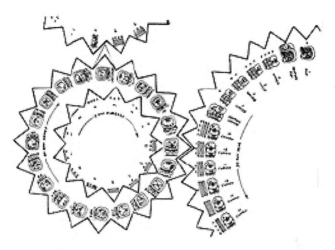

The Theorized Wheels of Time Untime

However, it is a proven fact that the Maya did have a remarkable complex calendar and number system for tracking time. Without getting into the complicated mechanics of understanding the Mayan calendar, we will touch only on the basics because the Maya understood 17 different calendars based on the cosmos. These calendars, some which calculate back as far as ten million years, are so difficult that one would need to employ an army of astronomers, astrologers, geologists, and mathematicians, just to work out the calculations.

It is fortunate for us that we need to work with only three of these calendars, the Haab, the Tzolk'in, and the Mayan Long Count. Of the three, the Tzolk'in is considered the most important because it has the most influence.

The Haab, or Vague Year, of 365 days is similar to our modern calendar, consisting of 18 months of 20 days each, with an unlucky five-day period at the end. The secular calendar of 365 days had to do primarily with the seasons and agriculture, and was based on the solar cycle. The 18 Maya months are known, in order, as: Pop, Uo, Zip, Zotz, Tzec, Xuc, Yaxkin, Mol, Chen, Yax, Zac, Ceh, Mac, Kankin, Maun, Pax, Kayab and Cumku. The unlucky five-day period was known as *uayeb*, and was considered an ominous time which could precipitate danger, death and bad luck.

The ancient Tzolk'in (pronounced Zol Keen) is the divine or religious calendar of the Maya used to determine important activities related to life events. It was used to name individuals, predict the future, decide on auspicious dates for battles, marriages, and so on. Each single day had its omens and associations, and the inexorable march of the 20 days was like a perpetual fortune-telling machine, guiding the destinies of the Maya. It consisted of 13 months, each month being 20 days long. This calendar uses the sacred numbers of 13 and 20. The 13 represents the numbers and 20 represents the sun or day glyphs. It was composed of 260 days called the Sacred Round and "Short Count" calendar. It paired the numbers 1 through 13 with a sequence of the 20 day name glyphs shown below. For example, 1 IMIX would be similar to Sunday the 1st, followed by 2-IK or Monday the 2nd, etc. When you get to 13 BEN, the numbers start over again, thus 1-IX, 2-MEN, 3-KIB etc. It will take 260 days before the cycle gets back to 1-IMIX again. (13 x 20) Within this calendar are four smaller cycles called seasons of 65 days and there are also Portal days that create a double helix pattern using 52 days and the mathematics of 28. In the 260-day ancient Tzolk'in and *Dreamspell Tzolkin,* time does not run along a line, but moves in a repeating circle similar to a spiral. The Portal days apparently were capable of measuring interdimensional and cosmic time. The concept of zero was also understood by the Maya, who wrote it like a shell glyph. Even trying to explain the basic Mayan calendar can become a very complex thing. The name, meaning, and symbols can vary in different Maya dialects, further complicating translation. Even the colors on the glyphs have meaning. The elaborate glyphs were a formal writing system of the Maya.

IMIX	IK'	AK'BAL	K'AN
ee mesh	*eek'*	*ok bol*	*k' on*
waterlily, world	wind	night-house	maize

CHIKCHAN	KIMI	MANIK'	LAMAT
cheek chon	*kee me*	*ma neek'*	*lamot*
snake	death	hand	Venus

MULUK'	OK	CHUEN	EB
mul ok'	*ak*	*chew*	*ineb*
water	dog	monkey	tooth

BEN	IX	MEN	KIB
ben	*eesh*	*men*	*keeb*
reed	jaguar	eagle	soul

Tzolk'in Sun or Day Symbols

The "Calendar Round" or "WHEELS of TIME" are best described as two interlocking gears, one smaller than the other. One of the gears is called the Tzolk'in, or "Sacred Round" and the other is the Haab. As both these theoretical wheels turned, so in theory passed the Mayan calendar cycles. Neither the Tzolk'in nor the Haab system numbered the years. It took 52 years for the Tzolk'in and Haab calendars to move concurrently through a complete cycle, called a Calendar Round. Smaller cycles of 13 days (the *trecena*) and 20 days (the *veintena*) were also important components of the Tzolk'in and Haab cycles, respectively. The traditional Maya in the highlands of Guatemala, Belize, and other parts of Central America still use the Sacred Calendar or Tzolk'in for divination and religious purposes. When a Mayan child is born, a reading is done by the "day keepers" of the Tzolk'in to forecast the child's destiny. The day glyphs determine the destiny, such as occupation best suited for a person, and if they do not follow the destiny the calendar determines, it is believed that the person will neither find success nor fulfillment in life. A child born on a bad day received its name on a good day, to rule out all harmful effects of the bad day. This is not to be confused with an astrology forecast because the Tzolk'in calendar bases its readings from an entirely different system not based on the astrology signs.

The linking of the Tzolk'in and the Haab calendars resulted in a longer cycle of 18,980 days, or approximately a 52 solar year cycle. Because the 52-year cycle was inadequate to measure the continual passage of time through the ages, it became necessary to devise another new calendar, called the Long Count. The Maya calendar uses these three (Tzolk'in, Haab, and Long Count) different dating systems in parallel. For example, a typical Mayan date looks like this: 12.18.15.2.6, 3 Cimi 4 Zotz

12.18.16.2.6 is the Long Count date

3 Cimi is the Tzolk'in date

4 Zotz is the Haab date

Theorized Tzolk'in and Haab Calendar Wheels

Using the Mayan Long Count calendar a day was called a "kin", and still is today. A 20 day month was a "uinal", one solar year was a "tun", 20 tuns a "katun", and 20 katuns a "baktun", 13 of which take us back to the starting date of the Mayan Long Count calendar, August 13, 3114 B.C. The term "long count" means to calculate or count the days since a certain day or date. Why this particular date? Because it was the end of the 4th Sun and the beginning of the 5th Sun. On August 13, 3,114 B.C. the sun conjoined The Sacred Tree or the

Milky Way marking the end of the 4th Sun. Approximately every 5,125 years the sun aligns with the center of the Milky Way Galaxy or Sacred Tree. When this occurs it marks the end of a Sun. The Great Year was then divided by these lesser sun cycles of 5,125 years to produce 5 world ages. The first 4 world ages have been destroyed. We live in the 5th world age that is predicted to be destroyed by earthquakes in December 2012; the first four having being destroyed by jaguars, wind, rain, and water. It is believed that the Long Count calendar was begun by the pre-Maya around 355 B.C., but there is reason to believe that the Long Count was being perfected by at least 200 years earlier. The Chichimecas either brought the knowledge of the ancient Tzolk'in calendar to this continent when they arrived here from the Middle East, or were given the knowledge from the Nephilim, or obtained it from Quetzalcoatl during his early travels in South America, Central America, and Mexico. The *Book of Mormon* actually records one of the Lords (Quetzalcoatl) early visits to the Nephites/Toltecs/Zapotecs/Mulekites of ancient Mexico in *Mosiah* 27:7, probably between 100 and 92 B.C. Due to the complexity of the Mayan calendar, only the priests were capable to work the calculations necessary to predict growing seasons for crops and various astronomical events for religious rites. It was also consulted as a type of astrology forecast on a particular day by individuals seeking advice. For the priests it was a sort of "job security" to be the only ones able to do the calculations. By knowing when to plant, when to harvest, when the rainy and dry seasons would occur, knowing the times of the equinoxes in relation with the movement of the sun, and other astrological events such as predicting eclipses, etc., gave them total power and control over the people. It appeared to the people that the priests had a sort of "magical power" given to them by the gods. Where did the Preclassic Maya acquire the knowledge of the calendar, knowledge of the cosmos, and knowledge of the spiritual dimensions? Without first reading *The Ark of Millions of Years* Volume One, it will be impossible to fully understand the answer. If the *Book of Mormon* is an ancient Toltec record, then the *Book of Mormon* people, namely the Nephites, Lamanites, Mulekites and Jaredites, can be correlated by current research to most likely fit the Toltecs (Nephites), Zapotec/Xicalancas (Mulekites), Nonoalca Maya of Classic Period, 200 A.D.- 900 A.D. (Lamanites), and Olmecs (Jaredites). When one does this, then the *Book of Mormon* changes its perspective and becomes an exciting read.

According to ancient traditions, the Toltecs/Nephites were learned in the arts of astronomy and other sciences. They were alleged to be the ones who gave the calendar system to the Preclassic Maya. There is much supporting evidence to indicate some of the Toltecas were a branch of the earlier Zapotecs, also Nephites/Mulekites, their culture dating to 500 B.C. The *Book of Mormon* states the Mulekites (Zapotec/Xicalancas) and Nephites (Toltecs) united to form one nation, possibly around 300-200 B.C. Archeology records give supporting evidence as they show the two cultures had a close relationship because Toltec cities had living quarters for Zapotec visitors and Zapotec cities had living quarters for Toltec visitors. The Zapotecs had a system of writing, a dot- and- bar system of numbering, employed a 365-day solar calendar called *yza*, and used a 260-day sacred calendar called the *pyie*. These two calendars also interlocked in parallel to create a 52 year cycle called a Calendar Round. Oral traditions say the Zapotecs and Toltecs had a similar writing and numbering system which they shared, later to be perfected by the Toltecs. In fact, the Zapotec writing system is considered to be the oldest and the basis of all other Mesoamerican writing systems unless the Olmec symbols dating to 650 B.C. prove to be an earlier form of writing, still under debate. On the other hand, the *Book of Mormon* states the Nephite culture (Toltecs 500 B.C.) were preceded by the early Zapotec/Xicalanca culture (Mulekites 600 B.C.) by 100 years, which statement remains yet to be proven, and they (Nephites) brought with them a system of writing. The earliest Zapotec writings show up around 500 B.C. We cannot date Toltec writing, for the manuscripts which were read by Ixtilxochitl, those found by Boturini, and interpreted by Veytia, have disappeared. The Toltecs merged as a nation about 700 A.D., maybe springing from the Teotihuacán culture. Much of what we know about the Toltecs is legendary. These findings do not mean the Toltecs/Nephites didn't use a writing and numbering system much earlier, but instead the findings in legends indicate they were the founders of civilization in Mesoamerica, even founders of writing, astronomy, medicine, arts, agriculture, used a numbering system and were reputed to be the founders of a calendar system. Legends say the early Toltecas were an advanced people in knowledge, particularly in the sciences. A clue is found in the *Book of Mormon* wherein it states that the Mulekites/

Xicalancas/Zapotecs were much more numerous than the Nephites/ Toltecs. Because the Toltecs/Nephites were fewer in number, they may have existed as a minor culture perhaps within the larger culture of Chichimec Toltecs and were accounted for as Toltecas, assuming the *Book of Mormon* people were the Toltecs, Zapotecs, Olmecs and Maya. For example, within the United States are many sub cultures (Chinese, Mexicans, Germans, Irish, Polynesians etc.) but they are all called Americans. Also, there appears to be distinguishing names of Toltecs. There are the Toltecs (possibly Nephites) and there are the Chichimeca Toltecs. This finding indicates a sub culture amid the Toltec nation. Again, the *Book of Mormon* supports this theory as it gives an account of the Nephite destruction as a nation in 385 A.D., the result of warfare following a long process of extermination by their enemies, yet 315 years later, the Chichimee Toltecs as a culture dominate the scene. Some Mulekites (Xicalancas) appear to have merged with the Zapotecs, therefore we will call them Zapotecs hereafter. As one can see, more research needs to be done in this area, if we are to find the answers. Quetzalcoatl is also attributed to have given knowledge of the calendar, writing, making books, and architecture to the Maya as founder of their religion. The early Maya called him Kukulcan, the Mayan word for feathered serpent. The Zapotecs, Toltecs, and Aztecs called him Quetzalcoatl. He was also called Ehecatl and Yolcuat.

It is altogether possible that the Toltecs/Nephites/Zapotecs/ Mulekites and Quetzalcoatl worked together to perfect their calendar system and passed the knowledge on to the Preclassic Maya, for it is now known that the Maya adopted their calendar system from an earlier culture. Legends speak of Quetzalcoatl having lived among the Toltec/ Nephite/ Zapotec/ Mulekite people for various periods of time and in different locations, which suggest that he traveled and lived among various tribes. *The Book of Mormon* recorded one of these visits in 3 *Nephi* chapters 11 through 17. In addition, *The Book of Mormon* in *Mormon* 9:32, and verse 34, validates that the Nephites/ Toltecs brought with them to this continent a system of writing which was later changed into a system that only they understood. The Preclassic Maya probably patterned their terminology and style of writing after the Toltec/Nephite/Zapotec/Mulekite style; however the placing of the characters to form the words would be different (Mayan glyphs).

The Aztecs used a sacred calendar called the Tonalpohualli, a 260-day calendar borrowed from the Mayan Tzolk'in system with some modifications added. This ritual calendar was registered in the Tonalamatls (*Book of Days* or *Book of Fates of Men*), a green-fold bark paper or deerskin codex's. The most famous example of this calendar is the Aztec Calendar Stone, more correctly called the Aztec Sun Stone, the centerpiece of the National Museum of Anthropology in Mexico City. The Aztec Stone was carved during the reign of the 6th Aztec monarch in 1479. It has a diameter just under 12 feet, a thickness of 3 feet, and weighs almost 25 tons. In the center of this stone is the sun god, Tonatiuh. He is surrounded by symbols of the five world creations. The outer ring contains the sun or day glyphs. Encoded in the central panel is the date 4 Ollin which correlates to the

Mayan end time date of December 21, 2012, when they anticipated the current world or the fifth age would be destroyed by earth quakes. Below is an incomplete illustration (missing its outer rings) of the Aztec Sun Stone by Robert Sieck Flandes, nevertheless it gives clear sight to the central panel. Below that illustration is an actual picture of the stone, taken by your authors in November 2005, in the Museum of Anthropology, Mexico City.

Stylized Aztec Sun Stone commonly seen in Mexico

The Aztec Sun Stone

Prior to the conquering of the New World, the Europeans believed that Native Americans were ignorant of astronomy, when in fact, it was quiet the opposite. The Native Americans employed a completely different concept of astronomy so foreign not to be recognized by European astronomers as astronomy. The great difference was that European astronomers tracked large objects, in direct courses, such as the sun and moon, whereas the Native Americans tracked small objects relative to large objects creating a very complex but accurate cosmic system, **so accurate that the solar year can be measured to within minutes.**

How did the Cherokee (real names Ani-Yun-Wia and Shawandasse) come into possession of the WHEELS of TIME UNTIME? According to Cherokee legends, the Cherokee originated anciently in South America (maybe from MU?), and migrated northward. After migrating into North America, the Cherokee migrated back and forth from Mexico twice, making the Ozark Plateau their home the second time about 800 to 1500 years ago. This fact has been proven scientifically by Dr. Tim Jones, a Cherokee descendant, who holds doctorate degrees in both archeology and anthropology from the University of Arizona. While in Mexico, they apparently came into possession of the calendar device having been in contact with either the Maya or Aztecs. It may have been a gift or even taken by force during one of the many Mayan or Aztec wars. Maybe the Cherokee took a copy of the Aztec Sun Stone? Another possibility is they might have had an established trade route with Mesoamerican tribes and exchanged goods for the calendar device. The Aztec Sun Stone does appear to be a wheel within a wheel without moving parts. Other than the Aztec Sun Stone and Indian Medicine Wheels, no other wheel like calendar device has ever been found to date in the ancient Americas. Apparently none of the calendar devices have survived 1500 years and oral traditions do not give an accounting as to what happened to them. Perhaps the Spanish destroyed some of them when they burned the Mayan records, believing them to be tools of the Devil as knowledge of the Tzolk'in was lost in the Yucatan after the Spanish conquest. Maybe the stone Medicine Wheels of Native Americans are a crude copy and remembrance of the former intricate device? It seems that the Medicine Wheels are a calendar like device considered sacred by the Native Americans. The Tzolk'in calendar survives today in the form of a chart.

In the chapter *The Future World* of Volume One, the prophecies of the Incas, Mayas, Aztecs, and Cherokees are similar because these peoples at some time in the past came together, exchanged knowledge, and possessed or acquired the WHEELS of TIME device. Nothing much would have been said of these calendar devices because they were considered so sacred to the priests that they would not have been publicly displayed, noting such devices could also weaken their prominence as diviners if important dates and events could be predicted by merely turning the wheels and reading the corresponding information engraved on that notch. The complex part was the interpretation thereof, which perhaps the priests made appear more complex than it really was. Priests were given high status and were supported financially and materially in all things by the common people. They wanted for nothing. So why give away your trade secrets and risk losing it all?

The Mayan Long Count calendar was used by the Maya of Chichen Itza to measure the movement of the Pleiades, which movement was used to check Precession movement towards the 2012 end time cosmic event. One complete Precession cycle of 26,000 years is called the Great Year which marks the end of the "Precession of the Equinoxes." Precession was known by ancient Babylonian and Egyptian astronomers of the Middle East, as did Tibetan astronomers in the Far East. It was also known to the Maya, Aztec, Olmec, and

Peruvian astronomers in the Americas. This is an indication that perhaps a WHEELS of TIME device, or round calendar charts, may have been used anciently by Middle and Far Eastern astronomers. The Olmecs were using the Tzolk'in Calendar as early as 679 B.C. It was probably in use much earlier. They either brought the knowledge of the Tzolk'in calendar to this continent when they arrived here from the Middle East, or were given the knowledge from the Nephilim, or obtained it from Quetzalcoatl during his early travels in South America, Central America, and Mexico. The Tibetan calendar is so similar to the Mayan that traditional scholars now speculate that they share a common origin. In fact, the calendars of the ancient Near East in the third and second millennium B.C. included a 364-day calendar, a 360-day calendar, and a 365-day calendar, which same calendars were all present in ancient Mesoamerica. The evidence is clear. Someone with advanced knowledge of astronomy has visited peoples of this planet and left calendars as a signature note. Many world cultures share similar calendars. Who were the bringers of knowledge after the cataclysm of 9,500 B.C.? They were none other than the Sumerians, the Nephilim, and the pre-mortal Christ who traveled the world with the Shining Ones.

Your authors previously speculated that the Toltecs and Quetzalcoatl perfected the calendar, which according to oral traditions, they did just that by either devising or revising a Long Count calendar, later adopted by other Mesoamerican cultures, some Native American tribes, and Peruvians through contact. It is entirely possible that the Olmecs also brought or even devised the Long Count calendar, later to be perfected by the Toltecs. According to oral traditions, the Toltecs made a revision or adjustment of their most likely Long Count calendar system in 6 A.D., when a mass planetary conjunction occurred. This adjustment is consistent with the *Book of Mormon* wherein it states that nine years after the birth of Christ (4 B.C.), the people adjusted their calendar system, the beginning of 6 A.D. or the end of 5 A.D. (3 *Nephi* 2:7-8).

Mayanists have bestowed the name Tzolk'in on the Mayan version of the ancient Mesoamerican 260-day calendar. The name Tzolk'in is modern and was coined based on the Yucatec language, with an intended meaning of "count of days." The actual names of this calendar as used by the pre-columbian Maya are not known. "Tzolk'in" is merely a transliteration into Yucatec of the Quiche name, *ch'olk'ij.* Quiche day keepers still make auguries using the *ch'olk'ij.*

Your authors feel that the Tzolk'in calendar has ancient roots that may have originated with Abraham (2,000 B.C.) or even Shem, the son of Noah. *The Book of Jasher* tells that Abraham lived and studied under the tutorage of Shem for 39 years. This was the source of Abraham's wisdom as Shem was the most intelligent man of his time who understood the physical and spiritual dimensions and their interaction with each other. *The Zohar* discloses that Abraham was the most learned man of his time in the arts and sciences and especially in astronomy and astrology. He had a calendar like device that he wore around his neck and frequently consulted. It is said that people would come every day, even kings, to seek a forecast and reading from the tablet. *Genesis* 25:5-6 records that when Abraham grew old, he gave all that he had to his son Isaac. But unto the sons of the concubines, he gave gifts and they departed unto the east country. *The Zohar* discloses that these were occult gifts (the Tzolk'in and maybe the I Ching) taken to the east countries by children of his concubines. Most certainly this calendar device was highly valued by Abraham and his children who most likely understood how to read and forecast from the calendar. In time, copies were made and the knowledge spread to the Tibetans, Egyptians, Babylonians and maybe Chinese astronomers, for a tablet form version of the calendar was used in those regions anciently, each culture having a different name for the calendar. From there it was carried to ancient Mexico by the first settlers from the middle and far eastern countries, who were known collectively as the Chichimecas, whom the Olmecs branched off into a separate nation very early on arrival. Later the Nephite/ Toltecs/Zapotec/Mulekites received the calendar knowledge and with Quetzalcoatl perfected it and passed the knowledge to the Preclassic Maya. Perhaps the use of the wheel form version, meshed with the 365-day Long Count, was the perfection of the Mayan calendar on this continent, noting no tangible evidence has ever been found to support our theory (as yet). Readers are referred back to the chapter *The Giants* in Volume One, for a history of the Chichimecas.

The Mayan Long Count calendar ends on 13.0.0.0.0 = December 21, 2012. The Winter Solstice occurs at precisely 11:11 am GMT and the End of the Age is marked by the sun rising out of the mouth of the Ourobourus, exact hour unknown, but presumed to be a morning hour. The Maya view this as the end of their calendar and the end of time as we know it. There are many who think that time will continue on without incident, that the end of Precession is just a zero point in time for the Maya who will restart their calendar once again.

Recently E. J. Clark revisited the ruins of Chichen Itza, Yucatan, Mexico, and had the opportunity to converse with a knowledgeable university educated Mayan guide. E. J. asked the guide what the Maya believed was going to happen on December 21, 2012. He replied, "Boom! Its all over, the end of time as we know it, is gone." He further said that all the Maya dreaded and feared this upcoming date and that their calendar would not restart time.

Most of the world reckons its time with the Gregorian calendar and are not too concerned with the 2012 date but the Tzolk'in calendar possesses a little known capability that other calendars lack. It has the ability to predict events and dates in other dimensions that effect events in this physical universe and unlike other ancient calendars in current use; it has **never been in error.** In fact, it is from this ancient calendar that Aztec prophecies were current *four generations* before the coming of the Spaniards and was the record predicting the arrival of the bearded white men with sharp swords, strange garments and casques on their heads, who would arrive from across the sea in ships with sails, destroy their gods and the Aztec empire during the reign of Montezuma, **accurate even to the very month, day, and year of April 22, 1519. Not only did the calendar predict the month, day, and year it also gave accurate descriptions of the coming white**

men and what would happen when they came. The Aztecs put up no resistance because they believed them to be gods.

There is no doubt that the Persian Magi (wise men) of biblical times knew of the impending birth of Christ associated with the Star of Bethlehem through prophecy foretold by the calendar. In ancient times every astronomer, prophet, magician, magi, priest, and king consulted, studied, and searched this calendar for impending prophetic events, for associated signs in the sky, and for good or bad days to perform certain tasks. Every king had his own personal court astronomers and priests who consulted this document on a daily basis and reported back to him.

Sometimes wrong interpretations would cost court astronomers and priests their very lives. Furthermore, if Abraham or Shem designed this calendar, then it certainly would add credence to its reliability in accuracy. When I (E. J.) learned what was predicted for the 2012 date, by this particular calendar, I immediately sat up and took notice, for it is another missing piece of the puzzle that just fell in place. It is the reason that the Maya all fear and dread this date, and I might add, rightly so. And it is reason enough that all on this planet should be fore- warned. We will continue this chapter in the chapter titled *The End Times.*

UPDATE

A badly corroded and shattered device, coined the "Antikythera Mechanism," was recovered in 1902 from a Roman shipwreck, now housed at the National Archaeological Museum of Athens. Recently it was analyzed by digital imagery and X-ray tomography. The findings were released November 30, 2006, at an Athens conference and in the journal *Nature,* which findings were also reported by Dan Vergano in USA TODAY. The following is the article written by Dan Vergano:

"The "Antikythera Mechanism," an ancient Greek astronomical calculator dating to about 100 B.C., possessed a technical sophistication centuries ahead of it time, an international research tram reports.

"The actual design is superb, almost jaw-dropping," says study leader Mike Edmunds of the United Kingdom's Cardiff University. The mechanism is now at the National Archaeological Museum of Athens.

Badly corroded and shattered and an object of fascination for scholars since its recovery in 1902 from a Roman shipwreck, the device "stands as a witness to the extraordinary technological potential of ancient Greece," the study concludes.

Analysis of the device by digital imagery and X-ray tomography shows it possessed 30 hand-cut bronze gears. Intricately connected, the gears enabled predictions of eclipses and other astronomical phenomena, probably down to within a few hours.

The ship carrying the mechanism sank off the Greek island Antikythera in about 60 B.C. Originally housed in a roughly 12-by-7 inch wooden box, the bronze-doored calculator was probably on its way from the island of Rhodes to Rome when it sank, Edmunds says.

With one dial in front and two in back, the hand-cranked device replicated cycles of the sun and moon's appearances in the sky over a repeating 76-year pattern, the study suggests, as well as the planets' motion. The reconstruction supersedes an older, simpler model of the mechanism and shows the ancient Greeks invented differential gears and miniaturized mechanism in ways unseen until the Renaissance.

Although Rhodes was known for shipping, "the device had no navigational use that I can see," Edmunds says. Instead, the mechanism encapsulated several hundred years of ancient Greek innovation in astronomy starting about 400 B.C., says classicist Stephen White of the University of Texas-Austin. Around 200 B.C., a trove of Babylonian astronomical measurements revolutionized Greek astronomy, culminating in work by the legendary astronomer Hipparchos, who lived on Rhodes around 140 B.C. He devised the device's mechanized eclipse cycles.

The scans have roughly doubled the number of inscriptions spotted on the device, which may be the study's biggest achievement, says classicist Reviel Netz of Stanford University in Palo Alto, Calif. "Essentially we now see there are two major inscriptions: one telling us about the machine, the other telling us about the theory underlying it." Classic scholars will debate and revise the inscriptions, starting at a conference underway in Athens, Edmunds says, "We hope the study makes museums return to their collections to look for more such devices," he says.

"We now live in a completely new age for the study of antiquity," Netz says. The ancients were inveterate inscribers, he says, but much has been lost. New technological breakthroughs make it possible now to recover those writings, and they change completely our picture of antiquity." Netz says "Generally speaking, (they show) it was much more sophisticated than we have once thought."

Your authors feel somewhat vindicated by the above findings because it was a Wheel of Time device used anciently by the Greeks who probably learned the knowledge from the Babylonians who in turn most likely carried similar devices to Mesoamerica. The theorized Mayan Wheels of Time Untime now become more of a probability.

Antikythera Mechanism (main structure)

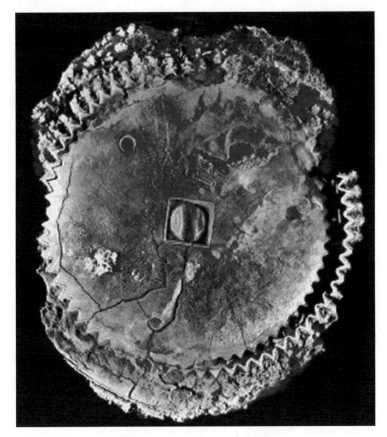

2005 X-ray imaging of Device

Similar devices are mentioned in ancient literature.

Cicero mentions two separate machines similar to the Antikythera mechanism.

The first was built by Archimedes and brought to Rome by the Roman general Marcus Claudius Marcellus after Archimedes' death at the siege of Syracuse in 212 BC. Marcellus had a high respect for Archimedes and this was the only item he kept from the siege. The device was kept as a family heirloom, and Cicero was shown it by Gallus about 150 years later. The motions of the sun, moon and five planets were shown by the device. Gallus gave a 'learned explanation' of it and demonstrated it for Cicero.

And when Gallus moved the globe, it was actually true that the moon was always as many turns behind the sun on the bronze contrivance as would agree with the number of days it was behind in the sky. Thus the same eclipse of the sun happened on the globe as would actually happen. *Cicero, De Re Publica I 21-22*

Archimedes' device is also mentioned by later Roman writers Lactantius, Claudian, and Proclus in the 4th and 5th centuries.

Cicero also says that another such device was built 'recently' by his friend Posidonius, "... each one of the revolutions of which brings about the same movement in the sun and moon and five wandering stars [planets] as is brought about each day and night in the heavens..." *Cicero, De Natura Deorum II.88 (or 33-34)* Later, similar devices are described in Arabic sources. The early 9th century *Kitab al-Hiyal* ("Book of Ingenious Devices"), commissioned by the Caliph of Baghdad, records over a hundred mechanical devices described in Greek texts that had been preserved in monasteries.

So we know of three such devices. It is probable that the Antikythera Mechanism was not unique, as shown by Cicero's references to such mechanisms and because of the sophistication exhibited made the device unlikely to be one of a kind. More parts of the Antikythera Mechanism have been found. So far 30 gears have been discovered and it is proposed that 37 gears did once exist.

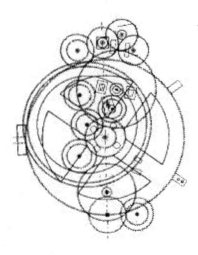

Schematic of the artifact's mechanism

The device is remarkable for the level of miniaturization and complexity of its parts, which is comparable to that of 18th century clocks. It has over 30 gears, with teeth formed through equilateral triangles. When past or future dates were entered via a crank (now lost), the mechanism calculated the position of the Sun, Moon or other astronomical information such as the location of other planets. The use of differential gears enabled the mechanism to add or subtract angular velocities. The differential was used to compute the synodic lunar cycle by subtracting the effects of the sun's movement from those of the sidereal lunar movement. (from Wikipedia, the free encyclopedia)

The End Times

This is a continuation of the chapter, *The Future World* Volume One.

The fact that we are now living in the end times has long been attested by many prophets who lived in ages past. It is a time long awaited by people of all religions. It is a time of culmination or winding down of events. It is a time of great expectations. It is a time of spiritual awakening. It is a time of rapid technical advancements. It is the time of the beginning of the glorious Age of Aquarius that will usher in the great millennial age.

Your authors are going to present a scenario, taken from many ancient sources, depicting the end time events. Are these events going to happen just as we present? We don't know. We do know that if what we present doesn't come to pass, it will come to pass in the near future. This is the time of preparation for future prophesized events that must occur shortly. Some *Bible* prophecy for the end times has already been fulfilled.

Just as prophesized for last days in *Ezekiel 36:24, Ezekiel 37,* and *Isaiah 66:8,* Israel was reborn as a nation on May 14, 1948. The biblical prophet, Jeremiah, in *Jeremiah 31:35-36,* records that the Jewish nation would exist as long as the world stands. It is after the time that Israel becomes a nation in the latter days that Ezekiel in *Ezekiel 38-39,* foretells the pre-millennial Gog-Magog invasion of that nation. This is not to be confused with the Battle of Armageddon, a much later event. The military campaign of Gog and Magog against Israel involves a few nations whereas the Battle of Armageddon involves all the nations of the world.

The prophet Ezekiel foretold that several Arab countries namely, Persia (mostly Iran and parts of Iraq), Libya, Ethiopia (North African nations), Russia, and maybe Turkey, would quickly mount a massive military campaign against Israel in the latter days. It is foretold that Russia will be drawn into this war by a "hook in the jaw" which will virtually drag her into this conflict against her will. This invasion will come from the north. The purpose of the invasion is to take spoil and will happen while Israel is living securely in the land whereas the purpose of the Armageddon Campaign is to destroy all the Jews. Ezekiel mentions several allies while other nations stand in opposition to the invasion. It appears that the nations of the West offer only diplomatic intervention without military aid in response to the invasion.

One only has to read the newspapers or watch the news on television or news websites to see the unrest, turmoil, suicide bombings, assassinations, failed peace efforts, and hatred being generated toward the Jews in the Middle East. War and rumors of war are blowing throughout the region, especially with the U.S. invasion of Iraq and Afghanistan. Almost daily, television news channels show mobs of Muslim protesters in Middle East countries shouting Death to America and Kill the Jews. Russia is aiding Iran to develop a medium range ballistic missile. Syria and Iran have been purchasing Soviet war aircraft and anti-tank weapons. In the mean while Israel has not been sitting idly by watching their neighbors arming. They have accepted delivery of advanced American F-151 fighter jets and are deploying an anti-missile system. Additionally, a high wall is being constructed by Israel between her borders and Palestine, further enraging the Palestinians. Although Israel has relinquished some land to the Palestinians, in agreement with Palestine to stop terrorism in Israel, it will simply not be enough to satisfy Palestine's long range plans for its country. The new found peace will hang by a thread. In a few years this could escalate easily and explode into the Gog and Magog invasion, seemingly over night. The situation is much like a powder keg just waiting for the spark to ignite it. Your authors see this event possibly happening within the next five or six years.

The outcome of this military buildup is given in *Ezekiel 38:18-23.* Biblical scripture makes it clear that no nation comes to Israel's aid. Perhaps they will protest but not offer to help because this would pose a threat to their economic existence, or maybe a peace treaty has been negotiated and to send aid to only a threat would be deemed unwise. For what ever reason, Israel stands alone, without military aid, to face the onslaught of invaders. Since no nation comes to Israel's aid to defend her, God sends a great destructive volcanic earthquake of fire and brimstone that utterly destroys the advancing armies. Only 17% of Russia's army survives the vengeance of God. So great is the destruction of war weapons that it takes Israel seven years to clean up the mess and seven months to bury the dead corpses of the enemy forces. God will use this attack to show his might and glory to unbelievers. He pours out his Spirit upon the house of Israel so that they might know that He is the Lord their God and neither will He hide His face any more from them.

After the event of the attempted invasion of Israel takes place and Israel's enemies are destroyed or at least they back off, the world relaxes as tension in the Middle East dies down. Israel then begins to rise, as a nation, unified in might, power and glory. She has finally earned the respect of the nations. But, it will be a short-lived false peace, lasting only a few years.

In the meanwhile the "Signs of the Times" have been increasingly manifesting as hurricanes, tornados, drought, ice storms, wild fires, floods, mud slides, earthquakes, tsunamis, typhoons, violent tempests, blizzards, extreme temperature variations, volcanic activity, famines, and pestilences in greater frequencies. As of this writing of October 12, 2005, there have been over 140 earthquakes at magnitude of 5 or higher, in the last 30 days. If you include any scale earthquake, there were more than 400 in that same 30 day period. The frequency of these earthquakes is staggering. The Indian Ocean earthquake that caused the devastating December 24, 2004, tsunamis was the second largest quake in recorded history, having a magnitude of 9.15 and was the worst tsunamis ever recorded in terms of lives lost. At least 232,010 are reported as either dead or missing. During that quake, the magnitude was such that the earth's rotation was actually slowed briefly! In spite of all the so-called "natural" occurring disasters, these occurrences will be perceived as normal, no worse than past occurrences, simply the hazards of living on a planet under going climatic changes and global warming.

The Mayan end time date of December 2012, is approaching. By now the media has made the world educated to the up coming event. Astronomers will be readying for the celestial alignment with their telescopes aimed toward the Milky Way. Scientists will be assuring everyone that it isn't the end of time, only the winding down of Precession. Some observers will be looking for the return of planet X (Nibiru) to return and wreak havoc to our solar system. Soothsayers and prophets of doom will be everywhere. Religious leaders will be assuring their congregations that the Antichrist hasn't made his appearance yet. They will point out that the Jewish temple hasn't been rebuilt and much of prophecy hasn't been fulfilled, therefore the end of time is not yet. Besides, everyone is accounted for as being present; there has been no "rapturing." Hyph will build up for black tie Precession Parties, since it will be 26,000 years before the event comes back around. Spiritualists will be looking for humans to reach a higher level of spiritual consciousness that will somehow change the world back into "The Golden Age." The 2012 alignment has even been predicted to change human DNA into12 strand DNA, producing a new breed of humans of a "higher order."

Most all pragmatics will then agree that the world is probably on the cusp of a new age, beginning with the restart of time once more, having reached the Mayan zero point in their calendar. There will be countries that will produce the ancient charts of the Babylonians, Egyptians, Norse, Celts, Tibetans, Chinese, and the East Indians, whose charts will also agree that we are entering an age very different than what the world has known since the birth of Christ. They will further point out that this 2012 alignment was thought of as being a significant transformative event for human beings on this earth. However, most of the world will turn a deaf ear, either not believing or simply un-interested in ancient charts. After all, we live in a more scientific world and nothing earth shattering is predicted to happen. The world will go on as in the days of Noah with eating, drinking, marrying and being merry. Precession is only an astrological event that will start over and end again 26,000 years into the future. The times are for the most part are good and finally there is unheard of peace and prosperity in the Middle East. Technology is at its zenith. Medical miracles cure many diseases and life spans are extended. Is not this the long awaited Age of Aquarius that is beginning to manifest?

Let us briefly review what is going to happen on December 21-23, 2012. For the first time in 5,125 years, the winter solstice sun will rise to conjunct the intersection of the Milky Way and the plane of the ecliptic (pathway of the sun), forming a cosmic cross within the Milky Way. At this point the sun will be in the opening of the "dark rift" in the Milky Way, which contains a supper massive spinning black hole. The Earth however, will make a three day transit through the "dark rift" passing directly in front and through the center of the magnetic axis of the super massive spinning black hole. Although the actual body of the monstrous black hole, located in the exact center of our galaxy, is still approximately 24,000 light years away from Earth, its energy path (magnetic axis) is directed toward and fills the "dark rift" region. That is why the area is devoid of light and dubbed the "dark rift." Radio telescopes, aimed at the "dark rift" in 2003, confirmed that indeed a monstrous super massive black hole does exist in the center of our galaxy. The ancient people referred to this area as the "cosmic sea" and believed that the black hole functioned as a doorway between heavens, universes, or dimensions. The term they used for the black hole transdimensional portal is an Oroborus.

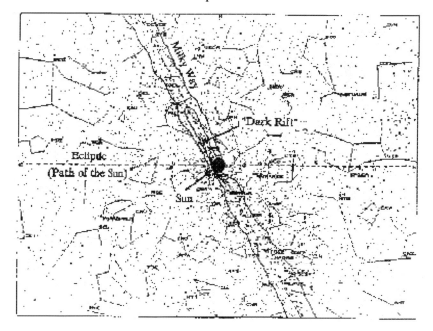

Ecliptic Path of the December 21, 2012 Sun. Note the rare astronomical alignment with the winter solstice sun directly in the "dark rift" of the Milky Way.

Stela 11 from Izapa shows Cosmic Father in the "mouth" of Cosmic Mother, the "dark rift" or "birth canal" in the Milky Way. This is an image of the celestial alignment that culminates in 2012 A.D.

This alignment of the sun in relationship to the black hole "dark rift" is called the Sign of the Suntelia Aion, meaning the End of the Age, and is symbolized by the Ouroboros. The Ouroboros is a tail eating dragon or serpent. The word Ouroboros is a Greek word meaning "tail eater" when translated into English. The Milky Way was perceived, by ancient peoples, as a great dragon or serpent of light that ate its tail every 26,000 years. The Sun will appear to be rising out of the mouth of the Ouroboros, which event occurs on December 21, 2012, exact hour unknown, but presumed to be a morning hour.

When this event happens, it marks the End of the Age. On the same date, the Winter Solstice occurs at exactly 11:11 am GMT.

Below is an Aztec seven segmented Ouroboros, the seven segments representing the seven principles of the creator. The seven aspects of the creator are identified as wisdom, understanding, counsel, might, knowledge, fear of God, and Christ. Christ was known to the Aztecs under other names. Another definition of the seven aspects or seven principles of the creator is "the unseen and unwritten laws of the universe that rule the behavior of manifested matter." Below it is a Greek style Ouroboros. There are two types of Ouroboros. One type has the serpent holding the tip of its tail in its jaws, forming a static circle that represents an endless round of existence or one eternal round.

The second type of Ouroboros is a serpent that is swallowing or devouring its tail and has dynamic meaning. It represents the gateway between our temporal universe and higher spiritual universes. The Milky Way Ouroboros where our sun conjuncts in 2012, is of the second type or the Greek style as seen in the second illustration below.

Aztec seven segmented Ouroboros

Greek style Ouroboros devouring its tail

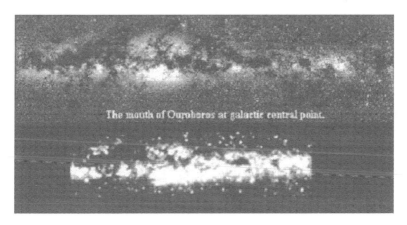

The above picture is the Milky Way Ouroboros as it will appear in 2012.

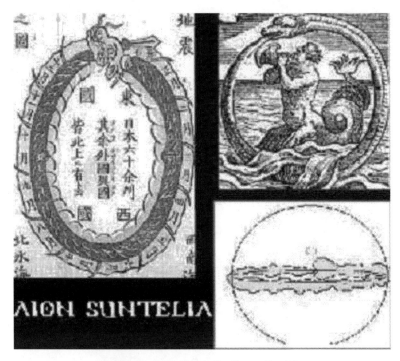

The End of the Age, the Suntelia Aion

The lower right hand illustration is our Sun rising out of the mouth of the Ouroboros. The Greeks called the End of the Age the Suntelia Aion. The End of the Age is when the sun rises out of the mouth of the Ouroboros when viewed at galactic central point near Sagittarius in 2012. An Age is typically 2,160 years between each transit of the zodiacal signs, by the sun. In 2012, it will have been 2,160 years since the earth entered the Age of Pisces. We are currently in the cusp or dawning of a new age, the Age of Aquarius. In 2012, the old Age ends, the result of Precession of the Equinoxes, and the new Age of Aquarius officially will begin. The earth is also completing one Precession cycle of roughly 25, 920 years, rounded off to 26,000 years. One complete cycle is called an Aeon, therefore it is the end of the Fifth Age and the end of the 26,000 Precession cycle, called an Aeon or Great Year, sometimes referred to as the Platonic or Plato's Year. It is also the end of the Mayan/Aztec Fifth Sun. Therefore the year 2012 marks the end of three great Ages. It is the end of the Fifth Age; however the beginning of the new Sixth Age is seemingly different because of the transit of the sun rising out of the mouth of the Ouroboros. When the sun makes this transit, the earth will be entering the "dark rift." Scientists do not know what is going to be the effect of the spinning black hole on our sun and planet but below is a sample of what has been predicted by various peoples and ancient writings.

The Maori believe that a removal or dissolving of the planes separator (veils) will occur allowing the merging of the physical and spiritual planes. Ancient historians and especially Plato referred to a cycle of catastrophe at the End of the Age (Suntelia Aion). Some Maya timekeepers believe that the world will not end but will be transformed. Other Maya believe that the second coming of Christ will occur and time is no more. They both agree that we are traveling through the 13th Baktun cycle (1618-2012 A.D.) This cycle is known as "the triumph of materialism" and "the transformation of matter." Maya Timekeepers of Guatemala teach that we have been through fire, earth, air and water ages already. The next cycle (beginning December 21, 2012) will be ether (spiritual) or the Fifth Age (note their number of Ages are different, depending on the tradition). There is further evidence in the traditions of other major civilizations, namely Egyptian and Vedic peoples, that this alignment was thought of as being a significant transformative event for human beings on earth, a transformation of human beings into something completely new. Spiritualists have taken this to mean DNA changes creating a newer higher level conscious being.

For certain sects of Gnosticism, the Ouroboros is even identified with Christ by transformation of the mere "quick soul" into the higher form of a "quickening spirit." In other words, terrestrial humans will change into spiritual beings. It will be the start of a New Age which requires people to make a change physically. It will be a spiritual evolution followed by the Golden Age.

The magnificently engraved lid of the sarcophagus of the giant Mayan King, Pacal, encodes the cosmic cross of 2012. The cross is represented by a huge foliated tree or sacred cosmic tree. The Mayans believed the serpent constellation called Draco will also cross the Milky Way during the 2012 cosmic event, giving the appearance of a foliated cosmic tree as engraved on many Mayan steles and Pacal's tomb lid. When this alignment occurs, the ancient Maya believed this was a sign of the End of the Age and the time of the resurrection. Pacal's tomb lid is telling that he expects to be resurrected when the cosmic foliated tree appears in the Milky Way at the End of the Age in 2012.

Your authors believe that the 2012 date is a culmination of events that have been leading up to that date since the union of the polarity occurred. When the spirit and temporal earths united millenniums ago, they were in relative harmony. Each planet has a unique frequency or pitch to its vibration. When they united their vibrations created a new harmonic sound, much like a harmonic cord in music. Over time, due to negative forces or vibrations over powering the positive forces exerted on the planet, harmonic discords began occurring which makes the harmonic vibrations sound out of tune, creating a new sound. The newly created sound is a wobbling sound, called a modulation that forms when two vibrations are out of phase with one another. This new vibration is having a degradation of the harmony between the spirit earth and the temporal earth and can cause destructive forces of great magnitude. The modulations will be violent and will result in the crust heaving and waving like wind through a field of barley. The crust is very thin compared to the mass of the earth. If one overlays the thousands of volcanoes on the earth, you get the potential for something very amazing. When the seas heave themselves out of their bounds, the volcanoes match perfectly with where they will crash. Add to that the potential for a super storm from glacial melting and you will have a disaster of cataclysmic proportions.

We are seeing this exact thing happening with dramatic increases (since 1980) in numbers and magnitudes of earthquakes, hurricanes, tornados, fires, droughts, violent storms, tsunamis, typhoons, floods, extreme weather variations, volcanic activity, and mud slides. There is only a very small chance that weather, sea levels, and ground stability will be maintained over the next seven years. It is because the two planets are vibrating in different modulations and are out of phase with each other. They are no longer vibrating in harmony, and are in danger of separating that is causing natural disasters to occur in increased frequency and magnitude. Below is a graph made and kept by the International Disaster Database showing the increase in the number of natural disasters since 1900.

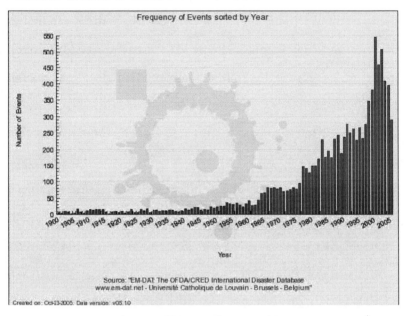

Earthquake Trends of the last 25 years

When the sun aligns with the spinning black hole in 2012, the earth will enter the "dark rift" of the Milky Way. Our Earth will pass inside the center of a magnetic axis created by the black hole. It may be darkened with a great cloud of black interstellar dust for 60 to 72 hours during its three day transit of the "dark rift" region because this region is filled with dark non-luminous nebulous clouds. The suns corona may be affected resulting in super solar flares of plasma energy that could scorch the earth in minutes. The earth will shake with extremely powerful forces coming from above and not underground. Many religions refer to the "great shaking" of the earth in the End Times.

One example is found in the *D&C* 118, as follows, "......I will not only shake the earth, but the starry heavens shall tremble." Another example found in *Haggai* 2: 6 states, "For thus saith the Lord of Hosts; Yet once, it is a little while, and I will shake the heavens, and the earth, and the sea, and the dry land." Even the greatest of prophets, Isaiah, foresaw the event as recorded in *Isaiah* 24:20 as "The earth shall reel to and fro like a drunkard, and **shall be removed** like a cottage;" (bold type added) (cottage = tent). When the "great shaking" occurs, the spirit earth, already in the process of separating, will fully separate or as Isaiah states, "shall be removed," from the temporal earth, rise and pass through the spinning black hole Oroborus into the fourth dimension, returning back in much the same manner that it arrived. Why didn't Isaiah state the spirit earth? Because he understood the **true** earth, the original creation, to be the spirit earth. We now can fully understand the biblical phase "at the last day" of the **true** earth in this universe or dimension. Linear time is no more for the "raptured" **true** earth because time will be measured differently in the fourth dimension. However, it is not the last day for the temporal or physical earth left behind in this universe.

Finally, we are understanding the words of Isaiah in ful-fillment of a prophecy which says Isaiah's prophecies shall be understood in the last days.(*Book of Mormon*, 2 *Nephi* 25:8)

In biblical terminology this is the *translation* or *transfiguration* of the earth. The *D&C* 63:20-21 speaks of a day "when the earth shall be transfigured." The spiritual part of the temporal earth will be changed from a telestial into a terrestrial state. In more modern terminology it is the "rapture" of the earth. The term "rapture" is not found anywhere in *Bible* scriptures. It is a modern term denoting the condition of being "snatched or caught up or removed." Anciently, it was called "the change or time of the change," "the cosmic transformative change," "the removal of earth," "the renewal of earth," and later, in more modern times, coined the "rapture," but it all means the same thing. Terminology meaning changes throughout the years. The important thing to remember is the concept of "rapture" was understood by the ancients. It is not a new concept but rather one of the oldest beliefs which we will prove in Volume Three.

The authors have meticulously arrived at this conclusion from the Tzolk'in calendar, both the ancient and *Dreamspell* versions. Remember that the Tzolk'in has the ability to predict time and events in the spiritual dimensions. The *Dreamspell* version predicts that during the 2012 cosmic event, the earth will pass into the fourth dimension and ascend into heaven. It further states that humans will be changed or transfigured into galactic bodies of living light. The ancient Tzolk'in version predicts a trans-dimensional re-birth, renewal, or cosmic change of planet Earth into a new beginning or Golden Age, following a time of cleansing or purification. The ball game played by the Maya is actually a cosmic reenactment of the upcoming 2012 sequence of events. Proof of this will be found in our Volume Three, now in the writing stage. We know that temporal things cannot enter into the spiritual fourth dimension without having first undergone a change such as translation because temporal things are not designed to endure spiritual conditions. The Tzolk'in calendar predictions must be taken seriously because of all the ancient calendars still in use, it is the only one that has **never** been in error.

If this event takes place then it will be the period following the opening of the sixth seal spoken of in *Revelation* 6:12-17, or "rapture" of not only spirit earth but of other righteous beings and believers described, in the *Bible*, as the church. The "rapture" comes for the church so that they might escape the great tribulation that is to follow on the temporal earth. It is also the resurrection of the just or the first resurrection. It will be a time of relative peace when the non-believing world will be caught off guard, being willfully ignorant and not discerning the "Signs of the Times." The trump sounds and will only be heard by believers and righteous souls, both living and dead. All will meet Christ in the air and will be taken into heaven (the fourth dimension) with the spirit earth. Simply stated, they will be "raptured" or translated with the spirit earth into the fourth dimension.

The *Rapture* is not to be confused with the second coming of Christ. The second coming of Christ occurs after the tribulation, therefore **it is possible to predict the time of the *Rapture*** using time measurement of the great Ages and the Mayan calendar. An upcoming chapter, *The Ages,* will teach how time is measured by the Ages. In fact, it was **meant to be predicted by this generation!**

It is in the fourth dimension that the great millennial 1000 year reign or Golden Age will take place, but it is not the highest heaven.

After the millennial reigns, then the spirit earth, along with its translated inhabitants who are worthy of the highest heaven, will transcend or rise and return to the highest heaven or universe, passing through the gates of heaven, until it reaches its final destination in the celestial heaven or universe of God. Once there, the spirit earth with its translated inhabitants will undergo yet another change in the twinkling of an eye. They will be changed into glorified celestial eternal beings that will live forever with the Lord.

In *Matthew* 13:39-40, *The Holy Bible in Modern English*, Ferrar Fenton's translation, Jesus clearly tells his disciples when the harvest of the righteous takes place as follows: "......the harvest is the **completion of the age"** [Suntelia Aion]. Simply stated, Jesus said **the harvest is the end** [Suntelia, ending period] **of the Age**. We have established that the End of the Age {Suntelia Aion} is December 21, 2012. It appears that we now have the *Bible,* with the words of Christ, and the Tzolk'in calendar, and Mayan Long Count calendar supporting each other in what is to occur on the 2012 End Time date.

The Mayan Long Count calendar ends on December 21, 2012, and will not restart again because the Mayans believe that humanity will no longer need a calendar depicting linear time for we will be moving to a higher dimension where time is measured differently. The ancient Mayans were only partly correct when they assumed the temporal earth would enter a higher dimension....it is the spiritual nature or the spirit earth that will enter the 4th dimension, not the physical planet.

When the sixth seal is opened (each seal is currently believed to represent an approximate 1000 year time period), *Revelation* 6:12-17, and *D&C* 88:87, both say there will be a great earthquake, the sun becomes black as sackcloth, the moon turns red as blood, the earth shall tremble and reel to and fro, the stars appear to fall, mountains and islands are moved, and the heaven is opened. This could describe what will occur in the 2012 alignment when the earth, sun and moon enter the magnetic axis of the spinning black hole (signs in heaven).

The spinning black hole would be perceived as "heaven departed as a scroll" or a portal or gate entry into the next universe or dimension (heaven opened). The sudden enveloping darkness and great destructive shaking of the earth will strike fear into the hearts of all men. All people will seek protective shelters and non-believers will cry for the rocks to fall on them rather than to face the great Day of the Lord's Wrath. It will be the equivalent of 72 hours of terror in pitch black darkness. Also, it is generally believed that we are now living near the end of the sixth seal period of a thousand years, which ironically fits the 2012 *End of the Age* date. Since these events have not come to pass, at this writing, and as we are near the end of this age, the 2012 date becomes more probable for the date of the End of the Age or Suntelia Aion, as found in the Mayan calendar.

Since the "rapture" is spiritual in nature, those people left behind on the temporal earth will not see any of what happened with their natural eyes, but they will figure out very quickly what has happened when so many people simply vanish off the face of the earth. It could be that there may not be as many souls "raptured" from the living as expected. Not all believers will qualify to be harvested with the more righteous. These will be "fence riders," professing faith but not valiant (lukewarm) in their testimonies and non tithe payers. Those left behind will turn to their sacred records and learn what is to befall them during the following years of tribulation. Some will repent and become valiant believers keeping a presence of the church on the temporal earth through tribulation till the second coming of Christ.

It is during this same sixth seal opening period or shortly after the "rapture" that the sealing of the 144,000 from the 12 tribes of Israel takes place. It is generally believed that the 144,000 will give guidance and leadership to the church, being designated "first fruits" during the tribulation years. Again, your authors will depart from traditional belief concerning the 144,000 thousand. We believe that the 144,000 are called to serve, give guidance, leadership, and foremost to prepare the translated spirit earth, along with it's newly resurrected and translated souls, for the great millennial reign of Christ. It seems contrary after being translated to remain in a sinful world. Instead, why not extend their lives for 500 or more years as indestructible mortal beings? Their translation occurs during the time of the resurrection of the just. This event may take place in secret without the public world realizing it happened. Sometime later, in the not so distant future, Babylon the Great will fall. This will be the collapse of the world economic, political and religious system as we know it. The chapter, *The Watchers* will cover how these events could come to be.

It is impossible to give exact interpretations of the book of *Revelation*. It seems that none of the many religious denominations or religious theologians can agree as to when or in what order the prophecies will be fulfilled. There are the pre-tribulationists, middle tribulationists, and post-tribulationsts. Some are pre-millennialists and some are post millennialists, in addition, there are the historical and the dispensational millennialists. They all present valid arguments for their beliefs, yet nothing "is" or has been carved in stone. Because of differing opinions, we have elected to give a broad over view of prophetic events, rather than an in-depth step by step study of *Revelation*.

It is not the intent of your authors to preach religious doctrine, but rather present a possible time line of events that could affect the destiny of the creation, as seen through the ancient texts, traditions, and restored knowledge of the union of the polarity.

Much of the book of *Revelation* is symbolic, written in prophetic language, and difficult for most, if any, to fully understand. This is further compounded by the fact that many predicted accounts by various biblical prophets are not in chronological order. Therefore we will speak in general terms, such as...... sometime after the "rapture" has taken place, the opening of the seventh seal happens. Immediately after the opening of the seventh seal there is a space of ½ hour. If you calculate this mathematically, using the knowledge that 1000 years of man's time equals a day to God, the ½ hour space would equal approximately to 20 years. Therefore, it could be in a few years, 20 years or many years later, after the opening of the seventh seal, when the world economic and financial system, called Babylon the Great in *Revelation*, collapses overnight. What could cause this collapse? Two things, the first scenario which we present in this book below or perhaps the catastrophic global earthquake itself which scenario will be presented in our Volume Three, now in the writing stage.

The following four paragraphs are opening statements taken from an editorial analysis by Rolf A. F. Witzshe, based on the ideas and presentations by the American Economist Lyndon H. LaRouche Jr., written in 2002.

"This premise has been largely rejected by society from the mid 1960s on. It has been replaced by the notion, which has actually been conjured up in much earlier times, that wealth can be created by purely financial means. This notion was popularized together with the "post-industrial society" doctrine. Today, we are facing the end result of the folly of embracing this doctrine.

Let's examine this folly that literally became law from the mid 1960s on. At around this time the myth had been promoted globally that wealth can be created by financial speculation. One doesn't need an industry, so it was said. One doesn't need production of physical goods and infrastructures. It has been said that it is more profitable for society to concentrate on financial speculation, to let your money work for you. Indeed, huge profits have been drawn from spectacular financial practices.

The only problem is that non-productive processes do not produce the slightest bit of wealth for society, except for the predators within the economic system. The huge profits that have been drawn over the years by the countless financial 'industries' were not profits in any fundamental sense derived from increased production that enhanced the status of society, but were in fact predatory profits that were quiet literally stolen from the living of society by clever means. In real terms, these predatory profits were stolen from the physical economy that supports the living of society. The global economic collapse is the direct outcome of this process.

We also face a corresponding world-financial collapse. Huge financial equity portfolios have been created over the years, consisting of numerous types of financial aggregates. These have been considered to represent wealth, while in real terms they represent nothing more than a financial claim against the tangible wealth produced in the physical economy. The problem is, the physical economy has been collapsed below the break even point. People are dying. Instead of producing surplus profits for society, the physical economy can no longer produce enough gain in its economic system to maintain its own operation and the needs of society, much less satisfy the astronomical financial claims that stand against it, which renders the financial claims literally worthless."

Witzsche continues:

"The economic collapse that this overloading of the economy set in motion is becoming acute now, even though it has been going on since the mid 1960s. The collapse began gradually at first, but as the parasite (the predatory financial system) grew into a monster parasite, the physical collapse accelerated.

At the present time, the infusion of new money to keep the speculative system alive is greater than the financial aggregates that this infusion is trying to protect.

The chief reason why the parasite remains protected at all cost, is the illusion of wealth that society sees in it. In real terms, the fancy financial portfolios that society has labored to build for itself in stocks, bonds, and other debt holdings, aren't worth the proverbial red nickel since the productive economy, that there are claims against, has been bled to death to create this imaginary wealth.

This is where we are now. For as long as the living of society is sacrificed to keep the parasite alive, things will get worse and more and more people will pay the price with their life, which is already happening on a much larger scale that the death toll inflicted by the September 11 destruction of the World Trade Center towers in New York. Society has deprived itself to such a point that people are dying at ever increasing numbers in the quiet recesses of their private living, because of the parasitic deprivation, especially in the nations of South America.

The currently outstanding debts have become literally unpayable. An economy that has been so severely depleted of its economic strength that it is collapsing at an ever greater rate, that can't even sustain itself, will never produce the surplus wealth required to satisfy the debt claims. Even huge corporations that once were deemed as solid as the rock of Gibraltar are collapsing under unpayable debt loads in times of a general economic collapse. And the debt load is huge.

At the present moment it will take approximately 25 years of intensive effort to build itself out of the depression that has already begun, and to get back to the level of prosperity that existed in the mid sixties before the collapse process begun. This rebuilding task is so huge that it must be pursued as a global effort in which the best capabilities and resources, and the greatest development needs arc brought together

The bottom line is, that we face the potentially brightest future we ever imagined with virtually infinite resources at out hands, or a new dark age that no person living today will see the end of it. We are at the cross roads at this stage. At this critical juncture we face the potential also for huge wars as the masters of the present system aim to draw attention away from the impending systemic collapse, as if this would solve anything. Nevertheless, the potential for these huge wars is very real, and so is the potential for these wars to become nuclear wars. The irony is, that the USA is insanely pushing for a world engulfing war that it lacks the economic resources to sin (estimated at a cost of two to three billion dollars a day) in times of the country's worst economic crisis. The U.S. military has the residual resources to start such a war and to cause huge damage, and set the world on fire with it, after which anarchy will likely reign by which global economic development becomes an unfulfillable dream for a long time to come."

What Witzsche has written above describes a chillingly accurate description of the economic and financial health of America and global societies in 2005. The world is teetering on economic and financial disaster. If the economy of one big nation should collapse, the resulting damage would resonant throughout the world, taking many other nations with it. This situation has not gone on unnoticed by Lucifer. He, according to biblical scriptures, is the evil driving force behind our present world system. He has been working behind the scenes to gain complete control of the world, both of the political and ecclesiastical kingdoms. Lucifer has declared that this world is his and he will not give it up without a fight. This is more clearly outlined in the chapter *The Watchers*. He has a short time to accomplish complete dominion of both kingdoms in the hopes of defeating the return of Christ.

With the help of his demonic forces and the fallen Watchers, Lucifer has been carefully orchestrating a plan to gain complete control of this planet since the crucifixion of Christ. When the world's economic and political system collapses, a new world leader will emerge to offer solutions. It is said that he will have a "dark or fierce countenance" which we interpret as being dark complexioned, stern looking and of Middle East extraction. The prophet Daniel wrote he "does not regard the desire of women." This could imply that he is either celibate or a homosexual. He probably will be an apostate Jew and more than likely come up out of the Common Market of Europe. Jewish tradition is that he will be a descendant out of the tribe of Dan through his maternal lines. This man will be well known and trusted in the international political and global financial system.

Empowered by Lucifer, he will come to power with intrigue and political maneuvering "but he shall come in peaceably," and will obtain the kingdom by flatteries.

His solution will be a one world government, made up of many nations… a sort of United States of Nations with an elected head of government; maybe a world president will sit at its head. The new world government will be marketed as a New World Order enacting a motto of "All for one and one for All." His solutions will include a one world currency, one global financial system, one global military force, and one global political system. By his charm, charisma, education, knowledge of world affairs, promises of solutions to the world's problems, and gift of eloquent speech, he will take the world by a storm, being hailed as a brilliant genius. His popularity will sweep him into the elected office of President of the New World Order. *Revelation* 13:2 symbolically identifies this man as the first beast (the Antichrist of Christianity (false Messiah) or Armilus of Judaism). Tenth century opinions held that the Antichrist would be the literal offspring of Satan and of a virgin. Don't laugh. Remember the Watchers mated with mortal women in the past and produced a race of giants. If it happened in the past, it could happen again. *11 Thessalonians* calls him the son of perdition (son of Satan). The seat of government and capitol of the New World Order will be centrally located in Rome. This government will be the last resurrection of the Roman Empire and the final embodiment of Babylon.

Once in office the new world leader will form a close alliance with a religious leader, identified in *Revelation* 13:11-12 as the second beast (false prophet). Together they will enforce the separation of church and state and attempt to form a global religion. There will be no public prayer, no school prayer, no public display of anything that might be construed as religious. All mention of God will have to be removed from walls of government office buildings, allegiance pledges, government documents, and the name of God will be removed from all currency. Constitutions of every state nation will have to remove or strike the name of God from their constitutional documents, necessitating the rewriting of many constitutions. The name of God will be erased from public music. Even tombstones must erase the name of God or any reference to Christ. Only pertinent information such as name, date of birth, date of death, and relationship to family members buried in family plots will be allowed. Civil marriage ceremonies will not mention the name of God; neither will God's name be on the marriage certificate. Baptisms will not be permitted in out door lakes, rivers, or streams, as this will be construed as public display of faith.

Religious parades celebrating religious feast days and other religious events will not be permitted. Secular music and Christmas Carols will not be allowed to be broadcasted on radio or television airways. All *Bibles*, *Qur'ans*, *Popol Vuhs*, and other sacred books must be carried in a manner to conceal religious identity, such as carrying in a suitcase in public areas. In public areas, the wearing of Christian jewelry, such as a cross on a gold chain, will not be permitted. Any hair style, hat, turban, yarmulke's, tattoo, clothing etc., associated with religion will not be permitted in a public setting. Religious television and radio broadcast programs will not be allowed. Religious activities will be mandated to observances within the confines of religious buildings or in non public areas. Same sex marriages will be legal. The violation of separation of church and state mandates will carry severe consequences.

The nation of Israel apparently likes the new world leader, even to thinking he is the long awaited Messiah. Israel likes him to the extent that they sign a seven year treaty with the new world government. The treaty will allow them to re-build their temple and once more revive their ancient rituals of animal sacrifices on altars. This treaty will exempt the Jews from prosecution when animal sacrifice is performed on altars in public view.

At first the New World Order will bring an upsurge in the world economy that will last for 3 1/2 years. Global unity will be hailed as the key to universal prosperity and peace, therefore it will be viewed that religion must also be unified. The New World Order government will stress that millions of people have been brutally killed in religious wars, all in the name of God. To keep peace, it will be argued that a form of a unified global religion will be an absolute necessity. Tensions will begin to rise when a concerted effort is made to globally unify religion. The Arab world will bulk at attempts to coerce it into religious unity, as will Christians in other nations. At first there will be out cries of disagreement. Senators will take their message to the world president, asking him to rescind the decree for a one unified global religion. He will tell them a unified religion is for the good of all people. He will profess a strong belief in God and will convey back that he and the false prophet are doing the will of God. The false prophet will claim to have had revelation from God that this is His will and may even conjure up some miracles to convince the people and sign seekers.

The Muslims will not buy it. Agitated by no show of support from the European nations, the Muslim nations will attack and destroy Rome which destruction will flatten all of its seven hills to the level of pancakes (note: Biblical and Torah literature refers to Rome/Europe as Edom). This will be a complete surprise, probably using guided nuclear missiles backed up by air raids. Christians and believers will take advantage of the situation and will rise up in civil disobedience in each of their united nation states. This rebellion will escalate into a Third World War.

Enraged, the world leader/Beast/Antichrist will turn against those who oppose him. Empowered by Satan, the Gates of Hell will open and will assist him to overcome his adversaries. He will display unheard of military might and genius that will bring his foes to their knees. When he defeats all his adversaries, one fourth of the world's population will have perished. At long last, the world is now completely in his control. It will now become one nation under Satan. Then, the unexpected happens. He will be mortally wounded by an assassin. Empowered by Satan, the false prophet will heal his wound and will bring him back from the clutches of death. The world will be stunned and will proclaim "who is able to make war with him? Who is like him?" The world will have to accept him as their leader or else face death (*Rev.* 13:3-4).

The Antichrist will set his sight on Jerusalem. His armies will overwhelm the city and once subdued into submission he will set up his new temporary head quarters or place of ruling power within the confines of that city. Once established, the Antichrist will annul the treaty he formerly made with the Jewish State. All temple sacrifices and daily oblations will be stopped. He will enter into the inner most sanctuary, the Holy of Holies, of the rebuilt Jewish temple and declare himself to be a God. He will exalt himself above all other gods, even the most high God. The Jews will allow him to be enthroned in their temple believing that he is their long awaited Messiah. When the Antichrist desecrates the Holy of Holies, he is the abomination of desolation, spoken of by Daniel the prophet. This event will take place approximately midway of the tribulation years.

Many events will occur at the midpoint of tribulation as follows: God sends two witnesses, dressed in sackcloth, to testify of Christ to the church and Jews. They will be like a spiritual light house to guide men to Christ and repentance. *Revelation 11:3-6* states if any man tries to hurt them, fire will proceed out of their mouths and will kill them. They will possess supernatural power to control rain, power to turn water into blood, and power to smite the earth with all plagues, as often as they will. Not even the Antichrist will be able to harm them during the days of their prophecy. They will be a painful thorn in his side. *St. Matthew 24:16-20* admonishes the Jews in Judea to flee into the mountains for safety, leaving all possessions behind, when they see the abomination of desolation stand in the holy place. A remnant of Israel will flee into the mountains to Bozrah/Petra in western Jordan for safety. There they will be divinely protected and "nourished" by God in the "wilderness" desert areas during the tribulation. The midpoint of tribulation years will be the beginning of the sounding of the seven trumpets and their judgments (*Rev. 8:7-12, Rev. 9:-13, Rev. 11:15*), followed by the sending of the three woes (*Rev. 8:13, Rev. 9:7-12, Rev. 11:14, Rev. 12:7-9*), and the emptying of the seven bowls of wrath of God upon the earth (*Rev. 16:2-16*). Each trial and judgment will be worse than the previous one. The last 3 ½ years of tribulation will be a time of trouble, the likes to which the world has never seen or ever will.

From the moment the Antichrist sits in the Jewish Temple of God and exalts him self above the most high God, it will be exactly 1,260 days till Christ returns to the earth.   Previously unable to unify the world into one global religion, the Antichrist, now in complete control of the world, will outlaw all religions except the worship of himself and his image. He will place a statue of himself in the Temple of God and demand that all worship it. The false prophet, empowered by Satan, will perform great miracles and wonders such as making fire come down from heaven on the earth in the sight of men. By the same means of those miracles, he will have the power to give life to the statue so that it may talk and deceive the people into worshipping it and will cause that as many as would not worship the image of the beast should be killed. All people who worship the Antichrist will receive a mark, the name of the Antichrist, or the number of his name (666) placed on their right hand or in their foreheads. Without one of these marks, no one will be able to buy or sell. Those who receive the mark cannot repent and will be eternally condemned (*Rev.* 13:11-18).

Members of the church who refuse to take the mark will be forced into hiding for their very lives. Many will be hunted down and put to death by being publicly beheaded as an example for not accepting Lucifer/Antichrist as their master. The two prophets will preach against taking the mark, warning those who do that they will drink of the wrath of God's fury. Finally when they have finished their testimony, the Antichrist will make war against them, and shall overcome and kill them. Their dead bodies will be left to rot in the streets of Jerusalem while the wicked of the earth will celebrate their deaths. The rejoicing of the wicked will last 3 ½ days when the Spirit of life from God will enter the dead bodies of the two prophets bringing them back to life. A great fear will fall upon the merry makers as they witness the ascension of the two prophets into heaven. At the same hour a great earthquake will shake Jerusalem even as it was at the crucifixion of Christ. Seven thousand will be killed. Those Jews who have accepted Christ and his gospel will give glory to God (*Rev.* 11:3-14).

"The second woe is past; and, behold, the third woe cometh quickly" (*Rev.* 11:14). The third woe is the burning of the vineyard which shall soon commence. Enraged by the righteous Jews and the righteous members of the church, Lucifer/Antichrist will seek to destroy the remnant. He will bring his armies against them into a place called Armageddon located in the valley of Megiddo and on the plains of Esdraelon. This war is a religious war to destroy all those who oppose the philosophies and decrees of the Antichrist. It is the final war between good and evil on this planet. If the battle is won, the Antichrist will have complete dominion of this planet for as long as the planet exists. There is much at stake here as Lucifer has declared that this world is his. The remnant of the righteous and the Jews is all that is standing in his way for complete dominion. Driven by the Antichrist, the plagues poured out on the rebellious armies of men will not cause them to repent. They will blaspheme God even more for their misfortune. The battle is a world wide conflict to rid the world of the righteous, however it is centered in the valley of Meggido and on the plains of Esdraelon. It is the final conflict that ushers in the Millennium. The wickedness of this day and time will exceed the days and time of Noah. The final war will be long with many battles, horror and bloodshed. Just when victory is seemingly within Lucifer's grasp, the Lord God will step in to defend his people. Two thirds of the armies defending Jerusalem will die; only one third will be saved. Jerusalem will be taken and pillaged and her women shall be ravished. The Lord then will seek to destroy all the armies and nations that came against Jerusalem and the righteous (*Zech.* 12:8-9). The tides of the battles will be turned against the wicked because the Lord will empower his people to defeat the armies of the wicked. Pestilences, plagues, and the sword of God, will be sent by God against the wicked armies that further aid in their destruction.

And then the Lord will suddenly appear in the heavens with great power and glory. All will see him. Those righteous souls who have died during the great tribulation and those righteous members of the church who have survived tribulation will rise and meet him in the air. These are they who had not worshipped the beast, neither his image, neither had received his mark upon their foreheads or in their hands. They will be taken as translated beings to the spirit earth to live with Christ during the millennial reign. They shall escape the great earthquake and burning fire, which will melt the very elements, at his coming. This is the second "rapture." When the feet of the great God touches the Mount of Olives, the mount shall cleave into or split in half exposing a great valley into which a remnant of the Jews will escape. It is this remnant who will come to know and accept the Lord as their savior and Messiah along with those who escaped earlier into the deserts of Jordan.

The great battle is over. The Lord then sends an angel down from heaven with a great chain to chain or bind up Lucifer/Satan and cast him into the great abyss or bottomless pit and shut him up for a space of one thousand years. A seal is set upon him so that he cannot deceive the nations during this time. The Lord then commences his millennial reign on the spirit earth now located in the fourth dimension. Its earlier translated inhabitants have been eagerly preparing for his coming reign with them and rejoice upon his arrival.

On the temporal earth the remnant of Israel will remain to repopulate the earth for one thousand years. It is the final triumph of Israel as a nation and as a people. There may be others who survive the destruction of Armageddon, although the scriptures are somewhat silent on this. It may be that there are remnants of Israel world wide that survive, perhaps remnants of the Ten Tribes, shall return during this time. Isaiah promised that a residue of Egypt and Assyria would turn to the Lord and be blessed of him. Perhaps this is the time of that fulfillment (*Isaiah* 19:20-25). Those who remain on the temporal earth will marry, have children, and rebuild homes and cities. They will live to be of great age and upon near death will be translated and taken to the spirit earth, now in the fourth dimension.

The curse will be removed from the temporal earth in that it will be a fruitful field once more and the fruitful field will be counted for as a forest. Man will no longer be required to eat his bread in the sweat of his face. The wilderness will be like Eden as will the rivers in the desert (*Isaiah* 51:3). Righteousness and peace will prevail because Satan is bound. Men are free of sin.

The spirit earth during the millennial reign is configured as it was in the beginning. Its land masses are all connected. There are no high mountains, only low lying hills. The seas are to the north and maybe the south. Its translated inhabitants will build cities, temples and churches. Families will be re-united. Children who died before the age of accountability will be raised by righteous parents or family members. Those children who died after the age of accountability but before maturity, who would have accepted the gospel had they been presented it, will come forth to be re-united with their families to have full opportunity to exercise their free agency to its fullest and partake of the blessings of the Everlasting Covenant. The millennial reign is preparatory for the receiving of further blessings prior to the great Day of Judgment. The curse is also removed from its ground in that it too will produce fruit and food in abundance. It is here that the lion will lie down with the lamb. The spiritual animal kingdom will be at peace with each other and man.

At the end of the 1000 years, Satan is again loosed for a "little season" on the temporal earth to test all later generations of those born during that time. This "little season" is presumed to be another 1000 years if the meridian of time is in the midpoint of history.

Again Satan will stir up and deceive the nations of the earth to rise up against Israel and Jerusalem. Once again war shall cover the earth and like before it will be Armageddon all over again. When the city of Jerusalem is again surrounded by Satan's army, fire will descend out of heaven and devour them. This is the post-millennial Gog and Magog invasion (*Rev.* 20:7-9). The Great War that began in heaven millenniums ago and that has continued on this earth has finally reached its climax. The war is over. The end has come at last. The final Day of Judgment comes after the last millennium. All will stand before the great white throne of God (*Rev.* 20:11-14). The resurrection of the wicked will then happen to face judgment. Satan, the Antichrist, and the false prophet will be cast into the lake of fire and brimstone as will death and hell. Fenton's *Holy Bible in Modern English* translation of the "lake of fire and brimstone" reads as "the fiery Lake burning with Divine anger."

Those on the spirit earth and those remaining on the temporal earth will face judgment, along with the resurrected wicked dead. Each will receive the degree of glory he or she has attained or can abide. Some will go into the second heaven to receive a terrestrial glory and some will go into the first heaven to receive a telestial glory. Only those who can abide the celestial law will remain on the spirit earth. When the great Day of Judgment is completed and everyone is assigned his place of reward, the spirit earth will ascend into the third and highest heaven, passing thru one of the many gates of heaven, into the spiritual fifth dimension, along with those who have abided and received a celestial inheritance. There, near to the throne of God, the terrestrial spirit earth will be changed in a twinkling of an eye into a celestial shining globe. Its translated inhabitants will be changed into eternal celestial beings; those beings that can and have abided the celestial law of heaven while in mortality or accepted and lived the celestial law sometime prior to or during the millennial reign. Once again Adam and his righteous descendants will regain dominion of the spirit earth forever. The shining world will join other celestial shining worlds described as foot stools of the Lord. It is the new heaven and a new earth seen by John the revelator.

According to John, there is no more sea when the spirit earth is changed into a celestial shining globe (*Rev.* 21:1). The *D&C* 29:22-25, states: "For all old things shall pass away, and all things shall become new, even the heaven and the earth, and all the fullness thereof, both men and beasts, the fowls of the air and the fishes of the sea; and not one hair, neither mote, shall be lost, for it is the workmanship of mine hand."

The crowning glory and jewel of the now celestialized spirit earth is when that great city, Enoch's city, the holy Jerusalem, descends upon the celestial earth and its inhabitants once more become a part of that world forever. It will become the capitol city of the celestial kingdom. Each gate of entry into that city bears the name of one of the twelve tribes of Jacob. The city is of indescribable beauty. It is a multidimensional cube, close to fifteen hundred miles in length and breath and height. The inspired account says that "the city was pure gold, like unto clear glass," and "the foundations of the wall of the city were garnished with all manner of precious stones." The twelve gates entering the city were of one pearl and the street of the city was pure gold, as it were transparent glass (*Rev.* 21:10-27). Remember the spirit earth was once its former place of residence (Re *The Garden of Eden,* Volume One). When the spirit earth receives its celestial glory, the temporal earth, in its telestial state, will be consumed and destroyed by fire. The planet will die. Later, it too may receive a resurrection and translation to reunit with its spritual counterpart in the celestial kingdom? (*D&C* 88:25-26) It may be that our entire solar system will be destroyed or even the entire temporal universe. But, more than likely, just our solar system. We base this on the knowledge that there are other worlds out there in the temporal universe, similar to ours that are also the children of God who are working toward their eternal salvation (*Moses* 1:28-29, 33-35). However, it is the end of our planet in **this** eternity that may be one of many eternities.

The *Dreamspell* Tzolk'in calendar reveals that the earth will ascend into the fourth dimension in 2012, and later will ascend into the fifth dimension or heaven (Shambala). It is the spirit earth that will do this, not the temporal earth. Using the Tzolk'in calendar as a time line for the above events it would appear that that the year 2032 may be the beginning of tribulation or collapse of the world economic system as we know it. We arrive at this date from the "rapture" of the earth in 2012, followed by a space of ½ hour, after opening of the seventh seal, which calculates into about 20 years or 2032. Assuming these dates are accurate, then the end of tribulation and the return of Christ would be around 2039/40. The temporal earth will then have about 2,000 more years of existence. If the Antichrist is on the earth today, he is a young child of about 5 to 8 years of age, assuming he comes to power at age 35.

There are many religious scholars who believe that most of the events described in *Revelation* have already come to pass in more ancient times. However, apocalyptic prophecy could not have been fulfilled prior to **this generation** because the state of Israel didn't exist prior to 1948 and most of the tribulation events in *Revelation* could not take place until the reinstatement of Jewish sacrifice. The end is near. The following prophecies have been fulfilled:

1. The rise of the European Union, the world's last empire (*Daniel* 7:7, Rev. 13).

2. The restoration of Biblical Hebrew as a living language (*Zephaniah* 3:9).

3. Personal ID chips, now widely used (*Rev.* 13:16-18).

4. Instantaneous worldwide communication (*Rev.* 11:9-10).

5. Explosion in knowledge in the last days. (*Daniel* 12:4)

6. Jerusalem a source of worldwide contention (*Zechariah* 12:2-3).

7. A peace process in the Middle East with many nations involved (*Daniel* 9:27).

8. A decline in moral behavior of society (*Timothy* 3:1-5).

8. The creation of the European Army (*Daniel* 11:38-39).

9. Terrible catastrophes and natural devastation increasing (*Luke* 21:25-26).

10. The Jewish temple ready for rebuilding (*Daniel* 9:27).

The only way we can possibly prepare for the 2012 event, assuming that the Tzolk'in calendar, the Mayan Long Count calendar, the *Bible,* and the words of Christ are correct, is to be the best person you can possibly be. If you are a Buddhist, be the best Buddhist you can be. If you are Muslim, be the best Muslim you can be. If a Jew, be the best Jew you can be. If you are Christian, be the best Christian you can be. Be the best of whatever law or religion that you abide. You will be judged by the amount of light, knowledge, and law you have received while on this earth and how you applied it in daily living.

The intent of the heart is measured. We are to exercise charity toward one another, that is, "love one another even as we love ourselves," simply stated "treat others as you would want to be treated." Be kind to each other. Extend a helping hand to those in need. Give a smile, say a gentle word, do a good deed everyday; that is all that is required. The big question is…when December 21, 2012 arrives, which planet are you going to be on? The spirit earth or left behind on the temporal earth? Having now been warned, it is up for you to decide. The decision is yours alone to make. It is less than seven years away as of this writing, July 9, 2005.

The Watchers

Who are they?

For most of us, they were first introduced to us in the *Old Testament*. They are discussed in detail in the chapter *The Giants* in Volume One of *The Ark of Millions of Years*. Approximately two-hundred fallen angels cast down to a lower universe were called the Watchers or the sons of God. They were off-worlders with intelligence and experience with transdimensional travel and the origin and destiny of mankind. Some were winged. Some had less-than-human features like full body fur or exceedingly long limbs. They were not of our creation, but rather were enemies of God. They knew the daughters of men and fathered many tribes of giants. They had immense power and influence over the anthropological development of man. Many of the tribes of giants became leaders, warriors, and predators. Like all children, some followed their fathers, and some did not.

**Ref: Steve Quayle files. Circus tours used giants as part of the show.
These men are about 9 feet tall.**

These giants—part Nephilim and part human—were very strong.
They could carry as much as five-thousand pounds in their bare
hands. Some were as tall as 36 feet, but could not survive well on
our Earth. On the higher Earth, they may have faired better than on
the temporal Earth, where the first created race of man thrived. The
most successful ones were around 12 feet tall, could run as fast as
a horse and cleave a human in two with one blow of a sword. They
grew to great height and strength when very young, but they did not
age well after the Union of the Polarity.

Hundreds of generations later, their genes have become recessive in many races and dominant in others. Occasionally, we see six toes, six fingers, multiple rows of teeth and excessive height coalesce in human births. Giants over the height of 8 feet do not live much past the age of 30 in modern times. Even those races that seem to have a propensity of 7-footers do not produce long life-spans, and display idiosyncratic genetic weaknesses that manifest themselves in a debilitating manner later in life.

The Watchers existed on both Noah's Earth, also called the higher Earth, and upon the primitive temporal Earth, also called the lower Earth. Prior to the *Union of the Polarity*, discussed in *Volume One*, they worked their mission of deception and corruption. On Noah's Earth they had corrupted the family of man so fully that the family unit was unrecognizable. Rampant incest, homosexuality and bestiality left the procreative process in a shambles. The process of procreation inside the bonds of marriage had been so completely disregarded by the general population that there was no hope of returning to the original plan of society. God sent a message to Noah that He was going to destroy the Earth by flood in a reclamation effort not unlike reformatting a corrupted hard drive.

As many of the giants did not follow their fathers' desires that they enslave or consume humanity, they consulted with prophet Enoch. They tried for a generation to convince God they deserved to be saved when the Flood arrived. Enoch went to the Lord many times on their behalf. Each time he returned with the same answer. They would not be spared the fate of the wicked.

The Nephilim, however, were off-worlders. They had the ability to leave the planet.

How did they survive the cataclysms?

Although the Nephilim are experienced and ageless, they can be captured for eternity. They can become trapped beneath landslides, cast into space with no means of propulsion, or held in prison. Cataclysms were sent to various planets in an attempt to expunge them from those worlds and erase the corruption they had sewn. Asteroids, Earthquakes, floods and even plagues were employed by God through various prophets to drive these evil doers out of existence. The giants, a hybrid offspring of Nephilim and human unions, feared the prophets. The Nephilim did not. Though they were committed to soiling the seed of man and corrupting whatever teachings or morals of the prophets, they were also committed to self-preservation.

There is clear evidence that they commissioned thousands of giants and many thousands of humans to build and maintain elaborate planetary alignment measurement systems to ensure a cataclysm did not take them unawares. Using the materials available on the planet, they designed elaborate and precise planetary measuring devices to detect the slightest shift in alignment of Earth with the stars and its neighboring planets. They knew that any change meant a cataclysm was coming. The Stonehenge (meaning *stone circle*) in southern England is only one of many such devices built with the strength of giants, the intelligence and precision of the Nephilim, and the sweat and blood of human slaves. These devices verified the position of certain star systems several times a year. This verification was reported to the Nephilim, who arranged their time on Earth accordingly. When the signs indicated there was a cataclysm coming, they would begin the long preparations to vacate the planet. They left the Earth prior to the Flood of Noah, and returned after the Flood subsided to rebuild their corruption.

All of these elaborate measuring devices had to be built out of existing materials. That doesn't make the design and construction any less of a marvel for modern man to behold. However, a great source of confusion for many is the reason why those structures were built. The reason is simple and has powerful ramifications. The Watchers couldn't control the cataclysms. Global floods, polar shifts, close passes by other large gravitational bodies, or sudden super-storms could not be prevented. They could only be avoided, if one could receive enough warning. Precursors of the arrival of such things had to be measured so the Watchers could make arrangements to survive. The slightest change in stellar alignment would indicate the Earth was moving out of position. The slightest difference in solar timing or in the position of the rising or setting of the sun would indicate a cosmic change. These changes were associated with cataclysms. The Watchers wanted to be warned lest they be destroyed. They needed to know when to leave. Leaving the Earth too soon would allow prophets a chance to guide the recovery of mankind. Leaving too late would mean the possible loss of life.

One cannot help but speculate on exactly how the Nephilim move from planet to planet, or even if they leave the planet in times of trouble. There are a few possibilities that are common ideas. They may remove themselves from the planet to a distance from which they can observe the cataclysm. The nearest natural satellite is Earth's moon. Would they rest on the surface, eating small snacks in their titanium can, or do they have a facility where they can repose? Suppose the moon is hollow, as many people speculate. Perhaps it is only partially hollow. We do know from spectrographic data, and from actual soil samples, that moon's soil is close to 25% oxygen by weight. Earth's own atmosphere is around 21% by weight. If one could simply create a pressurized environment on the moon—or inside the moon—it is quite feasible to supply that internal atmosphere with a suitable oxygen content directly from lunar soil. With unfiltered solar energy, some elementary chemistry principles and the right equipment this is completely possible. If one wanted to rest at a distance while polar shifts, volcanic upheavals, and global tsunamis cleanse the surface, this would be the perfect vantage point.

We also know that the moon has the most unique orbit in the known universe, relative to Earth. It revolves on its axis, but the rate of spin is exactly the same rate at which it orbits the earth. Hence, fully bright or totally eclipsed, the same side of the moon faces the Earth. From our vantage point we never get to see the other side of the moon. The moon's *albedo*—the percentage of brightness from reflected sunlight—is radically different between the side that faces Earth and the dark side of the moon. The side facing Earth is heavily marked with massive craters and covered with a dark layer of iron dust. The albedo of the Earth-side of the moon is about 10%. The albedo of the far side of the moon is over 60%. If the moon revolved any other way, we would have to wear sunglasses during the night of the full moon.

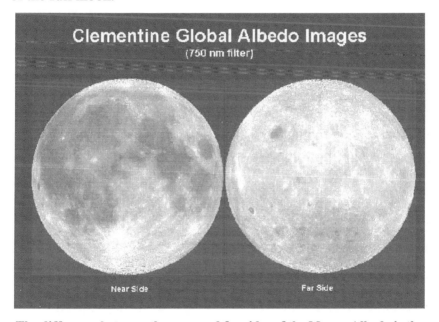

The difference between the near and far sides of the Moon. Albedo is the percentage of the Sun's energy reflected back out into space.

With a 750nm filter, one can easily see the difference between the two sides of the moon. Actually, the crust is much thicker on the far side of the moon. This fact makes the moon's orbit even more of an anomaly. The heavier side of the moon should be geotropic with respect to the Earth. The centripetal force of the moon's orbit is not nearly enough to ensure such a stable orientation. A difference of even one meter per year would change the Earth night forever. If the exact match of orbit and rotational speed—it has not changed since the two bodies were brought together—is not enough to wonder about, then consider that the moon is placed in orbit so precisely it completely eclipses the sun with only the corona revealed. The point is that there is excellent design in the placement and operation of the moon. The probability of this level of order and perfection occurring in a universe of entropy is so remote as to be immeasurable. How could the Nephilim not utilize such a perfect location for avoiding the cataclysms of Earth?

The other possibility is that the Nephilim have an ability to manipulate openings into other dimensions, from which nearly the same vantage point might be gained. This is a little more difficult for humans to conceptualize. We're used to three dimensions. Although science fiction film makers have made it easier for us to accept, considering the ability to physically slip through a portal to another dimension in the nick of time to avoid utter annihilation will earn one criticism that is not easy to outlive. Besides, other than perhaps physical preparation of one's body or psyche, why would the Nephilim require such elaborate and precise measurement devices to give them as much warning as possible? It appears that they required time, energy, and planning to leave the planet.

The ancients in Mexico had a perfect understand of the relationship of matter and energy. This statue depicts the wormhole open above the earth and the *phases* of the elements. Water represents the *Spirit* Earth and fire represents the *Temporal* Earth.

The other possibility is that the Nephilim did not leave the planet at all. They simply passed within it. You've heard the stories. The Earth is hollow. The Earth is hollow? Well, what evidence is there that the Earth is hollow? There is the famous Admiral Byrd story, where he ostensibly flew into the interior of the Earth over lush green fields, trees, and flocks of tropical birds. Unfortunately, there is no independent evidence of an opening into the core of the Earth. Yet.

There is plenty of evidence produced during every significant Earthquake, with hundreds of seismic phones listening and mapping the core of the planet like a giant MRI. What does it show?

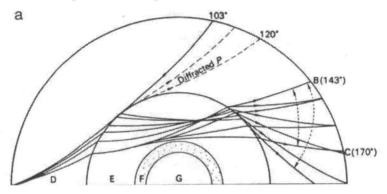

In the above seismic diagram (from a text book on seismology), D=Mantle, E=Outer core, G=Inner core.

The above diagram is the classical geological way of interpreting seismic waves generated during an Earthquake. They suppose from this data that the Earth's crust is about 800 to 1,000 miles thick. There is an interface that changes the velocity of the wave, and thus the angle of the wave. But, now look at the diagram below.

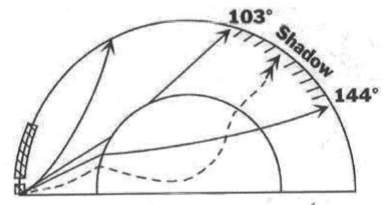

Observe the P wave strike the shadow zone in this figure[1]. Modern geologists are at a complete loss at explaining how this wave follows this pathway—see the dotted line—through a solid core counter-rotating in a liquid magma. They have made up exceptions and rules designed to support their molten core theory, rather than reach out for a more accurate explanation.

Consider an alternative theory that explains the seismic vibrations in the shadow zone quite well. See the illustration below:

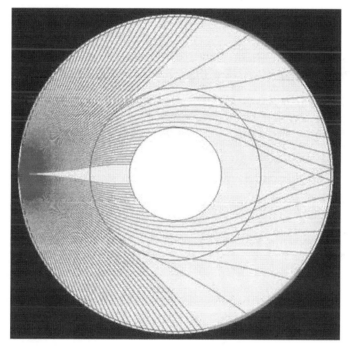

Earthquake vibration data re-graphed based on the actual signals.

In this figure one can see a theory proposed by Jan Lambrecht whereby the density of the core does not increase, but rather it decreases. In fact, the outer core and inner core described in the first illustration do not exist at all in this model. Still, the shadow zone is vibrated quite nicely without the insertion of *special refraction* adjustments needed to allow for these waves in the classical model.[2]

Think about it. The space shuttle orbits the Earth at an altitude of about 240 miles. If the crust was the same distance in thickness, that would leave about 6,100 miles of open space in which a core could be centered in an inner atmosphere. Could the core be a small star? Could it be a solid and warm iron ball spinning like the core of a planet-sized generator? Could it be a small black hole itself? The truth is we do not know. The seismic data collected over the past 20 years supports the hollow Earth model better than any other mathematical theory. The fact that the Earth has a wonderfully functional magnetosphere is evidence of a dielectric between the core and the crust. The differential between their rotational speeds is precisely what generates Earth's magnetic flux. This rotational differential simply cannot be possible with a solid core floating in molten magma under pressure beneath a solid crust.

Now, if there is a place for visitors to reside without being seen by surface dwellers, except when they're harassing radar operators, I suppose we need to discuss UFO's. They have been popularized by film and composition. There is scarcely a person who can be found who will deny their existence. I have not seen one. I have seen pictures, videos, drawings, and heard a thousand stories about their existence. The physicist in me knows that it is impossible for the occupants of a craft of any size to travel hundreds of years to Earth from even the nearest star system. There is no practicality, economy, or purpose in launching a craft half a millennia across open space to a civilization whose first radio broadcasts won't reach the closest stars for another ten years. That is unless those craft have another way of moving through space that uses technology other than simple space flight.

There must be a way for these craft to move across vast distances of space in a relatively short amount of time. There must be a way for activities on our Earth in our time to be known by other worlds, dimensions, or universes. We do not know if the Watchers use craft to move to and from Earth, or if they have a way of simply phasing to and from Earth. It appears from the preparation time they commissioned human civilization to provide them that they require a period of time to prepare for travel of this kind. The fact that they are fallen creatures apparently means they are not capable of travel to higher dimensions. They would only be qualified to exist in dimensions less than the one from which they were cast out. Beings from lower dimensions, lower vibrational capabilities, or lower glory cannot withstand the energy of higher dimensions. Beings must be transfigured by one with authority in order to withstand even a temporary exposure to higher dimensions.

So, how do the craft travel across vast distances of space and time to visit Earth so casually? The evidence points to a trans-dimensional method of travel. There seem to be two main possibilities that have support, albeit fringe support, from the scientific community. This evidence can also be classified paranormal. In any case, the organization of energy, time placement, and application is no casual matter. Unlike the imagined methods popularized by science fiction writers and television programs, moving from one universe, dimension, or phase to another evidently requires huge amounts of energy, planning, and experience to accomplish. It is no easy thing to arrive, leave, and decide to return to the same place in time and space.

It is believed by the authors that this has a basis in the theories that govern vibration, partial to the wave portion of the nature of matter. In the wave-particle duality of matter, there is a Heisenberg Uncertainty that the observer cannot state the absolute location or state of anything without affecting the very thing he is trying to observe. String theory in a nutshell says that the mode of harmony between frequencies results in matter. That is to say when two or more pitches of energy strings—so fine as to be measured on a quantum scale in Planck units of sound—harmonize perfectly, the result is something solid in a particular dimension. Keep in mind there are at least ten dimensions in which this can mathematically occur. Humans, with their limited senses, have a hard enough time with three dimensions. Manipulating or controlling the frequencies might allow matter to move from dimension to dimension, and hence from universe to universe. There are rules to this movement, just like there are rules to mathematics. What is done on one side of the equation must also be done to other side of the equation in order to maintain balance. The entropy information of known matter is inextricably linked with the entropy of unknown matter shielded from the observer by some horizon. That horizon could be that of a black hole, a magnetic barrier, or behind a veil in some other dimension.

In other words, if a person could excite all the molecules in their body and spirit, they might be able to travel great distances and perhaps through time itself. Returning to the exact moment, or another moment for that matter, may be a result of experience and ability on the part of the traveler. There is a harmony between one's spirit and their body as they coexist in this dimension at any given moment. The presence of one's consciousness in a set of energy being observed is affected by the consciousness of the observer. Think of it like the edge of space. Space is called space because there is some countable and measurable energy or particles in that region. Wondering what is beyond that edge, where there is currently nothing but void, may have an affect on that space. Traveling to that region of void transposes that void into space, because the ions from one's rocket engines are countable. The movement of one's spacecraft through that void introduces energy in the form of heat, light, and even gravitational waves, which also turn the void into space. So, the void is unobservable without transposing the void into space.

It has been proven that the universe is expanding, and that the rate of expansion increases with each passing moment. It is reasonably guessed that the universe is not rotating. Well, this brings up a problem. Without the centripetal forces of a rotating body, constructed with mass, diameter, and speed of rotation, how can the rate of expansion accelerate?

If this is true, and there is some dissension by the authors, then there is additional energy and thus mass being poured into our universe from another universe or dimension. If the universe is rotating, and there is a fixed amount of matter in the universe, then there must be areas of void being formed as matter blazes off toward outer darkness in order to balance the equation. There actually are no such voids being formed. So how does the equation balance? Where is the rest of the matter? We affectionately call this extra matter and energy that appear to be filling the void *dark matter* and *dark energy*. We're also not able to directly measure either of these quanta, except through difference measurements. That is to say, one can tell the weight of one hundred marbles in a weightless bucket by first weighing the bucket with the marbles, then filling all voids in the bucket with water and reweighing the assembly. By subtracting the actual weight from the theoretical weight—as if the bucket was filled with only water—one can deduce the weight of the marbles. Weighing space is the same way, except we use a sampling of known area. The difference between theoretical and actual is huge without the balancing act described above.

The Watchers left both planets prior to the Flood, which culminated in the merging of Noah's Earth with the temporal Earth, known as the union of the polarity. Where did they go? How did they travel? We will do our best to offer some evidence in this chapter. The giants remained behind, and along with the almost total annihilation of wayward populace of mankind, 90% of them perished.

After the Flood, the watchers returned. Their pattern of leadership changed significantly, as the new race of mankind, developing rapidly as a hybrid of Noah's race and the more ancient temporal race of men, was more sophisticated. Although the lifespan of the hybrid was not nearly that of Noah's race, they possessed a spirit of discernment that was not so easily mastered by the Watchers.

The global dynasties of Atlantis and Mu were gone, but the core beliefs of how the Earth was created, their origin in the stars remained. This common origin for these symbols permeates every community for the rest of time. Even today, the symbols we use for professional or governmental icons have their origin with these ancient establishments. The almost genetic belief in the eternal nature of the soul acted like an anchor to which men attached their roots, so they could not be swayed easily by every wind of doctrine. In doing so they unwittingly aligned themselves with the very origins the Watchers had taught to their ancestors.

Some of the races kept themselves pure and would not allow any marriage outside their own people. The reason behind this pathway to freedom condensed into traditions, rituals, and even religions. From this, the Watchers had no success in turning the believers. The Jews by and large hold to this tradition, and thus their gene pool is vastly different than the rest of human society.

But, more importantly than the anthropological aspects of the rebellion against the Watchers, modern man will not respond to them the same as ancient man. Off-worlders were readily accepted by ancient civilizations as angels, gods, or the shining ones. The appearance of UFO's, aliens, or even direct contact with extraterrestrials has been satirized so much by the media that it scarcely raises eyebrows anymore. The reality of the existence of UFO's is so connected with mainstream psychosis, or even classified paranormal, that the general public would no more associate themselves with anything like unto worship of off-worlders than they would a dashboard icon.

Why are they here?

All is not love, peace and happiness in the universe. God is not loved by everyone. He has enemies. The Watchers are His enemies. They came to Earth, and in fact to all the creations of God, to corrupt or eliminate His plans, not simply to kill all humans. Murdered innocent humans are saved in heaven. This does not meet the needs of their dark master. They must either convince you to choose evil, or they will attempt to make it so difficult to make the right choice, that the wrong choice becomes almost your only choice. In ancient times they used idols, symbols, and huge engineering projects to teach mankind their idolatrous version of history. These practices were the gateway of distraction that led to the corruption of both the Temporal and Spiritual Earths prior to the Union of the Polarity that occurred during the flood of Noah.

The Watchers taught that the early races of man came from the stars. Although that may be partly true, they left out a very important part. The stars are not to be worshipped as gods. This strategy was known by God, and was of utmost importance to Him when speaking to the prophets. When He delivered ten commandments to Moses, the first two commandments pertain to this very warning, "Thou shalt have no other gods before me. Thou shalt not make unto thee any graven image, or likeness of any thing that is in heaven above, or that is in Earth beneath, or that is under the Earth: Thou shalt not bow down thyself to them, nor serve them..."[3]   They designed and directed the construction of the pyramids, Stonehenge, Mayan temples, and numerous elaborate measuring devices with which to watch and worship the stars from whence they came.   Even though they were made of primitive materials, they were built to extremely tight tolerances and specifications.

Those early races were also taught the art of war by the Nephilim. Killing for personal gain was an easy practice to adopt when the spiritual leaders to whom the people gave their allegiance glorified it so. The many tribes of giants whom the Nephilim spawned were also very warlike. In many records they were classified as cannibals. There methods of warfare were so brutal those who came against them had to master their fear in battle. This was made even more difficult for human warriors, because giants were capable of producing tremendous sound with their voices. They had special nasal cavities, multiple rows of teeth, and lungs six-times the size of human lungs. They could scream so loud the vibrations were known to move objects. This was called harmonic levitation. They could literally blow a man down with their screams.

The Nephilim also taught the early races to limit access to energy, technology, fresh water, and to hoard food resources. They taught them how to control commerce, develop classes of wealth and slavery, and also how to dehumanize their enemies with weapons of mass destruction. Ancient writings are full of their influence. Ancient carvings show their very close relationship with earthly kings.

Even though they were far more advanced than most humans, they were limited in number and had to work with the materials and abilities that existed here on the Earth at the time. It may have been impossible for them to teach ancient man all the skills they needed to make this Earth a paradise for them. It would be much like an engineer being stranded in a third-world country without electricity or a supply of sophisticated parts or tools. In a single lifetime, an entire village under his tutelage couldn't learn enough to build the first lawn mower or pocket calculator. He may know those things once existed for him, but he couldn't train enough people in all the component design and production processes to make any of those things.

Have the Watchers returned again since the Flood to try to influence mankind? Yes. They will never give up the planet or the race they are commissioned to eliminate from the collective of God's creations. So, why do they not step out into the open and claim the Earth as their own? Why don't they show themselves and their craft to the world? Actually, we don't see evidence of them ever working directly with the masses. They always worked through the leadership behind the scenes. They were much more effective with the art of delegation through greedy kings and rulers who would gladly sell out their people for ultimate power or even a promise of peace through superior firepower. If you'll remember, the Romans had global peace on the Earth for one thousand years. They ruled with such brutality and such superior fighting skills that history records only a skirmish or two during that millennium. In their effort to conquer the entire world, Roman soldiers were sent to remote areas where they had to fight against tribes of giants. Although the most battle-hardened and organized troops in the world, they were often pounded into the afterlife by giant warriors. The Romans had to develop special war tactics to defeat them. War machines were built that could hurl a single bolt twelve feet long weighing over 200 pounds for terrific distances. Some historians claim these machines were for breeching the walls of castles. But, the barbarian regions conquered by Rome did not build castles. These weapons were for killing giants.

The holy Roman empire also controlled the church and through that all the world's leadership as well. No one dared rise up against the vestige of power that smacked of divinity. A practice of economic shunning, or refusing to trade or even speak to anyone who was judged to be a heretic could bring even kings to their knees. No amount of wealth could help them survive. The state controlled religion wiped out the last vestiges of true holiness through mass beheadings, burnings, and hangings. Anyone caught owning scripture, memorizing or quoting scripture, or trying to copy down a few words was summarily hunted down and executed. Most of the greatest translators all the way up the 16th century were murdered by the state's church leaders.

William Tyndale spent his entire frail life translating the *Old* and *New Testaments* into English. His translations were not only very accurate, they were beautifully poetic and revealed the spirit of the song-like ancient Hebrew script. Rather than working from the Greek, and sometimes misleading state texts, he used the ancient

Hebrew texts made of solid lines of consonants, with no spaces or vowels. Extreme skill and a spirit for deciphering these manuscripts were required. He constantly moved and changed his name to avoid capture by church authorities. Finally, just after he completed his work, he was captured and thrown in jail. His health continued to decline. He was kept in a dungeon and only let out for two events. The first time was to stand trial for heresy, at which he was judged guilty for his translations. The second was to be led to a stake, where he was strangled and then burned. Fortunately, his work lives on as a major part of the King James version of the *Holy Bible.*

The Nephilim worked closely with ancient kings to assure them ultimate rule. In exchange, the Nephilim replaced god with idols, symbols, and their own version of creation.

Nephilim exerted tremendous influence over the kings of the Earth.

They have always been successful at manipulation through the divulgence of new technology to one side, and then deftly giving it to the other side as well.

One can see in figure above, the image of the winged Nephilim holding a *pinecone* over the back of the Earthly kings. The common interpretation is that the seeds coming out of the pinecone are bits of knowledge. It is just as likely, that these are not symbolic, but rather devices through which they manipulated the leaders of the world. The winged disc over the tree-of-life symbol is a crystal clear indicator of the intention of the guidance being offered by the Nephilim. The kings received knowledge of war, economics, engineering and social sciences. In exchange, their doctrine replaced that of the Creator according to plan. Opposing kings are given nearly equal levels of technology so that warfare is never too one-sided. After all, it is not victory that is the goal of the Nephilim, but war itself.

When the Nephilim appeared in ancient days they were heralded as angels and gods, probably because their abilities to travel and manipulate energy was so far advanced as to be considered only possible by a deity. When they come to Earth now, they are not heralded as deity. They are regarded as off-worlders. But, today they work as councilors behind the scenes with the various leaders of Earth. The leaders of the world have always learned much from beings who can travel through space-time as easily as we plan a trip across an ocean. Modern people who think about such things ask, "What exactly are they teaching the leaders of the world, and what do the Nephilim get out of teaching them?"

Indeed, spending and organizing energy to come here and bear this primitive world is an investment in something. They are either trying to educate mankind in how to live with the Earth in perfect balance and understand the potential value of the race, or they are feeding the greed and lust of Earthly leaders so the race can continue its cycle of self-annihilation. Recorded history seems to point to the latter purpose. A kind and benevolent, vastly more adept teacher would most certainly take control of the airplane before the student crashes into the ground.

The Gulf

The population of Earth is reaching the levels once enjoyed by civilizations like Atlantis and Mu. We are beginning to explore outer space, although we have not yet discovered how to enter transdimensional portals. Our level of weaponry has also progressed perhaps beyond that of ancient civilizations. Perhaps not. Ancient civilizations had global war with weapons of mass destruction. They were not mature enough after ten thousand years of development to restrain themselves from war. In the end, a series of three great cataclysms destroyed them all. Modern civilization is also quite capable now of global thermonuclear war. Will we pass the threshold of self-destruction and survive? Will we also suffer through cataclysms of volcanoes, earthquakes, and even perhaps cosmic encounters? Will we suffer the same fate as the ancients?

It appears than mankind has reached this precipice before and failed to resist the urge to leap. Our ancient ancestors either were not aware of the ramifications of global warfare with energy weapons, or they were fully aware and did not care. We would like to think we are a more noble race than they. But, when Oppenheimer's team tested the first plutonium bomb they actually did not know whether or not the free hydrogen in the atmosphere would be drawn into the chain reaction and set the atmosphere on fire. They ran a risk of killing every living thing on the planet with the first test. The yield of the bomb was estimated, based on the mass and atomic number of the enriched fuel. The actual explosion was so surprising that many of the team refused to continue. The nuclear leaders, including Einstein, argued that the power was too terrible as a weapon. Dr J. Robert Oppenheimer quoted ancient Sanskrit literature in an interview conducted after he watched the first atomic test. Quoting from the Bhagavad Gita: "'Now I am become Death, the Destroyer of Worlds.' I suppose we all felt that way," he said. He spent years trying to convince the American leadership that the benefits of nuclear research could meet the world's needs for clean energy for centuries.

Of course, the value of its power as a weapon was the only reason the research was funded in the first place. Twenty years later, it would be used as a means to generate cheap and clean electricity. The nuclear power plants built in the early sixties are still operating today. Economic and political pressures from all sides stopped the construction of nuclear power plants in the United States in the early eighties. There has not been a single yard of concrete poured in the United States for a new nuclear power plant since before there was such a thing as home computers. There have been more than fifty thousand nuclear warheads built instead. Many thousands of these are deployed all around the globe in strategic locations, some of them mobile and undetectable, in a diplomatic balancing act in an effort to maintain peace between super-powers with an insane philosophy called Mutually Assured Destruction. The very appropriate acronym is MAD.

Evidence seems to support the fact that our ancient brothers also could not resist the urge to use the power of the stars as a weapon. The textbook of Basic Radioactive Chemistry (C. Claire ed.) used by Tsinghua university has the following paragraph: "The natural uranium in the Oklo mine in Gabon, West Africa, contains an abnormal amount of U235. It is as low as 0.29%, rather than the normal 0.72%. Geologists theorize that many self-sustained nuclear fission chain reactions took place at this mine about two billion years ago. Thirteen nuclear reactors existed in prehistoric periods along the 200-metre mine bed, and they were comparable to the modern nuclear reactor in power and heat combustion. This mine had the capability of enabling self-sustained nuclear chain reactions...." This discovery, that shocked the entire scientific community in 1972, has already been forgotten by people today."

Harappa and Mohenjo-Daro

When excavations of Harappa and Mohenjo-Daro—shown above—reached the street level, they discovered skeletons scattered about the cities—shown below—many holding hands and sprawling in the streets as if some instant, horrible doom had taken place. People were just lying, unburied, in the streets of the city.

The 25-thousand year old corpses found at Harappa lay dead in the streets as if running from the radioactive blast that killed the entire city

These skeletons are twenty-five thousand of years old, even by traditional archaeological standards. Why did the bodies not decay or get eaten by wild animals? Furthermore, there is no apparent cause of a physically violent death.

Even though they are 500 times older, these skeletons are among the most radioactive ever found, on par with those at Hiroshima and Nagasaki. At one site, Soviet scholars found a skeleton which had a radioactive level 50 times greater than normal. There is only one way this level of radioactivity could be found in skeletons discovered in this arrangement. Thermonuclear war.

Other cities have been found in northern India that indicate nuclear explosions occurred. One such city, found between the Ganges and the mountains of Rajmahal, revealed huge masses of walls and foundations of the ancient city fused together, literally vitrified! And since there is no indication of a volcanic eruption at Mohenjo-Daro or at the other cities, the intense heat to melt clay vessels can only be explained by an atomic blast or some other unknown weapon. The cities were wiped out entirely. Purely because the evidence does not support the traditional anthropological dates of humanity, reporters have discarded the obvious data and substituted it with their convoluted theories.

While the skeletons have been carbon-dated to 2500 BC, we must keep in mind that carbon-dating involves measuring the Carbon daughters of Carbon 14, left to decay at a known half-life cycle. Additional radiation, either cosmic of nuclear may alter the decay by adding electrons and neutrons onto the structure and even shifting the mean subatomic weight.

Fortunately, in modern times a weapon like this has only been used twice. The theories that such a fission reaction could occur naturally are, in our opinion, at best far-fetched. Given the mass of Uranium on the planet—Radon daughters of Uranium emanate through the soil of almost every square foot of dry land—the odds of another reaction similar to this theory would be very good. Since there have been no recorded events like this, or irradiated fields where this has occurred, there is no other evidence to support such a theory. The ancient records support the theory that thermonuclear weapons were used by ancient warriors against each other, having the same devastating effects as those observed at Hiroshima and Nagasaki.

The actual radioactive plume from Nagasaki rose 11 km into the sky. It was a plutonium bomb. The skeletons of the dead were not as radioactive as those discovered at Harappa.

Many records indicate that the Nephilim managed to use their technology to enable them to live somewhere else on the planet, or even temporarily leave the planet, when these events occur. Ancient records seem to indicate that when cataclysms of cosmic proportions occur, the Nephilim exist before and after the event. In some ancient records, it seems the cataclysm was precipitated by God to wipe out the Nephilim who had so corrupted His plans. UFO's may be the very craft that they, and their genetic creations, use to move themselves and their cargo about the planet.

The Nephilim are masters of planetary domination. One might ask how a team of off-worlders, even with their skills and aptitude, could bring an entire planet into control without a blatant display of superior weaponry. It appears that when they come here, they have only the clothes on their back and what knowledge they possess. So how would they do it? They might pit one nation against another, providing only enough technology to maintain the balance of power. Both sides would spend vast portions of their budgets to gain a military advantage. Every form of research would be colored by the funding engines designed to that advantage. Such efforts would distract the most powerful to maintain its lead, and the lesser powerful to discover a way to unseat the former. Resources that could be used to peacefully explore the stars would instead be used to launch surveillance satellites or space-based weapons. Resources that could discover cures for disease and suffering would be employed to create, or defend against, microbial or viral warfare agents. Keeping the planet in constant turmoil and conflict is one way to assure the cycle of self-annihilation. Modern evidence indicates that at least remnants of such designed conflict is still responsible for global terror.

It seems, though, that leaders have come forth in the last fifty years who have recoiled from the use of such expenditure of energy. As long as they remain in power it seems that global thermonuclear war may be abated. So, how then would the Nephilim use their skills to bring this more reserved world into submission? The ultimate goal is to form a single government that could control everything. We fear this consolidation more than anything else. Or do we?

The Greatest Generation knows the weaknesses and prophecies of such a government. They would never allow the tools needed by such a leader to rule the world to be forged. The mark of the beast is a very familiar tool foreseen by many to enslave all of mankind to a single malevolent leader. Generation X-ers—those born to boomers—are much less swayed by the prospect of evil. When modern leaders speak of a one-world government, they use sweet tones and paint pictures of great economic benefits for the whole world. Still, it has meant the demise of every political leader who has floated the idea on national media. So how will the Nephilim accomplish their goal? How will the entire race of man be brought into this new and all-powerful system?

Here is how it will be done.

The Mark of the Beast

Since the design and utilization of the sale of stock and other forms of bearer bonds or securities as a means of financing, the civilized world works the exchange of currencies for good and labor. Locally, it has worked in some form or another since the first coins were minted, but exchange between one currency and another has always been an issue of conflict. When pilgrims came to ancient Jerusalem to worship at the temple through various sacrifices, they had to convert their money into temple script. That script could be used to purchase items needed by the pilgrim for his purposes. Such a pilgrim might have traveled from afar, and at no small expense come with a humble heart to pay some homage and absolve a sin or two, bless some particular crop, or petition the healing of some family member. Although perhaps taken aback at the horrific rate of exchange on the temple grounds, he would likely capitulate without much recourse. During at least one such pilgrimage, Jesus cleared the temple grounds of such profiteers with prejudice.

In modern times, we are plagued by the same forces of profit through manipulation of one's currency relative to other forms of exchange. The disruption upon the global economy of one government printing money to pay its bills or make massive capital acquisitions has caused more than one economic crash. The wealthy class of early twentieth century aristocrats controlled nearly one hundred percent of all the world's resources for more than forty years. There were the extremely wealthy and then the millions who worked for twenty-five cents a day and a box of potatoes. There was no middle class. The lucrative banking and stock exchanges of those days encouraged working people to put their money in the bank. Those banks would then purchase stock on the exchange, sometimes at ninety percent margins. This means that they could profit from stock upon which they had only made a ten percent down payment. If the stock went up, which it almost always did, they built value and reaped huge profits. If it went down, which it almost always didn't, they would be required to make the *call* and pay the debt in full.

All went well until the late 1920's. The world's extremely wealthy slowly withdrew from the Exchange so as not to upset the prices of stock. They kept all of the wealth in the form of debt-free land, oil, gold, utilities and cash. There is great speculation as to what actually caused the market to crash in 1929, but the results are irrefutable. The middle class evaporated overnight. Stocks that once sold for twenty dollars could be bought for a penny. The price of labor, goods, and services dropped so low that the wealthy were able to repurchase entire companies, and in fact bought entire governments for fractions of pennies on the dollar. One could conjure up pictures of the Great Gatsby or the Rockefellers to represent the class of individuals who were richer than any modern billionaire. They owned the oil wells, the trucks and trains that hauled it, the refineries, the stations that sold it, and set the price of everything so as to make it impossible for anyone to compete with them. If it wasn't for the Sherman Antitrust Act, they would still own the world. War only made them richer, while the sons and daughters of the poor provided fodder for global wars through a forced draft. Not surprisingly, the wealthy could buy deferments, thus keeping their legacy alive.

So, how could that happen again? Would we allow ourselves to be governed by a small group of corruptible men again? Not that generation. They still had the memory of working for twenty-five cents a day and all the potatoes one could carry home. They remember the soup lines and welfare projects that dusted the world while private steamships and caravans bore the wealthy from one casino to the next.

The design has necessarily become more sophisticated now. The currencies of the world are shrinking in number. The dollar and the Euro have replaced dozens of currencies. The International Monetary Fund has helped stabilize the inflations and depressions of smaller nations. Stock exchanges are more stable and have margin regulations in place to prevent catastrophic financial crashes. There is more real equity in the world, and the base of wealth is broad enough that no nation can completely fall economically. Still, the exchange rate robs billions of dollars in real profits from hard-working people all over the world. It is a major source of loss for many nations. Doing away with the exchange of currencies would most assuredly save millions of jobs and help every nation compete more freely and openly.

The formation of a single currency for the entire world would be a major benefit for the world. It is also a keystone of the Nephilim's design for planetary domination.

Some form of cash has been the form of exchange used by mankind for over ten thousand years. When you paint a house, mow a yard, program a computer, or fix a car your effort is exchanged equally for currency. That currency can be taken anywhere in the world and traded for something else. That is a simple concept. Cash is the most powerful force on the planet. It fuels our cars, builds our houses, and even serves as a form of speech. Trading it or withholding it has phenomenal effect on the planet. We cast out or elect new leaders with it. We propagate ideas that are representative of our own through radio, newspaper, and television because we buy the products from sponsors of those programs. If we cease to support those programs with our cash, they cease to exist, unless they are artificially supported by governments as propaganda outlets. Cash is also uncontrollable. It is the ultimate form of freedom. Save it. Spend it. Donate it. Your choice.

However, it has some costs associated with it. There are three costs that are unbearable for a free and peaceful society.

1. First, it is the means by which illegal drugs are distributed throughout the world. Forget about legalization as a means to eliminate the crime of drugs. Many nations have tried it for centuries. The addiction of an entire nation is no solace for making drugs legal. Opium addiction nearly cost the lives of an entire generation of China and Western Europe. Bales of cash are smuggled out of America every day to pay for tons of heroin, cocaine, and marijuana that result in more than 95% of the murders, auto accidents, and divorces. Without cash, there would be no drug business. Doing away with cash would stop the drug trafficking business cold. No one would scan a debit card to pay for a gram of cocaine. The funds would be seized, and the participants would go to jail.

2. Second, cash is the exchange of terrorism. There are many providers of weapons in the world. None of them will donate weapons and ammunition to rogue nations or terror groups. They certainly don't take credit. The only way to fuel an army of any size is with cash, jewels, or precious metals. Controlling these forms of exchange is the way to prevent rebellion against the system. The Economic Council of West African States (ECOWAS) prevents the sale of what is known as conflict diamonds to anyone outside the region. The influx of cash to purchase diamonds or other jewels is what fuels warfare in that region of the world. No one would electronically exchange cash for weapons. They would be captured before they finished unpacking the boxes.

3. Third, the cost of printing and maintaining cash is unbelievable. Millions of bills are printed every week to replace the worn and damaged bills in the banking system. There is an entire division of the government that deals with the creation, storage, and distribution of cash. Thousands of armored trucks travel every city in America carrying billions of dollars to banks and places of business so commerce can take place. The amount of money spent just handling cash is enough to pay off the debt of the entire state of California. Add to that the hundreds of millions of dollars in counterfeit

cash that is smuggled into America as a form of economic terrorism, and if there is no doubt we must eliminate cash from our society.

All electronic monetary exchanges, and all cash exchanges over $10,000 are currently monitored by the US Treasury Department. Do you have any doubts of this technology? Here's how it works. The next time you go to the grocery and take advantage of the barcoded discount card in your possession, consider this. Every item you purchase is tracked with that barcode. Your profile, including all the information you provided the grocer when you obtained that discount card, is collected and modified with every purchase you make. The amount of orange juice sold in a certain zip code to a certain age group is vital information to the grocer and the producer of the orange juice. It helps both of them adjust their production, stock, and advertising budgets for your exact market area. When your debit card or credit card is stolen and used by another person, there is an extremely slim chance they will match your purchasing profile. Within hours of that deviation, the card is deactivated. The process is so effective now, nearly every bank provides identity theft insurance free of charge. The only thing that would make the system more effective and less susceptible to loss is a better form of electronic identity.

As of the writing of this book, the proposal to eliminate cash from our society has not been completely implemented. It will be. The Nephilim have very carefully facilitated the capture of every single person inside the system. About ten percent of the population of America still works for cash. They mow grass, style hair, work on cars, and paint houses for cash. They buy everything with cash. They don't exist in the income tax system. They cannot be tracked through their banking habits, because they don't use banks. Grocery discount cards indicate their demographics. How much they spend, what they buy, and where they shop is known. With a little data matching, the system could even determine the most likely sources from whom they get their cash.

The core to the plan is that cash will be eliminated. The proposal will be sold to Americans using the three reasons listed above. This would mean that every single dollar would be absorbed into a completely electronic form of exchange. Don't think this is impossible. I doubt you could find twenty people tomorrow that have a hundred dollars in cash on them. The electronic debit card or credit card will buy everything from airplane tickets, to a small order of fries. Every single bank provides their customers with debit cards. The next generation will accept the elimination of cash as so logical and sensible, they'll think having cash is as useless as owning a buggy whip.

The beauty and evil of the plan, is that it will work. Drug traffic would be greatly curtailed through the elimination of currency. War on any grand scale would be virtually impossible. Costs associated with printing and maintaining the integrity of the actual bills and coins would be put back into the national treasury. But there is another value in bringing all the financial incomings and outgoings into the electronic world.

The revenues gathered by the government from the people's income is currently a system of *catch me if you can*. No taxpayer wants to render one more penny unto Caesar than is absolutely required. Even then, as a people we spend billions of dollars on charities and other tax-deductible organizations to defer as much of our earnings as possible away from the government. Nevertheless, each Spring we voluntarily submit our forms and documents concerning our private lives to the auspices of the Internal Revenue Service to validate our contribution. With the new electronic currency, no one will be able to exist outside the system of revenue. No one will be able to hide their income in the form of cash. No one will be able to spend a single penny without paying tax, and causing tax to be paid by the recipient. So besides lowering overall costs, the new system will vastly increase revenues. In short, the government will receive many times the income they ever received in the cash system.

The only challenge left in the system is a flawless form of identification. Retinal scans, fingerprints, DNA, implanted microchips and even tattooed barcodes have all been explored. Each one has its advantages and weaknesses. Although it is not the purpose of this chapter to weigh those values, it goes without saying that it all depends on the extent to which an enemy will try to defraud the system. Whether or not that threat exists to any amount or not, the Nephilim have one goal in mind. It is not the protection of all law-abiding citizens from identity theft. Their purpose is to make sure no man woman or child can survive without being fed and clothed through the system.

The implantation of chips under the skin is already practiced with farm animals and pets. It stores all the inoculations, birth genetics, and ownership records for easy access. It has replaced the ear tag for millions of animals already. It is also installed in some automobiles as a theft recovery device. It is installed in cell phones, credit cards, and even shipping containers for global location. The technology is being made faster, cheaper, and more foolproof each day. The *Greatest Generation* would never accept a subcutaneous implant. Even Generation X-ers would resist the implant. But, the generation born in the 1980's will accept the implant. The sales job will be so easy, there will scarcely be a human alive that won't support it.

Every State in America will require the implantation of identity chips in all farm animals. As of the writing of this book, this mandate is nearly universal. Every day the news is blasted with one kidnapping after another. Children, young women and boys, and even college-aged girls have always been kidnapped on a weekly basis. But since 2002, the major radio and television news networks have broadcasted these disappearances in an effort to save lives. The instant notification and tracking systems, currently known as *amber alerts,* can get the entire public to help find a missing child in a matter of minutes. A popular program called *America's Most Wanted* had a phenomenal record of facilitating the capture of hundreds of criminals.

The parent of every child enrolled in public school is encouraged to have their child fingerprinted, photographed and even supplied with ID bracelets for rapid identification. The GPS micro-chip implant would be the ultimate life-saver. Parents have been urged to supply their children with cell phones equipped with GPS—global positioning satellite—chips so they can be tracked by law enforcement for a speedy recovery. But, a cell-phone can be lost. The preferred method of security is to implant the chip beneath the skin. The instant a life is saved by one of these chips, there will instant national support for the implant.

Evidence of the workings of this plan is carved into the soul of mankind. It is to make it impossible for the people to rise up and commit heresy against the god-like Nephilim. A prophet, a writer, or a rebel leader will always be inspired to rise up against total government, even if the living conditions are tolerable. There is an innate spirit inside of every human that yearns to be free. It takes many generations of oppression and domination to break the will of a people to seek freedom, but individually that desire remains. Inmates in America are treated in such a way as to experience no daily pain. They have health care, meals, clean clothes, and facilities with which to rehabilitate themselves. But they are not free. Denial of breathing the air on a public beach ,or hiking in the green lowlands with friends, or watching a movie in a theater is suffering for the people incarcerated inside of those prison walls. They cannot escape. Neither will mankind be able to escape the auspices of the rulers of the world, when this plan is completely implemented.

What do we do? To whom do we turn for deliverance? How can this be avoided? Do we even want to avoid it?

The Gods

This chapter is a continuation of the chapters *The Lost Civilization of Mu* and *The Lost Civilization of Atlantis* in Volume One.

The *Book of Enoch The Prophet* identifies the leader of the fallen angels as Lucifer. It was at his bidding that the fallen angels, called the Watchers, came to both the spirit and temporal earths and to other worlds in this universe. Primarily, their mission was to corrupt the seed of man but they ended up corrupting the animal kingdom as well. Because they sought to undo the works of the Creator's hands, Noah's world was destroyed by water and the temporal earth, in this universe, was nearly destroyed by a great cataclysm. Ninety percent of all life on this planet was wiped out. It was the day the earth nearly died 11,500 years ago or 9,500 B.C.

Although their numbers were small, mankind did survive on this planet. Over the course of a few thousand years, the population of mankind had increased sufficiently to form the beginnings of new civilizations. However, they were hampered by the lack of knowledge and technology to make much progress. For the most part, mankind remained barbaric hunters and gatherers. The exception of course was Egypt, who had access to knowledge stored in the Hall of Records that jump started their civilization way in advance of other civilizations.

The Watchers returned to restore knowledge, the arts of civilization, including magic, and warfare to mankind world wide but again, their primary mission was not one of benevolence but rather to re-corrupt the seed of mankind here on this planet, under the direction of their chief, Lucifer. A short account of the fallen angels is given in *Genesis* but there are other accounts that give much broader details. Until recently these other accounts were considered myths or at least misunderstood. Your authors want to open the readers' eyes to the beginning of all evil and paganism on this planet after the Flood of Deucalion or Flood of Noah.

The most famous name from antiquity after the flood, from the pagan perspective, was the biblical character Nimrod and his wife, Semiramis. According to *Genesis*, Nimrod, which would include his wife, were the ones who started the worship of pagan gods, rather than the true Creator. As discussed in a previous chapter, *The Tower of Babel*, Nimrod was a giant demi-god or product of illicit sexual union between a fallen angelic "son of God" and a mortal woman. He is credited as the first "empire builder" and through force of conquest he established his empire over the whole of ancient Mesopotamia. Perhaps he is best remembered as the King under whose authority that mankind attempted to build the Tower of Babel. His Hebrew name was Nimrod, his Babylonian name was Gilgamesh, and his Sumerian name was Amraphel.

The Sumerian/Babylonian tablets closely parallel the *Genesis* and *The Book of Enoch The Prophet* accounts of the fallen angelic host of heaven and their leader, Lucifer. According to the tablets, Anu (God) was the father and supreme God of all the gods who rarely if ever visited the earth. Under his leadership, there were two other lesser gods that served important roles and had very close relationships with mankind in ancient times. Enlil was the first and most powerful god of the Sumerian pantheon, followed by Enki, also known as Ea or Eya, who was titled the "Lord of the Earth." The center of worship for Anu was within Uruk (biblical Erech) which was a temple/ziggurat dedicated to him and known as the E-anna, or "House of Heaven;" while Enlil's city was Nippur, where the gods had previously met for an assembly. The Annunaki, Sumerian name for the fallen angels or Egyptian *Shebtiu,* arrived in the southern marshlands of Sumer and founded Eridu. You authors estimate that these beings returned on earth approximately 8,500-8,000 B.C. Eridu was the sacred city of Enki, and according to Sumerian myth was the first city built by mankind after the flood., and the first place where the human tradition of "kingship" began. The first cities in Mesopotamia were established by the Anunnaki. Accompanying the Anunnaki were seven sages called the *apkallu,* who were sent by Eya to bring the arts of civilization to mankind and they also set up kings to rule over the people.

In the epic poem *Emmerkar and the Lord of Aratta* , we are informed that the sacred site of Eridu had first been established prior to the flood through Enoch, the son of Cain, and the Anunnaki. This event of course, would have happened on the spirit earth before the union of the polarity. After the union of the polarity, Eridu was re-established on the temporal earth. Enmerkar, a great king and contempory of Nimrod/Gilgamesh, was in charge of building a new "House of Enki" at Eridu as well as building an elaborate new temple/ziggerat to the nephertali goddess Inanna in Uruk. The nephertali goddess Inanna was elevated by Enmerkar as an equal to Anu (Lord of Heaven). No doubt the *apkallu* had set up Enmerkar as a king because he was known as the "son of Enki." Everything this king did, he did it in the name of his father. Enmerkar's son was Asar/Agga, who the Assyrians recognized as their state deity Ashur. Although Nimrod/Gilgamesh was a mortal giant king, he was deified in Sumerian dynastic times and elevated to the status of a demi-god. As a deified god he would have had a temple/ziggurat built for him and a new name, however to date, historians haven't found conclusive proof of what name he was deified under. We don't believe that he was Marduk or Enmerkar as these were sons of Lucifer. Nimrod was a mortal giant. The *Epic of Gilgamesh* tells of Gilgamesh's search for the elixir of life that would grant him immortality. End result is that he fails to find it. It is possible that he lived many centuries before dying a mortals death. Historians generally forget that the giants had extremely long life spans. Lucifer's son, Marduk, was an immortal. Positive proof of the true identity of Nimrod/Gilgamesh may never be found because the historical data is entangled with so many myths. Originally Nimrod had planned to dedicate the massive beacon tower, in Shinar, to Enki. Instead, he and Enki both suffered a great embarrassment when his plan failed and the tower was left half finished.

It was in Eridu that a temple/ziggurat was built and dedicated to Enki, where generations of priests called *en.si* could communicate with their god in the "dark chamber." Enki is acknowledged as "Lord of the Earth" by Jesus in *Matthew* 4:8-10, *John* 12:31 and *John* 14:30, and referred to by Paul in 11 *Corinthians* 4:4 as the "god of this world." The Sumerian god Enki is none other than the Sumerian representation of Lucifer or Satan.

Enki's big mistake was that he plotted to take over the pantheon of gods, installing himself as the head god on this planet and the entire universe. He thus was *"enthroned on the mount of assembly"* making himself *"like the Most High."* Simply stated, he made himself an equal to the chief supreme God. As God's equal he took the credit for creating man here on this planet, as told in the Sumerian tablets. Of course, he lied; he wasn't their creator, although he may have had a role in the planning of this creation, you see, Enki probably could genetically re-engineer Homo Erectus into Homo Sapiens or modern man, but he didn't have the power or authority to give man a divine soul. To make matters worse, Enki repeatedly *defied the Council,* and defied the will of God as decreed in the Council. Lest we forget, Lucifer/Enki was called the "Father of Lies" by Jesus in *John* 8:44. This would cost him severely as you will see shortly.

The *apkallu* originally decided that each nation would be led directly by a different member of the nephilim host. These plans quickly weakened with the introduction of new gods and the elevating up of the minor gods in the pantheon as powerful city-state deities in their own right. This necessitated the building of new ziggurats and temple-complexes in each city to accommodate the worship of these new gods. Eventually, the surplus of new gods created intense competition and warfare between the city-states as the gods tried to achieve mastery over their neighbors. Certain gods, through survival of the fittest, were able to gain dominance and reign supreme over their respective empires once more. The dominant gods and goddesses of Rome, Greece, India, and Egypt, and other nations were essentially the same as with the original pantheon of the Babylonians. That fact is well established.

The Babylonian epic tale, the *Enuma Elish,* introduces a new god, Marduk. He was created from the union of Ea, the Akkadian name for the god Enki, and Damkina. The epic describes the son of Enki/Lucifer as follows:

Ea begot him and Damkina bore him, father and mother;
he sucked the paps of goddesses, from his nurses he was fed
on the terribleness that filled him.

His body was beautiful; when he raised his eyes great lights flared; his stride was majestic; he was the leader from the first.

When Ea who begot him saw him he exulted, he was radiant, light-hearted, for he saw that he was perfect, and he multiplied his godhead, the one to be first and stand highest.

His limbs were immaculate, the making a fearful mystery beyond comprehension; with four eyes for limitless sight, and four ears hearing all; when his lips moved a tongue of fire burst out. Titanic limbs, standing so high he overtopped the tallest god; he was strong and he wore the glory of ten, and their lightnings played round him.

Enki/Lucifer exclaimed, "My son, my son, son of the sun, and heaven's sun!"

Marduk, the son of Lucifer, ascended to become foremost among the gods of the Babylonian pantheon, nearly one thousand years after Nimrod's reign. It was through his son that Lucifer was able to further his agenda for continued dominion over the pagan world. He was the Babylonian vegetation god, the biblical Merodach, and later known simply as Bel or Baal (Lord). The nephertali goddess, Queen of Heaven Inanna, was his wife. Enki/Lucifer, supposedly with the approval of the Divine Council of the gods, installed his son as both the new ruler over the earth, and over the entire universe.

The Sumerian version of Marduk was Dumuzi and Inanna. The Egyptian version of Marduk was Osiris and Isis. Both goddesses, Inanna and Isis were fertility goddesses. Dumuzi was the resurrection god and god of the dead in the underworld. He is the dying winter god who is reborn as the new spring vegetation or a vegetation god. The same is said about Osiris. He becomes the god of the dead and is the Egyptian vegetation god. Therefore it is evident that Marduk, Dumuzi, and Osiris were one and the same god.

The mysterious green man whose face is seen peering in several places in Roslyn Chapel, Scotland, is believed to be a vegetation god. It is possible that he really is a representation of Marduk/Dumuzi/ Osiris or the biblical Merodach.

The Sumerian Dumuzi was the biblical Canaanite god Tammuz, the Phoenician Adonis, the Greek Dionysus, and the Roman Bacchus. Understandably, the prophet Ezekiel was horrified to see the women of Jerusalem worshipping Tammuz (*Ezekiel* 8:14-15). Marduk's son was the god Nabu who was represented by the planet Mercury. The Egyptian version of Nabu was the god Thoth and the Greek version of him was Hermes, who were also represented by the planet Mercury. Nabu was also viewed as the scribe and messenger of the gods as were Thoth and Hermes. Therefore we can again conclude that Nabu, Thoth, and Hermes, were the one and same god. According to

Berossus, the Greek Titan Elder God, Cronus, was simply the Greek version of Enki/Lucifer and Zeus was the Greek version of Lucifer's son, Marduk.

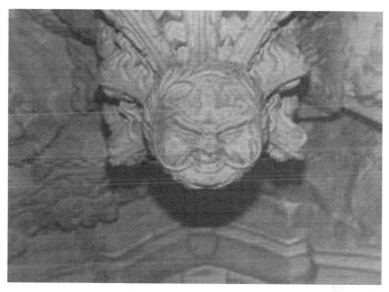

Roslin Chapel "Marduk depicted as *Green Man*" a vegetation god anciently by the Babylonians.

Greek mythology identifies Zeus as being one of the Olympian gods and offspring of the Elder god, Cronus. Zeus overthrew his father, Cronus, and became the head or supreme god. This is exactly what happened with Enki/Lucifer and Marduk. Marduk became the new ruler of the earth and universe, surmounting his father in power and glory. Lucifer's punishment for making himself equal to God was the loss of his powerful position to his son, Marduk, supposedly approved by the council or assembly of gods. Enki/Lucifer was dethroned by the assembly of gods in favor of his son. Marduk's wife, Inanna was known later as Ishtar.

During the Exodus, Moses repeatedly warned Israel not to worship the pagan gods of their neighbors or emulate them in any way. One of these gods they were warned about was the patron god of the Ammonites, Molech/Moloch/Merodach/Marduk because they sacrificed their children to this god. 1*Kings* 11:7 records that Solomon built religious structures in honor of many pagan gods, including one for the Ammonite god, Molech. Because Israel turned their backs to God by worshiping these pagan gods, the prophet Jeremiah predicted that God would hand over the children of Israel to the kingdom of Babylon as punishment.

Jeremiah 32:26-35 records:

"Then the word of the LORD came to Jeremiah: I am the LORD, the God of all mankind. Is anything too hard for me? Therefore, this is what the LORD says: I am about to hand this city over to the Babylonians and to Nebuchadnezzar king of Babylon, who will capture it. The Babylonian who are attacking this city will come in and set it on fire; they will burn it down, along with the houses where the people provoked me to anger by burning incense on the roofs to Baal and by pouring out drink offerings to other gods.

The people of Israel and Judah have done nothing but evil in my sight from their youth; indeed, the people of Israel have done nothing but provoke me with what their hands have made, declares the LORD. From the day it was built until now, this city has so aroused my anger and wrath that I must remove it from my sight.

The people of Israel and Judah have provoked me by all the evil they have done-they, their kings and officials, their priests and prophets, the men of Judah and the people of Jerusalem. They turned their backs to me and not their faces; though I taught them again and again, they would not listen or respond to discipline. They set up their abominable idols in the house that bears my Name and defiled it. They built high placcs for Daal in the Valley of Ben Himmon to sacrifice their sons and daughters to Molech, though I never commanded, nor did it enter my mind, that they should do such a detestable thing and so make Judah sin."

The historians, Cleitarchus, Diodorus Siculus, and Plutarch, all write in their histories that children were often offered as sacrifices to Baal-Hammon. Diodorus Silculus wrote,

"There was in their city a bronze image of Cronus extending its hands, palms up and sloping toward the ground, so that each of the children when placed thereon rolled down and fell into a sort of gaping pit filled with fire."

Diodorus gave another account of the Carthaginians, after suffering a defeat at the hands of the Greeks, when the nobles of Carthage blamed their defeat on their with holding their own children for sacrifice, offering instead only peasant children, to their god. They then immediately offered three hundred of their own children for sacrifice. As their children were cast into the fire, relatives were forbidden to weep, and Plutarch adds to the account writing, "*....the whole area before the statue was filled with a loud noise of flutes and drums so that the cries of wailing should not reach the ears of the people.*"

On this planet, following the union of the polarity, pagan religion began with Nimrod and his wife Semiramis. They followed and worshiped the chief of the "sons of God," that we know as Lucifer. The worship of the one true God was replaced with the worship of the fallen heavenly host. At one time, Lucifer was worshiped as a creator god and was considered a feathered serpent. For the most part, the old serpent religion was pagan, in that it recognized multiple creator gods (feathered serpents) rather than the one true creator God. To the ancients, any god who claimed to be a creator god was a feathered serpent. Most all of the ancient world was steeped in paganism, the exception were some of the descendants of Noah to Moses and the Israelite tribes. They alone continued to worship the one true God noting that pagan religion was a problem from time to time, even within their own ranks. Judah's prophets were always warning them against the worship of false gods. It is the first of the ten commandments...Thou shalt have no other gods before me.

We have dwelt primarily with the gods of ancient Mesopotamia, however we want the readers to understand that it was a world-wide irruption of nephilim gods, however it all began in ancient Sumer and Babylonia (Re *The Nephilim Evidence*).

As previously written in Volume One, the gods hated this planet after the cataclysm. It was no longer the paradise it once was. The planet now had awful climatic conditions, subject to terrible storms, earthquakes, floods, extreme heat and cold, and general miserable living conditions. Besides, they had accomplished their goal that was to corrupt the seed of mankind. Having accomplished this, most of them departed this planet leaving their giant offspring to rule for generations thereafter. Lucifer and his sons remain the **"Lords of the Earth."** and of the universe.

The Ages

Your authors have found that few people understand or even know about the Ages. Since much of the End Time events are focused on the culmination of the Ages in 2012, we feel perhaps this chapter will help the readers to better understand *The End Times* chapter and why keeping time of the Ages is so important in understanding prophecy.

The first step is to understand Precession. Precession occurs because the Earth not only rotates on its axis….otherwise known as the Axis Munde, World Tree, or World Pillar….it also wobbles. Chandler's Wobble is one of several wobbling motions that the Earth undergoes as it spins on its axis. It is a lesser wobble. A greater wobble is the Precession wobble. Its one revolution or circular wobble of the Earth equals 25,920 years; usually rounded off to 26,000 years. When one revolution of 26,000 years is completed, it is called a Great Year, Platonic or Plato's year, so named in his honor. A Great Year can then be referred to as an Aeon. In addition, the Earth's axis is inclined at 23.5 degrees. The central point of revolution is called the "pole of the ecliptic."

Due to the Earth's movement in its wobble, the Pole Stars will change gradually over the 26,000 years. In about 14,000 years, the Earth's axis will point directly to Vega, as it does now to Polaris. This slow movement is called Precession.

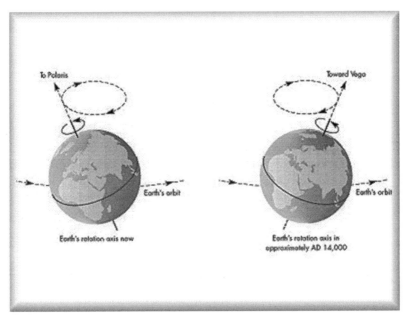

Precession of the North Pole Axis

Anciently, the sky above the Earth was divided into twelve constellations that represented the Signs of the Zodiac and the Twelve Ages; each Sign represented an Age. The ensigns of the twelve Zodiacal Constellations, representing the Twelve Ages in the Precession of the Equinoxes, appear to arch their way across the sky as if in royal procession. Over time, as viewed from Planet Earth, the constellations appear to slip gradually backwards, or Precess, thus the name Precession. The backward movement of the constellations is a slow one, moving at the rate of 1 degree per 79 years. Precession causes the coordinates of stars to gradually shift and over a few years add up to significant changes requiring periodical updating of star charts.

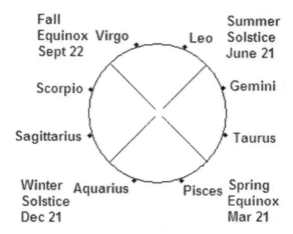

Platonic Year 4,000 years ago

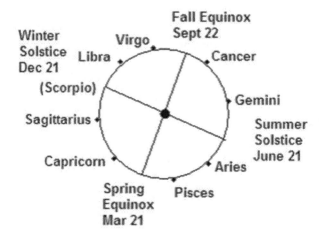

Platonic Year in 2012

The dot within the circle, in the lower illustration, is Planet Earth around which the Constellations of the Zodiac appear to revolve. The Zodiac Circle is divided into four quarters, seasons, or cardinal points represented by the cross. The Spring Equinox is in Aquarius, represented by a man. The Summer Solstice is in Taurus, represented by the bull. The Autumn Equinox is in Leo, represented by the Lion, and the Winter Solstice is in Scorpio, represented by the eagle. Between the cardinal constellation points are three Ages. For example, within the Zodiacal Season of Taurus there are the three Ages of Taurus (the Bull), Aries (the Ram) and Pisces (the Fish). Within the Zodiacal Season of Aquarius there are the three Ages of Aquarius (Man), Capricorn (the Sea Goat) and Sagittarius (the Archer) etc. Each Age is calculated at being approximately 2,160 years. The Ages move in a clockwise motion. The Fifth Cardinal

Direction, represented by a dot in the center of a circle, is the central point of revolution, the pole of the ecliptic. On the time scale, we have almost left the Fifth Age of Pisces and will enter the Sixth Age of Aquarius on December 21, 2012. Thus, it is correct to say present time is in the dawning of the Age of Aquarius. It is the end of two Great Ages; the end of the Fifth Age of Pisces and the end of one 26,000 year revolution of all the twelve Ages of Precession, called the Great Year. It is also the end of the Mayan Fifth Sun. If a Mayan Sun is considered an Age, then it is the end of three Great Ages and it is the end of the Mayan Long Count calendar. The significance of three Great Ages and the Mayan Long Count calendar ending on the same date in December 2012 cannot be over stated.

We have noticed some web sites that have the beginning of the Precession Year as starting in Leo, about 12,000 years ago. These sites are erroneous because the Mayan Long Count calendar identifies Aquarius as the starting and ending point for The Great Year. Precession was known before the great cataclysm. Noah and the Nephilim restored the knowledge back to the Chaldeans/ Babylonians, and the Egyptians regained the knowledge from the Hall of Records, following the cataclysm.

Thoth Tarot

The above tarot is an illustrated model of the Ages as conceived by the ancients. *Rota* is a wheel. Hence the word *tarota* or in modern terms, tarot. The solar system, with the planets revolving around the solar sun, is not a sphere. As viewed by the ancients, it is a wheel. The planet's orbits are elliptical. The ancients paid very close attention to the rim or belt of this wheel, and they called it the Zodiac. The above tarot illustration is showing the four cardinal points of the Zodiac, each sphinx head (cardinal point) represented by a bull, eagle, lion, and face of a man. They are pulling a chariot with a seated man holding the round wheel or belt of the Zodiac in an endless heavenly round of Ages.

Mythically, at sunrise on December 21, 2012, the Mayans believed that the Sun--their Father--rises to conjoin the center of the Sacred Tree, the World Tree, or the Tree of Life. The four cardinal constellation points (Leo, Scorpio, Taurus and Aquarius) will herald the event by aligning to form a cross in the sky. The sun has not conjoined the Milky Way and the plane of the ecliptic since some 5,125 years ago. The ancient Greeks called this solar event the Suntelia Aeon and it meant the end of the Precession cycle or Great Year. The Suntelia Aeon is the Age Christ was referring to when he told his disciples when to expect the *Harvest* of the righteous... "to be **completed** at the end of the Age" (Great Year) in 2012. (Bold type added). Another verse found in *Luke* 18:29-30, translated correctly in Fenton's *Holy Bible in Modern English*, the *Revised Standard Edition,* and the *Gideon Bible*, has Christ telling His apostles they will receive their full and final reward of eternal life in the **Age to come**. The apostles of Christ lived in the Piscean Age. The next Age or Age to come is the Age of Aquarius which officially starts on December 21, 2012.

Since the writing of *The Ark of Millions of Years*, Volume One, your authors have come to a better understanding of what is fore-told about the End Times. In Volume One, we did not fully understand what was going to happen to the Earth in relationship to the Mayan End Time date of 2012. We do understand now. The Great Ages are winding down to the Age of Aquarius, their starting point 26,000 years ago. A Great Year will then be complete. If the Tzolk'in calendar, the *Bible,* and the words of Christ are accurate in their predictions, then for some of us "raptured," it will be the end of time as we know it. For others left behind, it will simply be the continuation of the Ages and the re-start of Precession into another 26,000 year cycle of the Great Year or Aeon.

The Metamorphosis

You feel it too. Something is about to happen. It's not a single event, but rather the culmination of an anthropological process. There is a metamorphosis occurring in the human race. We are changing, evolving into the next level of being. Not all at once. There are a few thousand beings on Earth who's genes have been activated to allow a higher form of consciousness to occur. The ancient civilizations you now know about certainly appear to have been very advanced. The scientists of those days knew about the stars, planets, and even the mechanics of interplanetary travel. They knew about the union of the polarity, where two phases of matter came together to form this Earth from which we gaze into the universe. It appears many of them had also mastered forms of communication beyond the present that gave them insight into past and future events. Somehow most of them were destroyed.

Those on Noah's higher planet were also nearly completely destroyed. Their system of family, with a father, mother, and naturally born children were corrupted away by the teachings of the Nephilim.

Stone carving of Nephilim found in Roslin Chapel circa 1442

Angels sent to help men pray and help them on their mortal journey back to the celestial realm of their destiny, were seduced by the beauty of mortal women. They fathered abominations with humans and animals. Their crossbred human offspring were giants endowed with immense strength and intelligence. They had every advantage over mortal mankind, yet they had no souls. They did not have the inheritance or the potential for compassion and growth with which men were endowed.

They also had no enmity between their wills and that of the master adversary. His plan became their plan. Ultimately, the strategy of God was victorious. Mankind genetically starved the giants through forbidding their women, by covenant, the opportunity to breed with the angels or with giants. They also devised methods of warfare with sophisticated engines that allowed men to stand on equal footing with the giants in battle. Add to that the fact that giants did not live long. The gravity of Earth is too much for the physiology of giants. Their bones, organs, and immunological systems doomed them to early debilitating physical problems. While they were young and virile, they were practically invincible. But as they aged they, they became paralyzed or immobile. A proud and warlike race, they committed suicide rather than suffer the humiliation of being cared for.

Before the Flood, the Nephilim and their many tribes of giants were successful in corrupting nearly the entire race of man. It was their mission. Simply killing everyone while they were still innocent would only fulfill the Creator's plan. The Dark One's victims must be captured in such a way that their free will was defeated. They had no choice, but to succumb to the temptations, sparkle, glamour, and carnal pleasures of the mortal world. The plan was to taint their inheritance. If the Nephilim, their dark leader, and their offspring couldn't have a mortal experience worthy of inheriting exaltation, then the Creator's children would not have it either. It was a crime of galactic proportions. It was merciless and cold.

Many mortal kings, under the advice of these combinations designed to promise unlimited earthly power, took the brides of their enemies. This breeding was an exact copy of the efforts to rob every womb of its rightful heir. One can only imagine the fear that prevented their husbands from exacting instant revenge against their captors.

Under the inspiration of many prophets, and through revelation, mankind survived these crimes against humanity. They suffered. Yes. The suffering was necessary, in order to seal the doom upon the perpetrators. Those days were hastened, lest the entire Earth suffer the same global corruption and loss of salvation that occurred before the Flood.

Since the first stylus was laid to gold or clay, there has been a latent prophecy of a latter day. In this day, there would be land set aside for freedom. In this *New Jerusalem*, men would be able to worship God according to their own dictates. Such a land would come to pass. The Declaration of Independence would be dictated by an unknown visitor to Thomas Jefferson. That immortal document would be drafted once and once only in a single sitting. Although the Constitution would be debated for many days, that Declaration would stand without revision. The wording would be similar to another famous document, drafted and signed in 1215 called the Magna Carta.

The Freemasons were keepers of the *Flying Scrolls*, containing the patterns of liberty that would have to exist in order for the final stages of the Precession to occur. The Emerald Tablets, created by Thoth himself, may be copies of parts of the Flying Scrolls. It was so well known in those days, that when the land called America declared its independence, the British soldiers conscripted to defeat this rebellion could not fight against the prophecy. The nation set aside for the purpose of fulfilling this prophecy was being born, and nothing short of a miracle could make sure it lived.

Stone carving of Nephilim in Roslin Chapel carrying the "Flying Scrolls" that contained the instructions for rebuilding the Earth after the Flood.

Hundreds of thousands of people sold everything they had to board a small wooden ship and risk their lives to sail to the new world for this exact purpose. If they had nothing to sell, they sold the labor of their lives and the lives of their future children to reach this land. Was it easy? No. Did they always succeed or reach their goals? Certainly not.

The wealthy and powerful did their best to establish their prejudices and their methods of enslavement here as well. Those crimes were committed again and again. For nearly 300 years this nation struggled. It still struggles, but something very strange is happening now.

There is and always has been a line between good and evil. Since the passing of the days when cheating tithe-payers dropped dead at the base of the coffers, mankind has been doing the absolute minimum to please God. For six millennia, we have read of the dividing of the tribes of mankind. There were those who ate, drank, and were merry while those that obeyed the laws of God suffered under their whip. Like occupants of a global cabana, they laughed and drank and ordered the servants of the earth around to their pleasure.

Since 1830, the gathering of the saints has been occurring. What does that mean? Those who are willing to follow the will of the Father are being gathered. Lands have been set apart to receive those who were willing to live these laws. Since that time, those that seek power and wealth through secret combinations have sought to destroy these people. Many millions of innocent men, women, and children have been murdered to keep the vision of equality and exaltation from being fulfilled.

In the 1940's, six million Jews were systematically stripped of their wealth, their dignity, and murdered in every brutal method imaginable. The plan of evil was to exterminate them from the face of the Earth. This plan is eternal. Ever since they made the covenant to keep their heritage free from foreign DNA, they have been hunted by the followers of the ancient combinations set down by the Nephilim. To this day, half the civilizations of Earth are determined to complete the destruction of this tribe.

At the time of the writing of this book, more than 200 million children have been murdered before they every got the chance to breathe air. More than $2.5 billion was also taken from the young mothers of these children under what is arguably the most evil and corrupt genocide ever perpetrated upon mankind. Most cleverly marketed with keywords associated with freedom and healthcare, this billion-dollar butchery has nearly wiped out an entire generation of young people. Many nations practice this genocide, but one would not think the nation set apart as the New Jerusalem would have participated. Yes, indeed. Nearly 40 million of those babies were killed in modern times, with the full knowledge and suffering of its citizens.

Add to that the doubling of technology every 9 to 10 months. Almost all of the advances are being funded either by governments seeking new and more deadly weaponry, or by health organizations seeking to unravel the human genome. These weapons are manipulating the weather, geophysical properties of the Earth itself, or enabling commanders to disable their enemies with psychotropic vibrations. The range of effects go from mild paranoia or sleeplessness to schizophrenia and even death through cardiac arrest or organ failure. This can be done from any location to any location on the globe with complete anonymity.

Is there still evil in the world today? Yes. So what makes us any different than our ancestors who charged across the frozen tundra with battle axes in their hands? What makes us any different than the entire civilizations that migrated with their herds, their flocks, their wives and children with the express purpose of annihilating their enemies from the face of the earth? How have we changed?

Well, the gathering is nearly complete, at the time of the writing of this book. The Grand Division has begun as well. That line that separates good and evil was once manageable. One could live and play on the evil side all week, then jump back over to the good side on the Sabbath, sing some songs, pay some indulgences, and all was right with the world. Those days are past.

The line has gotten wider. If one is living on the evil side, there is not enough time to run back to the side of the righteous in a single week. We will have to make a choice. This is the core of this chapter. This is the metamorphosis of mankind. This Division will separate the children of God, just prior to the separation of the Earths into their two parts. One is vibrating at a higher frequency or glory. The other is vibrating at a lower frequency or glory. For nearly seven centuries, they have been in harmony as a physical Earth. We live here. We die here. We have our dreams and base all of our interpretations of the universe using ideas we have formulated while living here. As far as we know, no humans have traveled to other worlds and become educated under the tutelage of off-worlders. The off-worlders have always come here and taught those who have been chosen since the foundations of the Earth.

An ancient copper relief showing the tempting of Adam by Eve with the *fruit* through which she became a mortal being. His choice was to obey a lesser or greater commandment. All of this took place on the spirit Earth.

So, how is this done? What is the metamorphosis? How is mankind changing? Into what? A higher, more noble being? Yes. And, it is happening right before our eyes. Everyone can feel it. Some will deny it, because of the misery they have already suffered, but there are those who know what we know. There is a purpose and a *good* to life. In fact, there is a *good* that can be expressed or fulfilled in many ways. What are these ways? Well, there are five. All life can be placed into one of these modes of existence. I call them the five worlds of existence. Once these are explained, the best description of the metamorphosis of mankind will be added. Don't skip to the end. This is perhaps the most important message you will ever read.

World Number One

In philosophy, we often theorize about the *good* of a certain creed or methodology. In other words, when one is a model citizen of this philosophy, what will be their behavior? What will be their goal, or greatest desire, or their dream if they are seeking the reward of their lifestyle? This is what we mean by the *good* of a philosophy.

In World Number One, the good is the satisfaction from physical work. It might seem as though the crown of mankind's genius is the elimination of physical work from mortal life. Nothing could be further from the truth. There is a gift of pure happiness that comes from physical work. Physical labor is among the most satisfying activities for mankind. Humans, deprived of the opportunity to perform labor are among the most miserable creatures to behold. Their misery is so overpowering they will do anything, including ingest hallucinogenic drugs, alcohol, or even commit suicide to wash away their emotional pain.

Every time I go to the beach, I take a shovel and a bucket. I like to go when the tide is fairly low. Left behind the retreating cool and soothing waves is a treasure of wet sand. This is the perfect material for building sand castles. Using the shovel, a strong back, and any kind of design one can imagine, in a few hours the most amazing and unique sand castles can be constructed. An easy construction would never do. The work is hard. All of the struggles of life are washed away during the process. The sweat and the sun, the weight of the sand, and the design are all part of the good. If one were to involve children as part of the process, one could witness the therapy of work shaping and growing a child as well. For you see, it is not a castle one is building at all. It is a human being.

Even if participating in a contest with others to see who can build the best castle or sand sculpture, it is not the finished product that is the goal. The goal, the good of the activity, is the work of building the sand castle. The work itself provides the satisfaction that one is doing something.

When on the job, most people are very disappointed when the work of their labor must be redone, because of the mistake of another. But, this is because they do not understand the principle of work. Hand cutting stone, chopping wood, lifting weights, running a marathon, cleaning house, or tending a garden are all immensely satisfying. There is actually a *high* that can be obtained from this physical work. Hundreds of millions of humans know the pure joy that comes from work.

In this world, there is very little conscious thinking performed. In fact, there is an almost dream-state that is reached through the process of working hard. Endorphins are released in copious amounts. Seratonin is also produced in large amounts. These two hormones are unbelievably powerful in the human body. It seems unfair, but there is a process of uptake in the normal physiology of the human body. These hormones make us feel great. They actually can help the body heal itself, or more properly said, prevent it from harming itself. The high realized by the runner or the weightlifter is from these compounds. Joy and happiness are the treasures of life, and are largely derived from ones ability to produce and retain these hormones at generous levels. Possibly the largest profits in medical history are from patients who want to prevent their bodies from uptaking Seratonin. Tens of millions of people take Seratonin uptake inhibitors to prevent the depression that occurs when ones levels drop too low. All that may be needed, is a pattern of physical work to resupply the body with the hormones needed to keep the brain from feeling depressed.

HDL is the good cholesterol. LDL is the bad cholesterol. The lowering of the total cholesterol number is reported by many health professionals to be a good goal. However, the brain is made almost entirely of cholesterol. It is a tremendously complex and convertible molecule. The only safe way to lower the LDL and to raise the HDL is physical exercise. Lifting weights, running, riding a bicycle, or digging a garden by hand can replace a cabinet full of drugs.

The good of work is very good. The goal is not finishing, although there is great satisfaction is seeing the results of the work as a thinner waistline, a lush garden, or the most beautiful sand castle ever created.

World Number Two

World number two is the world of learning. The *good* of this world is learning new things, solving problems, or the act of discovery itself.

It is said that an intelligent brain trying to solve a complex problem radiates as much energy as 75-watt light bulb. This consumes as many calories in an hour as running or walking a mile. Besides the dietary benefits of an active brain, there is nothing in the universe that creates the kind of joy provided by discovery.

The contributions of every age have been recorded in every conceivable media. Whether in stone, metal, paint, chalk, or paper the ancients have tried their best to preserve their knowledge. It is through this ability primarily that man transcends the animal. Each human being starts life as an infant, and spends an entire lifetime learning new skills, new concepts, and reaching far into the unknown for answers to every question. The achievements of past generations are accumulated and passed along to the next.

All knowledge in not innate. That is to say, one cannot figure out everything without a source for the knowledge other than one's own brain. There are outside sources from which we can draw information if we are ready to receive it. When the end of all known knowledge is reached by a person, that person can reach out beyond himself to a maelstrom of information in countless forms. If he is able, he can withdraw from that experience with pure knowledge in his possession.

We would like to say something about sources of knowledge here. There are many sources for knowledge. Some are evil. Some are good. There are evil men who seek knowledge, just as there are good men who seek knowledge. The utmost care should be taken to qualify the source of knowledge before consuming that knowledge.

You make a conscious choice when you learn. The mind is the most powerful of human capacities, and is driven by the spirit of a person. The spirit of a person can either act, or be acted upon by the knowledge pouring into the mind. If we act, then we can accept, reject, or qualify the knowledge. In other words, just because you listen to a song full of foul language, power chords and screaming, it does not mean you choose to use such language or seek out the nearest body-piercing studio. Just because you watch an "R" rated movie full of death, explosions, and gore, it does not mean you will choose to use violence in your own life.

Unfortunately, even though we learn divine principles full of the mysteries of heaven, it does not mean we will choose to live righteously or seek the welfare of another human being. The Nephilim had every blessing of heaven. They had lived their lives and received their immortality, yet they succumbed to the temptations of carnality and chose eternal damnation rather than continue to live as angels.

This is what makes the world of learning so incredibly powerful. There is no boundary to human existence. We have the birthright to learn everything. We have what every race in the universe is seeking. We have the ability to transcend and overcome mortal life as a complete soul. There is no possible way this can be accomplished in ignorance. We must have all knowledge. Whether in mortal life, or in a later phase of our growth, we will have the opportunity to learn continually laid before us.

This is one of the most primal urges of men with souls. There is nothing more glorious and more exuberating than the discovery of new knowledge. It is why we develop language. It is why with that language we develop new languages of symbols and formulas and diagrams to compress knowledge into terms that can be manipulated into a more and more complete picture of the universe, time, and perhaps even God.

But, know this. Because it is this greatest treasure of joy in life, it is also the goal of evil to prevent mankind from learning anything other than those things that give it power. Hundreds of millions of books have been melted down, burned, buried, or erased by evil men trying to gain or regain power over the people. The early Catholic church systematically confiscated all knowledge in the known world. They killed those who knew it. They killed those who possessed it. They killed those who professed to know anything other than that which the church allowed men to know, or that which they themselves had fabricated and distributed. They fought or financed wars to keep ages of mankind so ignorant they could not read or think about anything except the dark and choiceless world of fear and homage that kept them in power and wealth.

It is only through the proliferation of knowledge that men remain free. The Gutenberg press was the greatest invention of the first 6,400 years of modern time. This one invention allowed pure knowledge to be learned by the people. Millions of people learned to read, using only the manuscripts translated and printed on presses throughout Europe and carried to all parts of the world. This greatly diluted the Catholic church's stranglehold on the minds of the world. Once the people had access to knowledge, neither tyrants nor suppressors could hold them slaves any longer. They began once again to see their potential. Within fifty years, the exploration of the universe had resumed. Within two hundred years, the stage was set for the establishment of the New Jerusalem and the restoration of the Gospel of Jesus Christ.

The next great invention was the Internet. This is the Guttenberg press of the twenty-first century. It only took ten years for the world to leap past institutional learning, once the Internet became accessible to everyone in about the year 1996. By the year 2010, there will be no need for a college diploma to secure ones future earning ability. The brightest minds of all ages now have full and unfettered access to all the raw and unfiltered knowledge in the world in every language. As fast as those minds consume existing knowledge, they are transmitting new knowledge, which in turn is being consumed by the other minds. The kings of curricula in the universities of the world have lost their monopoly on knowledge. People all over the globe are gaining knowledge so quickly that they will soon outstrip the knowledge of the doctors of tradition. New math, new science, and new music is being forged out of truth so quickly that they cannot maintain control of it.

The first cure for a virus will soon be found. All major diseases such as diabetes, arthritis, cystic fibrosis, and many forms of cancer will be cured. Human lives will be extended through healthy living and medical miracles to ages far beyond that of a tree. The quality of life will be better than any life every lived on the face of the earth in any age. All people will be able to each their fullest potential in mortal life, because they will have access to knowledge, the energy and food to pursue it, and the freedom to enjoy the fruits thereof.

That sounds like a fantasy world to us now. But, it is true. This is the core of the metamorphosis. Without this advanced knowledge of mankind's relationship with all lives—living and long since dead—in the universe, this will not be possible. But truth is truth. This is the destiny of mankind. And all the evil in the universe will be organized against it ever coming to pass.

The time will soon come when the Grand Division will result in two great armies arranged against each other. There will be those who know the value and the good of learning. And, there will be those whose sole design is to destroy any freedom of choice or any ability to learn truth from off the face of the Earth. They will seek to discredit those who have learned on their own. Only those who have successfully paid their pay through their halls of tradition will be allowed to call themselves learned. The knowledge kings have decreed that they must maintain control over knowledge, lest they lose their place in line for the awards of men.

As long as the Internet provides free access to the libraries of the world to those who thirst for knowledge, the foundations for the Metamorphosis can be built. If the foundations can be built, then the leaderless revolution of the masses breeding new knowledge amongst their interactive minds will overwhelm any king's ability to stop them. As a race, through this revolution of knowledge, we may realize the solution for transcending the animal inside us. We may at last see our true selves as spiritual beings merely having a mortal experience.

World Number Three

World number Three is that of mischief and evil. It might be a little confusing how there could be a "good" to this world. There is a level of satisfaction that comes from this kind of activity. In a survey of violent patients of a criminal psychologist, it was revealed that there is extreme gratification experienced by persons hurting another person. In at least six case studies the male perpetrators received an erection immediately after punching another person. Similar studies indicated that serial killers murder not through a feeling of anger or an insatiable desire for revenge, but rather for the dose of adrenaline or feeling of euphoria that overcame them during the act of murder. The rush of satisfaction was not unlike that of an addictive drug being pumped directly into one's veins.

It gets worse. Because of the aggressive nature of people in this world of existence, they may quickly rise to positions of power and influence. The apathetic nature of the peaceful people on the Earth supports evil leaders into office as surely as if they had donated their life savings and carried banners for their campaigns. History is full of these leaders who somehow construct a level of indoctrination. Indoctrination is intrinsically different than *instruction*. Instruction involves the free agency of the student to accept or reject the teaching. Learning from instruction is a process of thinking, and critical examination, and testing. The student invariably comes away with his own flavor or interpretation of the lessons, able to build upon that knowledge for his own ends. If every chemistry student learned the science like a clone of his or her instructor, we would still be trying to turn lead into gold and wearing long black robes and a pointed hats with stars on them. No. Each student stands upon the educational shoulders of the knowledge he has assimilated and reaches ever higher into new frontiers.

However, with indoctrination, the lessons are not offered as a matter of choice or left open to interpretation. Instead, the subject— we cannot think about them as a student at all—is forced to recite the doctrine over and over until he can repeat it with exactness and confidence. There is no room for individual thought or action. The mass of subjects becomes one in purpose and process. No matter which member of the mass to whom you pose a question, you will receive precisely the same answer.

In order for indoctrination to be successful, all individuals must be brought into submission to the doctrine, or they must be destroyed. The ancient philosophy is, "Any nail sticking up is hammered down." This pertains to the ancient Japanese social tradition, which does not allow for stupidity or brilliance. Instead, everyone will wear the same uniform, sing the same way, walk in single file, cut their hair the same way, and will not display any behavior that causes an individual to be distinguished from the mass.

In order for indoctrination to be successful, it must begin at very early stages of development, or become the terms of employment or survival for the individual. The administrators of the indoctrination never practice their own doctrine. The leaders are the free thinkers. The leaders are the individuals with their finger on the button. The leaders are the ones who craft the message, outline the plans, and of course wield the power of the mass. Success comes only when the doctrine has been ingrained into each individual in the mass to the point there is no wavering, no questioning, and I suppose each of you have heard these words at some time in your lives; "You are not being paid to think. You are being paid to do what you're told."

When indoctrination is successful, the leader can step to the pulpit and add the force of his minions to each word he professes. This, as my little green friend would say, leads to the dark side. Only evil can come from such a system. And evil comes from only one source. That source has only one mission. That mission is to corrupt and eternally occupy all human life in the universe.

We have many ancient examples of indoctrination that was successful in sudden population control. That is to say, huge number of people were killed or brought into slavery. We will leave those to another book. There are two modern examples of indoctrination of the most heinous and evil kind that we will use for this story.

The first is the most horrible and evil example of indoctrination since Satan drew a third of the host of heaven with him to hell. In the 20th and the beginning of the 21st centuries, the art of war changed. Super-powers developed weaponry that was so powerful, that by 1945 traditional warfare was rendered obsolete. The instantaneous death of hundreds of thousands of Japanese citizens with two flashes of uncontrolled atomic energy changed everything. Since the earth cooled, men have lined up on either side of the battlefield and charged across the frozen tundra at one another with their battle axes, staves, swords, and hammers and hacked at each other all day until victory was achieved. Now, can you imagine yourself holding a sword in open battle and defending yourself against horsemen, archers, fireballs, and hordes of berserk fighters trying to kill you? Of course you can. But, can you imagine being ordered to charge against another group with the intent of killing every last man, woman, and child down to the last infant in order to take their lands, their homes, their and all their resources for your leaders? Perhaps not. Perhaps you have not been indoctrinated to that point of barbarism.

But, in 1945 traditional warfare became impractical. No longer could a million soldiers devise any strategy that would allow them to march against an atomic bomb. Traditional armies became obsolete. New atomic technology proliferated. Soon, both sides had a race to see who could build the most atomic bombs. It became apparent that a new set of battle rules needed to be developed. The art of war became the art of diplomacy with weapons. It was called Mutual Assured Destruction, or MAD for short. Both sides knew that if one pushed the button to deploy their weapons against the other, that the attacked would do the same. With no way to defend against these weapons, each side was assured they would be annihilated without reserve. There may indeed be a victory, but the winner would have lost so many people and so much infrastructure that the leaders would have to go back to raising their own food and washing their own clothes in a washtub by hand.

The race proved too expensive. The people, supplying the revenue for the race through confiscation of their wages, could not provide the economic machine it took to stay in the race. Shortly after the collapse of the Soviet Empire, the republics decided nuclear weapons could not be used again. Too many innocent people might be killed in the process. Armies had to find a more efficient and less collateral process to fight one another. Once again, armies were built in ranks and supplied with traditional equipment. Swords, and rifles, and tanks, and planes, and ships were once again lined up on either side of the borders. And once again dictators, those who dictate the doctrine to the indoctrinated, lashed their voices against the weak and innocent and sought to take the spoils of war.

By the early 1990's blind rage and greed empowered another tyrant to invade an innocent country and steal their wealth. This time, the Unites States was in a position to help the conquered nation. Within a few weeks of Iraq's invasion of Kuwait, millions of tons of armament and weaponry began positioning for the *mother of all battles*. Within months war had taken on a new face. Technology allowed the construction of new weapons that could be deployed with such accuracy that only the target was destroyed. That same technology allowed the public viewing of live warfare in the safety of one's home or office with popcorn and soda. Unlike the aristocrats who surried down to the battlefield with a picnic lunch of fried chicken, freshly baked biscuits, and celery to watch the first skirmish of the War of Northern Aggression, the viewer could not smell the stench of death or hear the screams of pain as the hell of war ripped human spirits from their bodies.

The viewer could simple turn it off, or switch to sports, or walk to the safety of their own kitchen for another glass of milk. The precision of destruction was pure entertainment. When a missile went down the ventilation shaft of a single building to destroy the enemy from 25 thousand feet, it was not unlike the perfect threading of a football through the chaos of defense gracefully into the hands of the offensive receiver's hands for a touchdown. The precise delivery of bombs were touchdowns. When a single bridge was destroyed with a single bomb without a single human casualty, a world-wide "Ooh," or ,"Ahh" could almost be heard as if the finger of God had reached down and smashed an insect without harming anything around it.

There was another lever of success in the new methods of warfare. One cannot build an army without money. Bombs, uniforms, food, and equipment cost money. The art of war added the color of manipulating the money so that enemies could not build armies. Much like cutting off the supply line and waiting for the soldiers to starve, great and marvelous technologies were crafted to keep money out of the hands of dictators. They were called sanctions. Revenue was stopped. Bank accounts were seized. The currency of the dictator was nullified.

With the combination of these tactics, it was thought that warfare had been made obsolete. One cannot underestimate the power of evil. Indoctrination never ends. A new weapon was built that would be successful against any defense. Like a pachinko ball, this weapon could bounce from pin to pin, innocuously through the obstacles until it reached its target and delivered its explosives.

Masses of ghostlike soldiers could be controlled through an almost unbreakable bond that keeps them applied to the task. The new doctrine would link the success of their suicide to their eternal reward in the heavens. Each soldier must be just like the other, precise and willing to complete any mission, demanding the sacrifice of his or her life without hesitation.

This new indoctrination would have to be thorough and begin at a very early age. The new dictator has learned the lessons of evil from the master of evil himself. First, every single person in the society must live in absolute squalor. If there is fresh drinking water, it must be drawn by hand and hauled by hand every day. Storing water would be forbidden. There would be no individual wealth allowed. Only the state would acquire wealth. There would be no travel allowed. There would be no access to news, weather, entertainment, or other activities that might weaken the grip of poverty even for a moment. All of these things would be labeled as evil and temptations of their enemy.

Next, the dictator must paint a picture of heaven that is so beautiful and so glorious that without exception, every human being desires it more than food or love or even life itself. Each child would be taught from birth that he or she had a single goal in life. That goal is to reach heaven through the suicidal extermination of the enemies of the state. To make sure that the indoctrination is complete, the dictator himself must be willing to murder without compunction. Family members, neighbors, and especially ethnic groups must be summarily taken to the public square and slaughtered or tortured so the masses can plainly see the difference between heaven and their present state of affairs. Neither executed people nor their families would ever see a single chilled grape in heaven. A few thousand executions a year is all that is normally required to keep a complete society in line.

Now, what does this have to do with the third world of existence? This is the *good* of the third world of existence; the world of mischief and evil. To be the dictator of such a land is the ultimate power on earth promised by the evil one. Each and every member of this world of existence is dedicated to death, pain, pleasure, and all replacements of inspiration such as thrills, adrenalin rushes, drug-induced stupors, and even raves of sex. And, when the armies of the peacemakers march forward to vanquish such a land, they will be surprised. When the armies arrive to fight, all they will find are innocent people playing ball or singing songs or having a party. There will be no soldiers. There will be no weapons. There will be no tanks or planes or ships to target. There will only be masses of people peacefully praying to their god. The dictator knows that national television will be showing the world how harmless and peaceful they are, and how their lives should be spared, and how horrible the soldiers are treating them by desecrating their holy ground with their unwanted presence.

And if the soldiers do not leave, then the dictator unfolds his war. This is where the indoctrination yields its treasure. In the darkness of their covenant with death and hell, the child-soldiers slide their bodies inside their weapons. In willing innocence they sift through the defenses of their dictator's enemy like cold air under the windward door, and they detonate their weapon. In a flash of smoke and metal they are translated to their heaven while the enemy is murdered. Like slashing at ghosts who suddenly materialize and slay a few of their comrades, the soldiers will attack the wind. Their search for their attacker is pointless. He is evil itself. He is in another dimension, fortifying the dictator's power. He is creating enemies of the soldiers with each explosion.

How does he do that? How do enemies breed when the soldiers of the dictator die with each attack? Ah, this is the master stroke of genius in this most evil style of warfare. Even more efficient than the indoctrination of the human missiles, is the utilization of greed. The dictator has ultimate power. He has received his ultimate reward for his covenant with the evil one. But, the evil one does not want one side to win or to lose. No no. His goal is to capture both sides in the conflict. He already owns the dictator. Now he wants to own the people who are attacking the dictator as well. He does this through greed. Since the society of the super-power is free and open, allowing each individual to seek after his greatest potential according to his own dictates, it makes the perfect breeding ground for greed.

A free and open society will always have at least two political factions. But unlike traditional enemies, they debate and posture and convince their constituencies of their benefits, instead of marshalling armies. But, power is power. Temptation is temptation. And greed is greed. The ruling party gets the blame for all things that go wrong. Credit for positive accomplishments is only given long after the historians get through with the story. The party that is out of power seeks to defeat the ruling party, because the ruling party has access to the money. Lots of money. All the money in the world. The ruling party wields the faith and credit of the nation. Now we have the stage set for the evil one to do his will.

As the dictator kills soldiers with his ghost bombers, the political party that is out of power will blame the ruling party for incompetence and poor leadership. If it appears like this political party of the super power is working with the dictator, you have become a very astute observer. It is worse than that. The greed and lust of this political party can be so great, that the leaders of this party covenant with the evil one to gain this power. Now you can see how the *good* in the third world of existence has destroyed so many civilizations before us. Both the dictator, the enemy of all that is good and decent, and the super-power's political leaders are sworn to follow the same dark lord to the death in order to be granted ultimate power and glory on this earth. Everyone hates. Everyone lusts. Everyone dies. The perfect plan has unfolded without flaw time after time until every last vestige of that civilization evaporates from the planet, and the survivors are reduced to hunting insects and gathering berries all day, every day, while they pray unceasingly to their god for deliverance.

World Number Four

World number four is that of depression. This is a world with many degrees of light and darkness. In can be surreal. In can be very real. More than any other world, it testifies to the dimensionality of the universe. Two souls can be in the same room at the same time, yet one will be filled with joy and peace and tranquility, while the other is filled with sadness and darkness and despair.

But, that is not the only aspect of this world. This world is the doorway to all creativity. How? Well, only individuals enter this world. I guess I should explain the process of *stepping in*.

There was a movie released called, *"Being John Malcovich."* In the movie, there was a great actor named John Malcovich who was played by John Malcovich. There was a puppeteer who was shown a transdimensional portal in a storm drain pipe that led to the inside of the head of John Malcovich. Now, the puppeteer was skilled at manipulating the movements of a puppet body, so he knew exactly what to do when he arrived inside the head of John Malcovich. At first, the eyes were like two holes in a black wall through which one could see whatever John was seeing as he went innocently about his movie-star life. The puppeteer was merely a spectator. But soon, the puppeteer learned how to manipulate John Malcovich. He *became* John Malcovich. This is the process of stepping in.

When the puppeteer's face was settled up against the inside of John's face, his viewpoint was quite different. He had peripheral vision. He had a full awareness of John. This is how a child changes from the animal to the human. When he finally steps in and becomes self aware, then a mighty change occurs. A sense of accountability for one's actions begins to impress upon the soul. The age at which this occurs varies for each individual. Some people never step in. They are blown around by every wind of doctrine. They are ruled purely by their passions and their appetites. If they are hungry, they eat until they are gorged. If they are angry, they yell and scream and stomp their feet. If they are lustful, they will fulfill their desire without reserve. They have no thought for tomorrow. They wait for nothing. They save for nothing. They consume everything and build nothing. They are the perfect fodder for indoctrination, as it turns out.

At the end of the day, there are two types of people. Those who act, and those who are acted upon. Those who are acted upon are usually not self-aware. They don't know who they are, where they are from, or what they can become. Those who act are awake. They realize that their actions affect others. In fact, if they have really caught the vision of being alive, they realize that their actions affect the entire universe.

But when a person steps in, they have special ability to explore. They can deprive themselves of things. They can set goals and reach them by directing their own energy in a manner that changes that energy into matter. A friend of mine once, in his lack of appreciation for the genius of our instructor, said, "Yeah, but if you really want to impress me turn peanut butter into eye tissue." The implication was that God was greater than science because He changed dust into a man. What he did not realize was that we, as self-aware beings in this dimension, can change a ham sandwich into a skyscraper or into a car that will cover a quarter mile from a dead stop in less than 4 seconds. We convert energy with the genius of our hands into other things. But that, of course, should not be worshipped. It does, however, take a genius to take the ability to learn with self-awareness to its eternal conclusion. A self-aware being will one day know as much as the Creator. Of that there can be no denial.

So how does this relate to world number four? This world is on the path to discovery. Consider it a canyon of blue through which one must pass to find knowledge beyond that which is known in the world. After all the music is learned, where does a musician go to find a new sound? He or she must pass through the canyons of blue to find the new sound. And when the sound is discovered, it must be brought back to the world and played or sung. Sometimes the journey is long. Sometimes a traveler can get lost, relatively speaking. You see, the canyons of blue are like a black hole. Black holes are probably the gravity engine that powers all light in a galaxy, and thus the universe. But beyond their horizons, time warps. That is to say, time inside the black hole is quite a bit different than time outside the black hole. During a single second inside the black hole, 10 million years may expire outside the black hole. It's the same when passing through the canyons of blue.

Travelers, who are self aware, can pass through the fourth world of existence many times in their mortal lives. The journey can no more be avoided than the womb for a soul to come to earth. It is a dreadful mistake for humans to think that in order for them to be happy, they must avoid the fourth world of existence. Drug companies make the majority of their profits in the 21st century by providing chemical assistance to avoid depression. It has even been called a disease, a chemical imbalance, or an affliction, from which you can never be cured.; only treated for the rest of your life. But, know this much. It is meant to be a journey, not a destination. Of course there are forces that, for purposes of explanation, are personified herein. Besides the traveler, there are two forces in the canyons of blue that must be explained.

The first is that of the Dark One. You might have seen him in your travels. It's a little hard to explain. Picture a black flame with yellow eyes. Size and shape? Depends upon the observer and the situation. It is most important to remember that he does not give off energy. He consumes energy from souls. There are certain rules about this encounter. He cannot kill the traveler. He can only convince the traveler to destroy himself.

The second force in the canyons of blue are the songbirds. These are giant white birds whose feathers make a peculiar sound during flight. When they are moving through the air, the wind moves through the fine fingers of their feathers and makes musical tones. It's not quite like music with a melody. It's more like the sound one would make running a quill over the strings of a harp.

Why are these two forces so important? Because they represent the two most powerful things a traveler will encounter while passing through the canyons of blue on the way to discovery or back. Sometimes travelers get lost or decide not to return to their world.

I hesitate to say, "reality," because after all, what is reality anyway. People who never travel to other forms of consciousness may never experience the kind of discovery mentioned in this chapter. They are asleep. Only those who are awake can experience the amazement of the universe.

When a mathematician reaches the end of all known math, and yet he feels that there is something more, he must reach out beyond himself to find the answer. Now, you might no think that a mathematician would be the sort of artistic personality that would reach out in the maelstrom of chaos for an answer. Even mathematicians, who you would think would simply derive one new equation from another, have a clear and incredible record of inspiration. I chose mathematicians because the reader might not think of them as particularly prone to inspiration.

Srinivasa Aiyangar Ramanujan was a ground breaking Indian mathematician. Living a mere 33 years as a result of tuberculosis, he was a child prodigy completely self-taught in mathematics. When his theories and proofs were discovered, he was at first considered a fraud, for he derived nothing, but rather simply wrote the finished product in his notebooks. It was said that he would have visions during prayer during which pure math was poured into his head. Once the world of conventional mathematicians caught up with him, he was heralded as one of the greatest to have ever lived.

**Ramanujan said "An equation for me has no meaning,
unless it represents a thought of God."**

Girolamo Saccheri (I am sorry to have no picture as the man was never portrayed as far as I can tell), born on the 5th of September, 1667, was the original discoverer of Non-Euclidean geometry. He also has a similar approach to exploration. "The exact problem with Saccheri's approach to geometry was that he began with a fixed notion of what was true and what was not true, and he set out to prove what he'd assessed as true to start with." (Gödel, Escher, Bach. Douglas R. Hofstadter Vintage Books, P. 452) His vision of mathematics enabled us to explore space. He expressed curved mathematics in ways no recorded method could. Where did he *see* these computations? How did he manifest the formulas from raw imagination? The answer is the core of the *metamorphosis*.

Bernard Riemann also lived a short life of 39 years, born in 1826. A student of Gauss, he did work in geometry so advanced that a least one of his theories, the Riemann Zeta function for example, still remains unproven and one of the most fascinating revelations in mathematics. His definition of space as a metric is one of the foundations for all theories of spacetime and transdimensional exploration.

**Bernard Riemann gave us new mathematics
that allowed us to visualize spacetime**

When he was 14, he was lent Bernhard Legendre's book on the theory of numbers. He read the 900-page book in six days. The universe would never be the same, as his work was always based on intuitive reasoning, rather than lengthy computations. At the age of

25, he was granted a PhD in mathematics. His theory of complex variables was heralded as, ..."a gloriously fertile originality." The day before his death, also of tuberculosis, while resting under a fig tree, his soul was filled with joy at the glorious landscape, he worked on his final work which unfortunately, was left unfinished.

Riemann mathematics allowed us to seriously consider parallel universes, multiple dimensions, and even faster than light travel. He postulated that *connections* are possible between two universes. Called Riemann's Cut, it is now a fairly standard proof all math majors will consider.

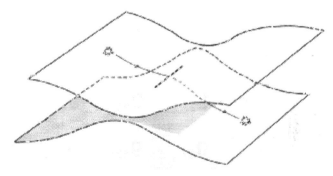

Riemann's Cut

The passing from one two-dimensional plane to another for a bug crawling on the paper is a simple matter of finding a point of curvature where the two universes come in tangential contact, discovering a cut, and walking through. One might be able to have such a journey there and back and testify to a possibly antagonistic audience of their experience. There are many credible testimonies of explorers who passed into warm tropical lands while traveling across the North Pole. Upon their return, nothing they could say would convince anyone of their reality. Perhaps they accessed a Riemann possibility and passed into another universe or another dimension and returned to tell about it. There are many reports of people, ships, planes, and even lands moving one-way through such a possibility, thusfar not returning to our presence. This visionary mathematician *saw* his solutions and was able to inspire the future of science well beyond our comfort level. Many of these concepts are still considered science fiction today. Who knows how close we are to sensing these realities?

Another noted genius, although not a mathematician, was Nikola Tesla. Born in Croatia on July 10, 1856 he lived to the age of 87. He had a way of intuitively sensing hidden scientific secrets and employing his inventive talent to prove his hypotheses. He vehemently claimed he received communication from other planets.

**Born precisely at midnight of July 9/10, 1856,
Nikola Tesla was the most prolific inventor in modern history**

It is said of him that human evolution made a sudden and massive

leap forward with the birth of Tesla. His flashes of brilliance were

prophetic and so far ahead of any natural progression that those few

men close to him claimed he saw visions of his inventions before he

built them. They always turned out exactly the way he drew them in

his notebooks. Edgar Rice Burroughs once said of him, "Tesla draws much of the inspiration for his ideas from poetry, literature, dreams, exotic spiritual beliefs, and visions that flash across his brain. Who knows? Perhaps if I pursue my interest in poetry and writing I might benefit from the converse: drawing my inspiration for writing poems and stories from imaginative science and futuristic speculations." (Edgar Rice Burroughs' *Remarkable Summer of '93* a docu-novel by Bill Hillman)

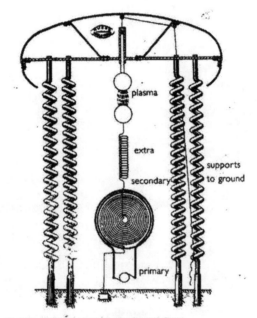

Fig. 6 Oscillating electrostatically charged dome.

The Tesla Coil Patent Drawing

Tesla's Coil proved to be the driving force behind high-energy electricity experiments that still dazzle the world. He was able to discover sources of energy that were powerful enough to deliver an entire planet out of darkness without pollution or depletion of any natural resource. He could have transformed the world into a civilization of light with no pollution, had the energy barons of the day not visualized an empire of power and ultimate control. To this day, all modern population centers must connect the existing energy grid, controlled by a handful of energy companies, burning fossil fuels, belching megatons of CO_2 into the atmosphere, and producing nuclear waste by the ton.

These are but a very small group of the brilliant minds who reached out into the void of the spirit, walking through the canyons of blue, and they each retrieved pure knowledge as if their heads were opened and it was poured in. Well, the experience of gaining the knowledge is, for the purposes of this chapter, not as important as the experience of disconnecting one's self from the physical world during the trip. That is to say, the ability to *see* beyond the physical 3-D world to a source of knowledge that acts much like memories rather than new science is the process that occurs in World number four.

That is one of the most remarkable and repeatable things about this experience. Humans demonstrate a disconnection with the physical world that, as far as we know, is singular in nature. We are the only beings on this planet that can do this. We are not the only beings in the universe that can do it. We may, in fact, be accessing and contributing to a field of consciousness that is accessed and contributed to by trillions of beings throughout the universe.

That is to say, one's soul is alone on the journey, but not alone in the field of *source*. It is only when we make these ventures that the thirst for purpose is addressed. Sometimes it is quenched, even flooded by knowledge that seems as if it was stored up for us for millennia and then released upon us like a bursting dam.

Other times, the landscape is barren, and the blueness of the canyons surpasses twilight even unto darkness itself. When we face ourselves in the fourth world of existence, we might find fear, anxiety, and even paranoia. We might hear music, see machines, or even other worlds. We most certainly will become aware of things beyond our physical existence. It is in this place where our attention turns toward our own self so completely, that we do not see other people. We may not see our jobs, our children, or even our own love during these travels. It is a completely individual experience. The first few times through the canyons of blue can be overwhelming, but don't despair.

Some feel as though they are acted upon by their surroundings. They feel as though there is a significant portion of their lives that comes at them like destiny; out of control and uncontrollable. In a survey of 100 people taken by the author, almost 80 percent felt as though at least part of their experience on Earth was *destiny* rather than made of their own choices or in their control. After *clearing,* only about 10 percent of those same people felt *destiny* had any part in their experience on Earth.

It is written, "Many are called, but few are chosen." In point of fact, that may be a mistranslation, for this is not at all what God wished to say. The proper statement is, "Many are called, but few choose." Becoming a chooser, rather than the chosen, is a process born from experience with traveling in the fourth world of existence. That is to say, one has made the journey to the realm of knowledge and returned completely to the place where he normally dwells. In doing so, he has been changed forever by the things that he learned. And the universe has been changed forever, because taking knowledge from beyond is a transfer of energy from one place in the universe to another. Not that there is any great loss to cause weakness in the supplying world, but that the mass of the knowledge withdrawn is determined by the drag or resistance against that withdrawal. This is exactly the mathematical relationship between string theory and mass. The mass of a thing is determined by its drag value. It is a quantum level of the perturbation theory. The more muscle it takes to lift an object, the heavier it is. And, we were always taught that the heavier an object, the more muscle it takes to lift it. Not so in physics.

The observation effect is such that the effect itself may be the creation of that thing. You see, there is such a thing as an empty void. Nothingness. But nothingness becomes space as soon in contains energy or particles. Open universe is thus created at an accelerating rate, in total chaos by the imaginations of beings like you and me. We are the creator-class beings.

In Superstring theory, one of the vibrations is called a *graviton*. If gravitons are present, then the strings of various energies begin to attract one another, forming particles of matter. These subatomic particles form protons, neutrons, and electrons, which in turn can be energized to form heavier elements. These react in predictable ways depending upon the energy to which they are subjected. The universe has been affected. Stars, planets, and even third-dimensional life-forms may be created this way as well.

So, what does this have to do with the journey through the canyons of blue in the fourth world of existence? One has to get the grasp of the expanse of this world. It is large enough to hold all the imaginations of every soul in existence. It contains the youngest and very oldest, encompassing all knowledge. It is this pool of energy into which we thrust our spiritual hands to grasp inspiration. We must be strong, because that knowledge can come from an infinite number of sources. All sources of knowledge come from not just light and darkness, but from an infinite variety of shades. Knowledge is not discrete. That is to say, it does not always fall into a category of darkness or of light. God has all knowledge. Even knowledge of evil. But, just because He knows, does not mean He has the capacity to act on it. His virtue is not cloistered, but rather the most tested in the universe.

So, when we reach out to the universe beyond time to get our answers or our new knowledge, be aware that we do not yet have experience of wisdom with that new knowledge. It has been tested by someone, but we know not by whom. Almost without exception, knowledge is imparted to travelers without the wisdom to use it. History has shown that those with the wisdom to use the knowledge are often not wealthy enough, or live in the right time period, or have the personal resources to develop the concept to a finished product. Instead, these individuals work for corporations or for governments. In all of these cases, the things they recover from the frontier of knowledge become the automatic property of the corporation or the government. History has also shown without exception that neither corporations nor governments have the wisdom to work with the knowledge confiscated from their workers.

From atomic technology to alternate fuel sources that would allow all people to be able to heat their homes cleanly and affordably, knowledge has always been collected and used for profit, rather than the benefit of mankind. The level of technology that the world has reached since 1945 is greater than perhaps any civilization in the history of the world, but it is not even close to the level we could have achieved if all the knowledge learned by individual explorers had been completely and freely disseminated.

Drug corporations can't afford to cure diabetes. Oil companies can't afford to allow high-mileage or alternative fuels to be mass-produced. Utility providers cannot afford for low-cost fusion devices to be manufactured so homeowners could heat or cool their homes without outside electricity. The dental industry cannot allow tooth decay to be cured. These innovations would put these corporations and industries out of business.

Well, back to the canyons of blue. As one might expect, the canyon is entered from a pass in the open lowlands. What people don't know, is that the canyon is a very long box canyon. The ridges of mountains that form the canyon are steep and extend well into the upper atmosphere of the fourth world of existence. The sun never gets directly overhead of the canyon. It is always twilight in the fourth world of existence. There is one way in, and numerous ways out. How many? Well, that is part of the *good* of the world.

When a person is the center of the universe, and his soul is turned in upon itself, the fourth world of existence comes into view. The further he travels into the canyons of blue, the closer he comes to passing through it and reaching the higher knowledge he is seeking. The first few times a person passes through, the going is tough. There is very little light or heat. The warmest thing in the canyon is the traveler. This warmth attracts two forms.

The first is the Dark One, the being who feeds upon the warmth of a soul. While the traveler is without his mortal body, he is vulnerable to disappointment and discouragement and despair. This is one of the places where virtue is tested. Keep in mind, this is not the place where the knowledge is gained. The sources of knowledge are onward an upward. As long as the traveler keeps moving toward is goal, the heat signature is not easy prey for the Dark One. He will try his best to convince the traveler he is worthless, and that his best solution is to destroy his connection with his mortal body, thus allowing all his energy to be trapped in the canyon forever. Always remember, it is the traveler's choice. His free agency is always maintained, as there is no worth to the dark one in a body that is killed against his will.

As the traveler moves deeper into the canyon, another force comes into view. This force is represented by the songbirds. These are avatars of the friends of the traveler. These can be mortal, immortal, or disembodied spirits who know him. They are large birds, with immense wingspans, capable of carrying many times their own weight. Although landing in the canyons of blue would mean certain destruction, they can fly overhead with the sounds of hope singing through their feathers. They may even swoop very low; low enough that the traveler can reach up and be plucked from the surface and carried out of the canyons to safety, but the grip must be that of the traveler. If he does not want to be extracted, there is nothing the songbird can offer, beyond the melodic sounds of the feathers through the cold wind of the canyons of blue.

Giving up, or surrendering to the temptation to remain inside oneself forever is a pathway to destruction. The person can either get completely lost in mental illness, schizophrenia, or even death. Being plucked out of the situation by a friend or a family member, represented by the songbirds, will cut the experience short, but leave it incomplete. Drugging the physical body to avoid traveling the canyons of blue leads to empty libraries the human soul desperately requires. Traveling through the experience of depression is a necessary part of the human experience.

Artists, musicians, and other intrepid explorers pass through the experience of solitary reflection in order to stretch their souls to the source of new knowledge. Some call it revelation. Some call it an Out of Body Experience (OBE). But from mathematicians reaching toward new math, to musicians searching for a new melody, they each record the same experience. Although my analogy may seem awkward at first, it has been supported by agreement by many travelers and explorers over the years. It is true and right.

Now, there might be yogic analogs, or correlations with sepherotic patterns, but this is the pure knowledge of the thing. This is the simplest description of the experience of spiritual travel, or non-physical exploration. I do not propose to massage or manipulate or "view" certain parts of the aura of a human to get there. Most of us do not know of such things, and have little patience for learning ancient sciences to understand the texts of ancient masters. We know what we feel. We know what we see. We know that we grow with each journey, and that the knowledge we have gained cannot be denied. We also know that with human words it is nearly impossible to explain. These images are better transferred directly to the human mind through telepathy, rather than broken into third-dimensional symbols. We have just forgotten how to function in this manner. We have *fallen* to a mortal existence where one must replace the pure images of thought into words and then back again without error; a process of art rather than science.

The journey through the world of depression is natural and expected. Taking drugs or filling our lives with thrills or adventures to keep our minds so full of noise that we cannot feel the journey blocks that human from progressing. Eventually, without fail, each drug-using individual loses the ability to deal with their thoughts, or to tolerate the emotional aspects of life. They satiate themselves away from the world of depression. They don't take the journey through the canyons of blue because they don't want to, or because someone has taught them that being there is a disease for which there is a cure.

Instead of trading the journey for long drug-insulated periods of one's life, we should be wearing a path through this world. With repetition comes confidence. Instead of dreading the extension of one's soul in the nether parts of the universe, we should be able to say to ourselves, "Hello old friend," and pass through to the point at which we can find the knowledge we seek. All of the prophets and have done it. Billions upon billions of humans have done it. The world of depression is as natural and healthy, if properly negotiated, as breathing for the mortal body.

The most important thing to learn in the fourth world of existence, is that you are *source*. There is no need to adhere to any religious ritual or creed. The only separation between you and God is the one you create from yourself. God is within you. You are His embryo. What you wish to become, the way you wish to look, the things you wish to accomplish in life are all within you and completely in your control. All you have to do is master your intention, focus your energy into that intent, and manifest the reality of that intention. It cannot be withheld from you, if you will but generate the amount of energy found in a mustard seed toward that intention.

Are there tools for learning how to harness this intent and manifesting it to create worlds? Yes, of course. The ancients had them. We have them again. Each single individual being can master these tools well enough to find peace, joy, and happiness in mortal life. You may even find your soulmate using these tools. We will discuss these in detail in Volume Three. For more information, research the subject of *Mer-ka-ba*.

315

This is but a piece of chapter of an entire work on this subject.

World Number Five

World number five I like to call the celestial world. I guess I adopted the name from Paul the Apostle. He speaks of three degrees of glory, the celestial being the highest. There is no requirement of perfection or holiness here in this world. In fact, it does not matter where one is on the ladder of life. It only matters in which direction you are going. You will know when you have reached a vibrational state sufficient to see what is in this world. The frequency of a person in this realm is able to perceive what is in higher dimensions. This world is the culmination of all the worlds of existence that a third-dimensional being can behold. Instead of being absorbed into oneself, spending nearly every waking moment dwelling on how the universe is acting on us, the soul looks outward toward everyone and everything else. The *good* of this world is the spiritual connection with every living thing. It goes beyond this, actually. The temporal and spiritual dimensions begin to make their presence known to this explorer. There is an almost overwhelming love that fills the body. It is as if you want to stop everyone on the street and say, "I love you." There is a very noticeable difference in the human that reaches this world of existence.

Although the physical body appears to be firmly ensconced in the material or third-dimensional universe, the awareness of energies around the body and those of others around the human being become evident and powerful. Auras, energy fields, and even psychic impressions make themselves known to the observer. The transition is often referred to as *the ascension*.

Ascension is the transition of a human being into a higher state of awareness or consciousness without experiencing physical death. That is to say, the soul is like unto a *translated* being without tasting physical death. Christians would call this a *Calling and Election made sure*. This is a point at which the individual human becomes totally aware of the god within their own being.

Around the 5th century, the translators of *the Bible* simply deleted any references to this divine portion of the human being. The eternal training of the intelligence known as *human* through a mortal experience was artificially and deliberately limited to a single lifetime with the specific purpose of firmly establishing fear as a means of managing the populace by the government. Also known as *the church*, this government imprisoned the human mind in a hopeless void skillfully manipulated by church leadership so as to quench any aspirations of mankind toward the divine nature with which it agreed to be created. 5th-century mortal lifespan had fallen to less than 5 decades, while infant mortality was nearly 20 percent. Man's ability to work with the Earth's bounty had been stripped from him through nearly a millennia of warfare and slavery. No leader could motivate an army to fight a church who claimed that opposition of any kind was blasphemy, punishable by eternal damnation.

Once the eternal nature of the human progression was written out of the ancient records by biblical translators and scribes, the dominion of the church was practically invincible. The principle of endurance to the end for one single mortal life all but dowsed the flame of hope in nearly every human being on Earth.

Now, this might sound a little strange, or a little uncharacteristically unscientific. But there is some quantitative evidence of this effect. In several major studies, the energy manifested by one in this world of existence has been measured to have a statistically significant effect. That is to say, data was collected using quantitative methods and treated to display the trends, patterns, and probability comparisons. Some things can happen. Some things can happen only in rare circumstances. And, some things can happen only after a three-foot deep snow in Death Valley.

Dr. Larry Dossey wrote a book, *Healing Words*. In this work, he reports on dozens of double-blind designs of experiment were conducted to determine the results of the application of a form of energy transfer commonly known as *prayer*. He quotes:

"The subjects in these studies also included water, enzymes, bacteria, fungi, yeast, red blood cells, cancer cells, a pacemaker cell, seeds, plants, algae, moth larvae, mice and chicks. Among the process that had been influenced were the activity of enzymes, the growth rate of leukemic white blood cells, mutation rates of bacteria, germination and growth rates of various seeds. Also affected were the firing rate of pacemaker cells, healing rate of wounds, the size of goiter and tumors, the time required to awaken from anesthesia, autonomic effects such as electrodermal activity of the skin, rates of hemolysis of red blood cells, and hemoglobin levels. It sis not seem to matter whether the praying person was in the presence of the organism being prayed for, or was miles away. Objects locked in lead-lined rooms and "cages" designed to block all known forms of electromagnetic energy were still affected."

"In one study by researcher Daniel P. Wirth, the effects of prayer on wound healing were studied. This was a double-blind study. Forty-four subjects were deliberately wounded with full skin thickness surgical wounds. They were not told they were going to be prayed for. None of the patients were told they were receiving any kind of a healing treatment at all. They were told to insert the arm with the wound on it through a hole in the wall for five minutes. The reason for this unusual exercise was explained to them to be for the purpose of measuring the "biopotentials" from the surgical site with a "non-contact device."

They did not know that the "non-contact device" was a person praying for their wounds. With twenty-two of the subjects the praying person was in the room praying, and with twenty-two subjects the praying person was not in the room and not praying. Several time during the study, doctors double-blinded as to which patients were in which group, trace the wounds on transparent acetate sheets. Then an independent technician, also double-blinded, would digitize the tracings into a computer for data collection. By day Eight, 100% of the wound sizes of the prayed-for subjects were significantly smaller than the non-prayed-for subjects. On day Sixteen, the result was measured again. By then, thirteen of the prayed-for wounds were completely healed as opposed to none of the non-prayed for wounds." (*Healing Words* by Larry Dossey, MD. 1993 Harper Collins Publishers)

There has never been a drug or a topical treatment that has had a 100% positive effect like these experiments. There are more studies that have generally the same results, but there is simply not enough room in this book for them. As a statistician, I am trained to be skeptical and to watch for tainted data. If either of the above studies took place in a Catholic hospital with the data collection performed by seminary students I would be doubtful. That would be sort of like a new study saying that three hamburgers a day could lower your cholesterol by 30% that was paid for by the American Beef Council. We try to be very aware of corrupted statistical data. These experiments were designed to report the results fairly and without any preconceptions. The odds of these effects occurring for any other reason except for the prayer that was being administered are somewhere in the realm of 8×10^{47} to one.

Now, these energy transfers have three levels. Bear with me here, especially if you're not particularly *churchy*. From lowest to highest in effectiveness and value-added, here they are:

Level One. The lowest form of energy transfers are the repetitious prayers. These include rituals, blessings on meals, and even rote prayers like rosaries or other recitations. These may have an effect on something, but there is no evidence that we have been able to find that these energy transfers have an effect other that the shear act of obedience to some deity of choice.

Level Two. The next level of energy transfer contains the prayers for real need. Prayers for success of crops, business ventures, a personal struggle to overcome some habit or gain some kind of understanding are in this level. These even include the spiritual expeditions into higher understandings of nature, metaphysics, and even higher mathematics. Transcendental meditation reaches into this level. Any type of extension of one's spirit toward some outside force or being that is performed with passion or great willpower qualifies. The point is, the soul is yearning for something in such a powerful manner, that all mortal efforts have been expended, and a supplication for supernatural efforts from an outside entity is being applied.

Level Three: As shown in the work done by Dr. Dossey in this chapter, this is the direct transfer of energy through prayer from one person to another. This is where the true metamorphosis occurs. This is probably the key that unlocks the universe and all its treasures for the explorer. It is this one level of energy transfer that seems to accompany all humans who have morphed into a being higher than an animal. This is the one indicator that the individual has changed, event temporarily, into an Earthling, rather than a tribal member ready to lop off the heads of other tribes in greed or anger. This level of energy transfer is for the welfare of someone else. The more remote the person is, the higher the level of energy transfer. Only with this change of heart can humans reach the fifth world of existence, or the third degree of glory.

Humans that are awake on this planet all feel that something is about to happen. With the agency of the collective vibrations of all humans on the planet, the race of man will once again be given a chance to decide whether the event is terrible or wonderful. It is physically impossible to have joy and peace if the more part of the vibrations, or spirit, generated by the energy transfers of humans is dark and of a lower more base content. It is like trying to pour a glass of water that is at twenty degrees below zero. Everyone knows that water at this vibrational level is a solid and thus cannot pour, except very slowly like a glacier.

No. Even pure water must be at least zero degrees Celsius in order for it to pour. The events that are going to culminate in 2012 will require a much higher vibrational collective from the race of man for them to ascend with the higher dimensional world. Many civilizations have come to this point and failed. Perhaps they did not know what we know. Perhaps they did not feel what we feel. It is our contention that ancient writers just like us tried many times to teach their societies that the peoples' thoughts would betray them.

They too tried to teach their people that this unconditional love and higher energy transfer from one to another for the welfare of a soul was what the race needed in order to overcome mortality.

But, planet Earth was still a binary planet then. It still is. But, in December of 2012, Earth will pass through a cloud of heavy dark energy, and the spirit portion of the Earth will begin to separate from the temporal portion due to the harmonic dissidence. The two frequencies will be destructively interfering with one another, and thus will not exist any longer in the same dimension. The souls that will leave with the spirit portion will be in tune with it. The souls that remain behind will not be in tune with the spirit portion. This event makes this precipice so important for the Earth that without assistance from the very strongest and noblest of our race, we will not survive it.

By reading this book, you have demonstrated that you have the capacity to accept the truth. By acting on what you have read herein, you will see the difference between light and darkness, joy and despair, the fifth world of existence and the lower worlds.

As always, we have our free agency. There is one thing that most people seem to overlook here. Not even God can act contrary to your free agency. And if He cannot, then no other being in the universe can either. Each soul has the right to become a sovereign being, with the power to choose for himself. It is confusing that one being would give up his ability to choose. But, we see people do this every day. In this act, they fall asleep. It is one of the purposes of this book to awake these sleeping souls, so that they will begin to become sovereign. This sovereignty is the godhood of the human soul. The realization of this godhood is the purpose of creation. Creation is the self-awareness of the soul, which occurred when the original soul reduced itself into at least two parts. Without at least two parts to the soul, it did not exist. Each soul divides into two mates, often called soul mates. Perhaps one of the greatest joys in the universe is the meeting of these two parts of the same soul at some future time, when each portion has gained some experience at mortal life. The rejoining of these soul mates can bring to the forefront the most powerful awareness in the universe.

This awareness is often called Christ consciousness. It can also be called the love of God. We emulate it. In point of fact, it was the only commandment that Jesus gave us, upon which all the laws of the prophets were hanged. Without establishing a church or a government, Jesus taught us how to reach a state of *being* through which we could achieve *ascension* using this consciousness. The greatest indignation Jesus expressed in known history was toward the Pharisees, who denied the godhood and eternal nature of the human soul.

This state of *being* is accomplished through learning and practicing completely unconditional love. It appears from the *Bible* that he was crucified and afterward accomplished resurrection into a higher body while retaining all His memories and experiences. 14 generations of careful planning provided the perfect conditions for perhaps the only individual in the universe capable of establishing this process by which mortals can accomplish this state. Joseph and

Mary were both well-trained members of the Tat Brotherhood, which taught for hundreds of generations the process of conception through an interdimensional copulation facilitating immaculate conception.

The only way for a mortal human to accomplish this without dying is through the process of *ascension*. There are many steps to this process, each of which are extremely powerful and require great effort on the part of the individual. One thing is clear. Not one nanometer of movement upward in this process can be made by the individual human, until a realization of the eternal nature of the spirit within is begun. The Biblical statement, "Neither do men light a candle, and put it under a bushel, but on a candlestick; and it giveth light unto all that are in the house," clearly describes three conditions.

First, the individual has a light inside of him. This means the human being has energy capable of lighting the way for others as well as himself. It means that he is a source of light. In fact, it means that he is *source* itself.

Second, the individual is shown two extremes by which he may utilize the *source* inside of him. He can hide it under a bushel, thus plunging his world into darkness. There is no enlightenment or ability to see beyond the ends of one's reach. This human practice has wasted more mortal lives than any other imaginable.

Third, once the human decides to unshield his light, he must decide how large the house is going to be. That is to say, how far will the human shine his light? Will he shine just far enough for him to find his way, or will he shine it far enough for others? Will the love of his light go far enough to help another find his way?

Through the teachings of Christ we may have the ability to inherit from our ancestors, unlike the Nephilim and those who appear to be prevented from advancing to higher frequencies through violation of the laws of the universe. Whether it is out of jealousy or a will to have what we have vicariously, they are dedicated to our consumption. Whoever appears like an ally to that effort probably is an ally to the dark one. Listen and watch, and you will be able to tell the difference.

Achieving this fifth world of existence also allows its inhabitants to access a power of discernment through extended sight. There is a Christ grid of energy surrounding the Earth. The mere acknowledgement of this will allow you to see the disguise peel off those who seek your destruction like an infrared camera reveals the living from the dead. If we say that evil exists, then listen closely. Evil, or rather absence of light, has an allergy; light itself.

Even more than this, the Christ grid can receive energy from each conscious being near the Earth. It can also be a source of energy for those who can raise their personal frequency to one with which it might constructively interfere. That is to say, if the frequency of the human soul is not raised to one that matches the period of the Christ grid, there is no awareness that it exists at all. Mere belief that it is there is not enough to partake in it as a source of power. There is a principle known as *glory* that is nearly universally misunderstood by

326

the human race. It ties inexorably into a much more familiar principle called *faith* by many religious traditions. Faith is nothing more than the power to utilize glory, which might be an analog of the Christ grid around the Earth. Belief is not faith. Belief is an extremely basic principle that, if held onto too tightly, can enslave people in ignorance and prejudice. Without it, humans can barely function at all, not even having the hope that the sun will rise on the morrow.

The desired amount of belief is that which can be likened to remembrance. That is to say, each human being has experienced hundreds and perhaps millions of years. In each of these lives, we have gained some experience. Some of that experience has been good and peaceful, and some has been horrible and painful.

All of these times have taught us something. Belief and faith are principles used by mortal beings to remember the lessons learned from these lifetimes just enough to help us continue to grow, but not so much that we are not surprised or amazed at the wonder of mortality. And, if we say that we are enlightened beings, then perhaps our mission is to flood the Earth with light. It is given to us to do this, and we have been asked to do this by the Christ. There is no force in the entire universe capable of stopping you from letting that light shine, except the free will of you yourself.

The authors are transferring energy to you with this book, with our thoughts, and with our prayers so that you will see the truth of what we have written. It is our hope that you have awakened a little more. So, let your light shine a little brighter. Find the good in people and help it to grow a little every day, and before long, you may have helped save the planet. Peace, Earth explorers.

The New Finds

In this chapter we would like to present some "new finds" that may be of interest to the readers. Each new find will be numbered and titled.

1. **Noah's Manuscripts** In *The Books*, Volume One, we traced the where abouts of the manuscripts that comprised *The Divine Book of Wisdom*. These manuscripts were copied by Noah's grandchildren and were carried to different parts of the known world to help restore civilization following the great cataclysm of 9, 500 B.C. The following information recently surfaced about those manuscripts and were according to the Akashic Records of the nephilim god, Thoth as follows: "Beneath the Etchmiadzin Monastery (in Armenia) were sequested texts of information written by the second and third generations of Noah; and beneath St. Jacob's Monastery were

texts actually transported by Noah." There is a tradition that certain "Books of Noah" were found by St. Jacob and kept for safe keeping at St. Jacob's Monastery, located on the north east slopes on Mt. Ararat, near the ancient town of Ahora, which was located at the base of Ararat. Other artifacts from the Ark were housed there as well. The Armenian priests in St. Jacobs venerated the memory of Noah and his family as the progenitors of the Human Race. Among the housed artifacts from the Ark was a sacred cross, which they claimed was made from wood brought from the Ark. Ahora, which means "planted a vineyard," and St. Jacob's were destroyed and buried by an earthquake in 1810. The town of Ahora and the Monastery of Echmiadzin were rebuilt. Did any of the manuscripts survive the 1810 earthquake and are they now housed in the Etchmiadzin Monastery?

2. **Mayan Ruins of Tulum** The ancient name of Tulum was Zama. Those of our readers who have visited the ruins, are first struck by the beauty of the fortified city which over looks the Caribbean Sea. Secondly, they are impressed by the size of the ruins in comparison to other Mayan sites---they appear to be in miniature. E.J. Clark had to stoop down low in order to enter some of the doorways. Why is this? Well, the city was built by "munchkins," something the Mayan

tour guides never disclose. These "munchkins" were a tribe of Pygmy or Dwarf size Mayans called the Alux. Mayan traditions say they were about 39 inches tall and inhabited parts of the Yucatan, Honduras, Peru, and even Tierra del Fuego. The Maya regarded them as a special creation of the creator; thus the little people were given many extra favors. These tribes appear to have died out, perhaps from diseases brought by the Spaniards. Several Mayan stone reliefs attest to their existence as pictured below.

Pacal Sitting on backs of Alux Dwarfs

3. Avebury Stone Circle Avebury Henge is located in England, near the famous Stonehenge Circle and Silbury Hill. Recently the profile of a well-carved sculptured face has been found on at least one of the major megalith rocks comprising the Henge. Other profiles have been found, but do not photograph well as the light must be perfect, and a three-dimensional perspective is required to see them. These stones are made of a very hard stone called Sarsen which is harder than granite.

Only diamond is harder than sarsen. Your authors believe that Avebury Henge was built by giants who once lived in the area. E J. visited this remarkable site in July 2005. She experienced a sensation of being extremely "heavy" while walking amid the stones.   Both your authors felt a similar sensation while at Stonehenge. The heaviness sensation was physically tiring. Could these well carved images be actual carved photos of themselves? The carvings are big. You be the judge.

Avebury stone face (profile 1)

4. Stonehenge Circle On the narrow outer side of trilithon stone 54, is a newly discovered carved face which faces west. The face has prominent eyebrows, a long straight nose, and well-formed upper lips. The image is best seen from afar and only when the light is right. This discovery was the subject of a BBC News announcement. On trilithon stone 53, an axe and dagger carvings were found 46 years ago. Is this face a tribute to one of Stonehenge's giant builders?

Avebury stone face (profile 2)

Avebury stone face (profile 3)

5. **Dead Sea Origin** Historical evidence indicates that the lower Jordan Valley in the past was much different from what it is today. The Dead Sea did not exist at the time of Abraham. In fact, studies of the accumulation of the salt content of the Dead Sea place the lake no older than 6,000 to maybe 5,000 years. The area of the Dead Sea used to be called the Valley or Vale of Siddim.

6. **Nagamaya** The Maya/Aztecs, according to their traditions, say that winged beings came and lived among them anciently. At first there were only 4, later more. These beings claimed to have come from the Pleiades. The Maya/Aztecs called

them the Nagamaya. The Aztecs, on their calendar, have 20 day glyphs which they named each glyph after one of the Nephilim/Nagamaya. They did just as we have done in naming our days of the week after them. We suspect that the Nagamaya taught them astronomy, therefore they named their calendar days after them. It is said that these beings took human form.

Now, the Nagamaya probably came to the ancestors of the Aztecs and the Maya, who were the Chichimecas, but were remembered in later generations. It was the Chichimecas who built Teotihuacan, probably with the help of the Nagamaya and their giant offspring.

Prologue

Will there be a Volume Three? Yes, because much more information just recently came forth concerning the End Times of 2012. That volume is already in the writing. Projected date of publication is the Fall of 2007. The hope we wanted to give you is in this book, and it is in your heart. You may hear doom and gloom from numerous prognosticators in the coming years about the year 2012. But do not despair. We have provided the world some view of the glorious and wonderful aspects of these times. The ascension of the human soul, the incredible love that is sweeping the world, and the unlimited potential of the individual are just a few.

Much of what has been written in this book was once common knowledge among the ancients. Down through the Ages wise sages, prophets, kings and magi ensured that the common people knew it and retained it by use of symbolism. Tragically, when the Gregorian calendar replaced many of the ancient calendars, much ancient knowledge was lost concerning the End Times. Even as late as the 15th century, Michael Nostradamus predicted "the dead to rise from their graves sometime near to the year 2007." As much as we hate to admit it, the ancient world was wiser than we are today, if for nothing else than displaying maturity with what knowledge they did have. What good is all the modern worlds' technology if we miss the mark concerning 2012?

The technology we possess is doubling at a documented 100% rate every four years! Unfortunately, we have demonstrated no such increase in wisdom with what to do with this technology. We are still digging up the planet and putting it into our gas tanks. We are still packing cubic miles of trash beneath our soils. We fund every new energy technology based solely on its ability to be used as a weapon. Instead of exploring space as a planet, we are racing to the moon as we speak, country-by-country, for the purpose of controlling the wealth of resources that may be there; not the least of which is widely reported to be alien technology abandoned on the planet. In 2024, the first manned expeditions are expected to return to the moon. Speculation on why the race is so heated, and as to what the winners will gain, is swelling like the ultimate technological tsunami. Obviously, that wave is expected to crash well after the 2012 End Times date. We will be right there on the first covered wagon that crosses the plains of Copernicus so you will have the truth in your hands.

We hope that our readers have enjoyed reading this book as much as your authors have enjoyed writing it. For us, every chapter was an adventure in re-discovering what was lost. Our mission was to restore to the world the ancient knowledge of the union of the polarity and to warn the world of the End Time date of 2012. Our mission is now accomplished; however much more on 2012 is to come in Volume Three. We want to thank our readers for purchasing our book series. Please go to the books web site, listed on front cover, and email us your comments as we value your input.

Index

Table of Illustrations

345

Made in the USA
Lexington, KY
16 January 2010